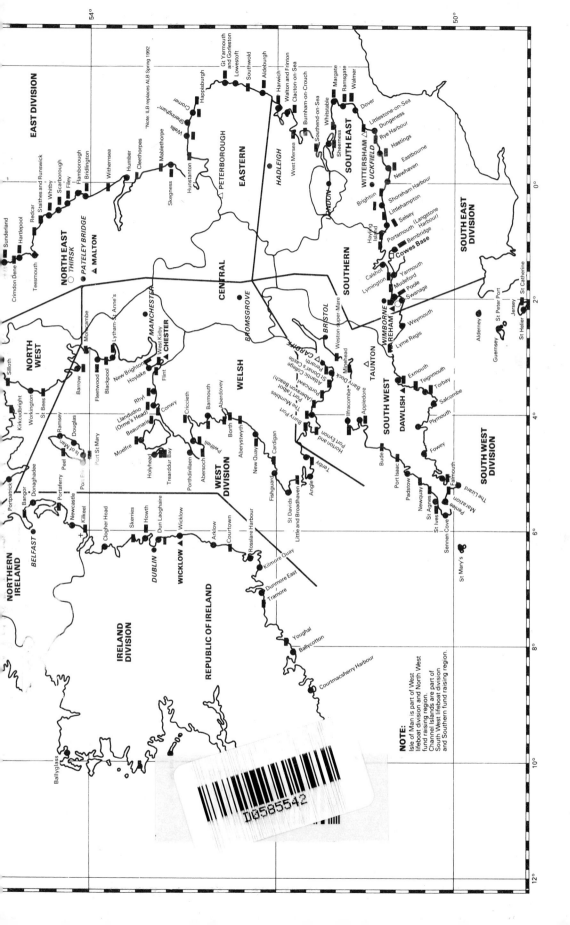

THE LIFEBOAT PRAYER

Merciful Father, all things in heaven and
earth are held within your loving care,
look with favour upon the Royal National
Lifeboat Institution.

Protect and bless the crews of all their
lifeboats and all who risk their own
safety to bring help to others.

Guide all who work for the Institution that
they may be faithful to the vision of its
founders, so that it may always be seen
as a beacon of hope and light to those
who find themselves in peril on the seas.

Through the same Jesus Christ, to whom
with You and the Holy Spirit be honour
and glory, now and forever.

Amen.

HEROES ALL!

THE STORY OF THE
RNLI

Patrick Stephens Limited, an imprint of Haynes Publishing,
has published authoritative, quality books for enthusiasts for more
than 25 years. During that time the company has established a
reputation as one of the world's leading publishers of books on
aviation, military, model-making, motor cycling, motoring, motor
racing, railway and railway modelling subjects. Readers or authors
with suggestions for books they would like to see published are invited
to write to: The Editorial Director, Patrick Stephens Limited,
Sparkford, Nr Yeovil, Somerset BA22 7JJ.

HEROES ALL!

THE STORY OF THE

RNLI

Alec Beilby

PSL

Patrick Stephens Limited

363 · 123

First published in 1992
Reprinted in 1992
Reprinted in 1994

British Library Cataloguing in Publication Data:

A catalogue record for this book is available from the British Library.

ISBN 1 85260 419 0

Patrick Stephens Limited is an imprint of Haynes Publishing, Sparkford, Nr Yeovil, Somerset BA22 7JJ.

Printed in Great Britain by Butler & Tanner Ltd, Frome and London

CONTENTS

FOREWORD
by Michael Vernon, Chairman of the RNLI

The work of the Royal National Lifeboat Institution and its lifeboat crews has inspired many books and articles over our long history and I am delighted that this latest book by Alec Beilby can now be added to the list.

I must say I envy the author the lengthy research he undertook, touring the coastline and meeting lifeboat people wherever he went. You cannot fail to end up an admirer of the organisation after so much exposure to the volunteers at the sharp end. Mr Beilby is no exception, his enthusiasm for the RNLI is reflected in every chapter which follows.

Clearly the book presents a story of our organisation as described by an affectionate but independent observer and Mr Beilby's views will not always be those shared by the RNLI. However, thanks to him a new opportunity is presented for readers to discover the many facets of the lifeboat service, to learn about its glorious past and to understand why it will continue to flourish far into the next century.

INTRODUCTION

"In the beginning God created the heaven and the earth." Genesis: Chapter 1, verse i.

It might seem ostentatious, even risky, to take the first words of the most read book in the world to start a work about the Royal National Lifeboat Institution, but those very words suit the purpose of this book well.

The institutions of man, unlike those of the gods, are seldom, if ever, the production of instantaneous creation. They evolve.

Often the evolvement of what in time becomes an established and much-cherished institution emerges after a period of gestation where the genes become the thoughts, aspirations and achievements of the many men and women who have fused them together. The result, as is certainly the case with the Royal National Lifeboat Institution as we know it today, is the birth of a healthy, well-adjusted and well-controlled body with a firm and dedicated sense of purpose.

Many thousands of lives have been saved by the people who are associated with the Royal National Lifeboat Institution. Certainly the men who put to sea in the lifeboats are the front line, but those who also serve the Institution, the boatbuilders, the local committee leaders, the craftsmen at the Poole depot and even the Chelsea Pensioners who collect money at the London International Boat Show each year, are all very much an essential part of this internationally respected and successful organization.

AUTHOR'S INTRODUCTION

The researching and writing of this book took almost exactly a year. The research involved travelling about 14,000 miles by road, air and ferry. Visits were made to 117 offshore (large boat) lifeboat stations ranging from Aith in Shetland to the north, Jersey to the south, Cromer and Humberside to the east and the Isles of Scilly to the west. Several factors quickly became apparent on my travels. First, the friendliness and enthusiasm of all those whom I met at the stations. Next, the modesty and reticence of coxswains and crew members to discuss their exploits, particularly in cases where awards were made afterwards. Finally, the help received from coxswains, honorary secretaries and others who, after a visit, sent photographs, paintings and, from Llandudno, a cartoon by Gareth the son of Coxswain Meurig Davies.

While not wishing to offend the many people who went out of their way to offer hospitality and help I should like to mention just a few incidents of this sort to emphasize the way things so often went. There was the visit to Brian Bevan's station at lonely Spurn Head, Humberside, with coffee at his comfortable home and the battle I had to prise from him details of his medal-winning services. On another occasion, having tea in the cottage of the legendary retired Isles of Scilly coxswain, Matt Lethbridge, listening to him expound his views on the safety of modern racing yachts; another memorable moment.

There was another occasion when, after a long tiring day covering the lifeboat stations south from Girvan on the west Scottish coast, I reached Barrow-in-Furness looking for somewhere to stay for the night. Barrow was grey and cold so I headed out of town. Suddenly out on the edge of Morecambe Bay, perched on a small island, I saw a lifeboat shed. I headed for it and found the Barrow station quite by accident. The Assistant Divisional Inspector, George Rawlinson, was visiting to carry out trials with the 'D' class inflatable lifeboat. A small hotel stood at the mainland end of the narrow causeway leading to Roa Island where the lifeboat shed stood. His work over, George Rawlinson, Coxswain Steve Hurst, some of the offshore and inshore boat crew and myself enjoyed a convivial evening, a great and pleasant surprise to me. I had been facing yet another night alone in one of the many bed and breakfast hotels that I visited on my research travels.

The visit to the south coast of Ireland was enhanced by the call at the home of Ballycotton's honorary secretary, Donie O'Sullivan, who had just heard he was to receive a gold badge for his work for the RNLI. Coffee and biscuits in front of a warm fire accompanied what the Irish call 'a good crack' about lifeboat activities and Donie's fears of the journey to the annual general meeting and presentation of awards in London the following spring. I hope my guide, Tom O'Sullivan, head of RTE, the Irish National radio and television organization, in Cork, managed to persuade Donie to make the trip. Until then Donie had never been out of Ireland let alone in an airliner.

I think it was the people as much as the places visited that enhanced the research. For example, Coxswain Hewitt Clark, at Lerwick, Shetland, who failed to tell me that he was to attend a special dinner and the presentation of an award for one of his exploits on the very night after I left the islands. I found out about this from the local honorary secretary, Magnus Shearer, JP, who came to meet me from his home on the island of Bressay across the sound from Lerwick. Watching Hewitt show a crowd of grubby school children around his immaculate lifeboat was another thing. If anything moved, they moved it. Later he told me that this local public relations job was harder than any night rescue at sea in a gale.

Certainly the places visited made their impressions. The loneliness of stations such as Aith, Spurn and Sennen. The beauty of Lochinver, St Davids and The Lizard. The man-inflicted harshness of Workington, Teesmouth and Coxswain Robbie Maiden's station at Hartlepool where, after an evening in the local pub he will offer broth and dumplings to any visitor whose constitution can take the treatment in the small hours. Heartburn and Hartlepool are a memory that will stay awhile.

The call and the night stop at Bamburgh, where the embryo of the RNLI came to life was something special. The little museum dedicated to Grace Darling and a quiet visit to her grave made the research more poignant as the low sun lit her ornate Victorian tomb while away to the east the Longstone lighthouse gleamed especially white. It was like meeting someone one had known a long time. There was a lump in the throat, a tear in the eye.

I could not visit all the offshore stations. Weather put a stop to my attempt to go to Stornoway and the other Hebridean stations but I knew the places from earlier visits. These gaps were filled by hours on the telephone to helpful honorary secretaries and coxswains as far apart as Galway Bay and Anstruther, followed by copious help from the Service Records Department at Poole. The visit to the Isles of Scilly was made by ferry from Penzance on one of the roughest days of 1990. The ferry company apologized for the rough crossing, which fuelled my thoughts as we passed the Tater-du light and Lamorna where the Penlee lifeboat had been lost with all hands. I would not have had the conditions any other way. It was this awful disaster, and the long talk on a quiet summer afternoon with Mechanic Eddie Madron in the Penlee lifeboat house a few years ago that set me about writing this book. As the flying spray threw rainbows into the sky I half closed my eyes and tried to imagine the scene on that dreadful night in 1981. I could not.

During a visit to one station a call came through from local Coastguards putting the lifeboat on stand-by. The tension was electric. The kettle was boiled, massive mugs of tea brewed, one crew member was smoking two cigarettes having lit a second when he had forgotten another one alight in an ashtray elsewhere. The coxswain, a few minutes earlier a jovial gag-cracker, became the man he really was as he picked his crew for the work. Dedicated, a little hard, paternal to the younger men who had answered the call, reassuring. His words as the call came and the crew headed for their boat was typical of the attitude.

"Right" he said, "let's go and look for the buggers and try and save them."

He chose six from the twelve men who had turned out for the call, or 'shout' as the lifeboatmen describe it. The look on the faces of those who did not go out was one of total disappointment with no sign of relief. That is the RNLI.

The lifeboat station visits, meetings with crew members and cheerful hospitality were one thing. Visits to boatyards where the lifeboats are built and finished were another. The same friendliness was there, the same enthusiasm and the same dedication to the task of giving the lifeboat crews the best of everything possible. No corners are cut, only the best will do. It was impressive.

Writing the book is a little like the old cliché about painting the Forth Bridge. The RNLI crews answer over 4,000 calls a year. As soon as one has described one event at a station another has occurred. What I have done is try and find something unique or typical for each station. It would be impossible to be up to date even if the publisher had managed to print the book yesterday. The only way to keep your news about RNLI rescues and other events up to date is to subscribe to the Shoreline membership of the Institution and thereby receive a copy of their magazine *Lifeboat*. You will then be able to add to this book and, at the same time, help those brave, modest people who form the crews continue their work.

Finally thanks to the hundreds of people who helped me gather the words to make the book and apologies to any who may feel left out. Be assured, the omissions were not intentional, but painting something as big as the Forth Bridge alone is as impossible as fitting all the works of the RNLI into one relatively small book. I tried.

Alec Beilby
1991

ACKNOWLEDGEMENTS

I should like to thank the following organizations and people who provided generous assistance beyond my expectations in the researching, writing and checking of this book.

The Directorate and Staff of the RNLI.
P&O Ferries (Scrabster to Stromness route).
Brymon Airways, Plymouth.
The Isles of Scilly Steamship Company.
Aurigny Air Services.
Tom O'Sullivan, *The Cork Examiner*, Cork.
Tom MacSweeney, RTE, Cork.
Rick Tomlinson, Port St Mary, Isle of Man.
Clarke Murdoch, Farnham, Surrey.
Ken Rayner, Isington, Hampshire.
Mike Heathcote and the staff at Andrew Kent and Partners, London.
Mr & Mrs Charles Telfer, Frensham, Surrey.
Gareth Davies, Llandudno, North Wales.
Lieutenant Commander Peter West, RN Public Relations Officer, Flag Officer Naval Air Command.
The Mariners Hotel, Frensham.
David Turtle, Manager, National Westminster Bank plc, Farnham.
Tracey Brooks, British Rail InterCity, Birmingham.
Melanie Mercer.
Ann Hughes.
Dr John de Courcy Ireland, Dublin.

I would like to add special thanks for help with material to illustrate the text to:

The Royal National Lifeboat Institution.
Chris Fairclough.
Maggie Murray.
Edward Mallinson.
Fred Walkington.
Dave Trotter.
Radio Times.
Scottish Daily Record.
Jeff Morris.
Mallory Maltby.
Robin Sharp.
Peter Hadfield.
Campbell MacCullum.
A M Ferry.
Peter Orme.
Whitby Gazette.
HMS Gannet.
Rick Tomlinson.
Focus Press.
Andrew Besley.
RNAS Culdrose.
Lord Greenway

Photographs frequently come down over the years in a form which makes it difficult or impossible to accurately trace their origin. If there are within these pages any such unacknowledged illustrations, I extend my apologies and thanks to the photographer or artist concerned.

MICHAEL VERNON, CHAIRMAN OF THE RNLI

Michael Vernon joined the RNLI Committee of Management in 1963. He was appointed Chairman of the Institution during the summer of 1989, succeeding the Duke of Atholl who had held the position for ten years. He is well qualified for the position having been a successful businessman as well as a keen amateur sailor. He was Chairman of the Board of Spillers Limited from 1968 to 1980 and still holds a number of active directorships. Sailing is one of his main recreations. He was Commodore of the Royal Ocean Racing Club between 1965 and 1969 and is a member of the Royal Yacht Squadron.

Apart from being Chairman of the RNLI he also sits as a member of the Boat Committee and the Establishment Committee. The post of Chairman is more than that of a figurehead. The work involves attendance at naming ceremonies, running the annual general meeting in London and other functions organized by the RNLI. When the Duke of Atholl was in the Chair he travelled the length and breadth of the country during the course of RNLI business. Michael Vernon is ably following in the Duke's footsteps.

Michael Vernon – Chairman of the RNLI 1989.

BRIAN MILES, DIRECTOR

Lieutenant Commander Brian Miles joined the RNLI in 1964 as Assistant Inspector of Lifeboats for Scotland. He was educated at Reeds School, in Surrey, and then went to HMS Conway Merchant Navy Cadet School in the Menai Strait, North Wales.

On leaving HMS Conway he joined the P&O Shipping Company as a Cadet, then served as a Deck Officer, mainly aboard passenger vessels. He then left P&O after ten years service to join the RNLI. Following his first appointment in Scotland he was put in command of a prototype 70 foot long offshore cruising lifeboat built on the Clyde for evaluation. This lifeboat operated in the Shetland and Orkney Islands and on the north-west and north-east coast of Scotland. Following a year evaluating this boat, he became RNLI Inspector of Lifeboats in Scotland between 1967 and 1970 before taking up the same position in Ireland.

Brian Miles is a lifeboatman's lifeboatman, making many friends among the crews he came to know well during those days so it was no surprise when, in 1973 he was appointed Assistant to the Director, then Captain Nigel Dixon, RN. It was a tough assignment, starting just one year before the 150th anniversary celebrations of the RNLI.

In 1978 he became Staff Officer Operations, a post held for four years until 1982 when he was then appointed Deputy Director.

The Director at the time of this

Brian Miles – Lieutenant Commander RD, RNR. RNLI Director from 1 Jan 1988.

appointment was Rear Admiral Wilf Graham, CB. The seeds were being sown for the final step up the RNLI ladder when, in 1988, Admiral Graham retired and Brian Miles took the helm as chief executive of the Institution. It was a natural and very popular progression with everyone involved in the many facets of the RNLI operation.

During his many and varied duties

which range from attending naming ceremonies at stations to attending many different meetings at Poole and further afield, Brian Miles travels thousands of miles each year in his work. Indeed during the nine month period of researching this book the author met him, quite unplanned, in the Shetlands, Tynemouth, Sunderland, Guernsey and the 1990 London International Boat Show.

He married his wife Anne at the same time as he first joined the RNLI in 1964. After 27 years of marriage she considers she not only married Brian but the RNLI as well, sharing the high spots and the tragedies over the years. While she feels part of the RNLI family she considers the RNLI part of hers, but then that is not an uncommon evaluation of the life of those who serve the Institution.

GEORGE RAWLINSON

George Rawlinson is one of the 'new boys' in the RNLI management team which includes eleven Inspectors and Deputy Inspectors of Lifeboats, who cover seven regions that divide the British Isles and the whole of Ireland. He joined the RNLI in 1990 at the age of 32. The Inspectors and their deputies travel round the offshore and inshore lifeboat stations in their respective regions ensuring that the high standards required from the RNLI in all aspects of lifeboat operations and maintenance are achieved by the crews. Not only do their checks cover the actual lifeboats but also the lifeboat houses and ancillary equipment.

In 1974 George left school and headed for a life at sea, joining the P&O Shipping Company as a Cadet, his first ship being the *Otaio*, which he joined at the age of 17 in New Plymouth, New Zealand. A four-year apprenticeship followed, ending with his gaining a Second Mate's certificate and a redundancy note from the company, not, he points out, due to his shortcomings in ability but because of a running down of manning levels in the Merchant Navy generally. After a time ashore he joined a shipping company based in Rochester, Kent, serving as Mate on a new coastal bulk carrier from 1981 until 1984 when he transferred to a cable laying vessel. Here he served sufficient time to earn his Master Mariner's certificate at the age of 29 after a period of time

George Rawlinson.

ashore at Warsash College, Southampton, where he sat his Master's examination.

He married his wife Lucy in 1983 and their first child was born in 1987, also the year when he went to Plymouth Polytechnic to study for a Diploma in Management Studies (Shipping). He had already been in touch with the RNLI about the possibilities of working for the Institution. Following this he joined a Scandinavian shipping company's British office as Operations Manager, but office life did not suit him. In 1989 he saw an advertisement for an Inspector's job with the RNLI, applied and was appointed in January 1990.

After four months of training he took over the post of Deputy Inspector, West Division, working under the Inspector, Jeff Mankertz, a former nuclear submarine navigator who, with George, covers the coastline from Tenby, in South Wales to the south and Barrow-in-Furness to the north. When he joined the RNLI George Rawlinson and his family were living in Berkshire but in the summer of 1990 they moved to Hereford in order to be nearer to the lifeboat stations on his 'patch'. He found the RNLI welcoming and received considerable help from other employees both before and after being assigned to his first posting. He admits that the work is demanding and the need for considerable self-motivation essential. He spends a great deal of time away from home. His wife says that she has a photograph of him so that she and the children know who he is when he manages to return home!

Discussing his work he makes the interesting point that it is easier to work with RNLI people who are doing the job because they want to rather than working with people who are doing a job because they have to do it.

He is full of admiration for the people who work for the RNLI particularly the fund-raisers whose efforts never cease to amaze him. He describes himself as a money spender in the RNLI hierarchy and always bears the fund-raisers in mind as he makes decisions to spend the money they have worked so hard to raise. He divides this admiration between these worthy people and the people who man the boats. During one visit to take an Atlantic inshore lifeboat on an exercise for the crew he became involved in a rescue of the crew of a small yacht that was in difficulty. The look of pure relief on the faces of the two people towed to safety said, for George Rawlinson, more than anything he could put into words. It simply summed up what the RNLI is all about. One feels that George Rawlinson, who ran away to sea at the age of 16, as he puts it himself, is going to be with the RNLI for some time to come.

Chapter 1

IN THE BEGINNING

The basic concepts of a nationally-organized body devoted to saving lives at sea probably came to William Hillary, the justly attributable founder of today's Royal National Lifeboat Institution, as he watched a fishing fleet being destroyed by a storm off the coast of the Isle of Man.

Like so many people who begat the embryo of something that foreigners often consider typically and eccentrically British, William Hillary was certainly something of an eccentric adventurer himself. He was born in 1771 which, coincidentally, was about the time that several organized local lifesaving stations were being established around the coast of Britain, but it was not for more than another fifty years that the efforts of William Hillary were to begin the co-ordination of these very local endeavours. He claimed to be of French descent and with adequate income to enjoy a reasonably leisured life, spent his early years as equerry to the Duke of Sussex, the third son of George III, with whom he enjoyed the social seasons and a tour of the Mediterranean. He was obviously something of a seafarer in his early days as he made voyages around several of the larger islands of the Mediterranean in open boats.

It was not as a seafarer, but as a soldier that Hillary made his name during his middle years. The Napoleonic War with France began in 1793 and Hillary raised his own local battalion of infantry in his then home

Sir William Hillary.

county of Essex.

The raising of the 1st Essex Legion of Infantry and Cavalry cost him the then enormous sum of £20,000, giving some indication of his wealth. The Legion comprised 1,400 men and was a well-respected force, but the war that earned him his baronetcy cost Sir William even more than the fee for his small army.

The French blockading of the Caribbean and the French threat generally to maritime trade left him in dire financial straits, even though Admiral Lord Nelson and his fleet had solved the French maritime threat in the West Indies and then defeated them at Trafalgar in 1805, ten years before the war finally ended.

Bloodied but unbowed by his financial situation, Sir William sold his Essex properties and headed for the Isle of Man where he settled in Douglas in a substantial house with views across the notoriously tempestuous Irish Sea. Shipwrecks and subsequent drownings were a common occurrence on the island's shores and it is certain that Sir William Hillary witnessed many of them, and indeed took part in rescue attempts to try and save beleaguered crews.

His self-imposed retirement gave Sir William time to think, and those thoughts continually returned to the business of rescue at sea. In 1773, two years after Sir William had been born, a paper had been written by the harbour authorities in Liverpool and an institution formed. This was given the curious title 'The Liverpool Institution for Recovering Drowned Persons'.

At about the same time a rescue boat station is thought to have been established at the entrance of the River Mersey just south of the town of Formby, in Lancashire. Fifty years later, across the water in his large house at Douglas, Sir William Hillary was having more positive thoughts. He was not pondering on how to recover drowned persons but how to recover shipwrecked persons before they drowned.

In 1823 he set off for London. Once there, he wrote an appeal to the nation for the foundation of a national co-ordinated lifeboat service. He made good use of the friends that he had made during his more affluent days to help promulgate his paper which he cleverly and thoughtfully dedicated to the King, George IV.

Among those he lobbied was Thomas Wilson, the Member of Parliament for the City of London, who called a meeting of some of the most influential people in the land on 12 February 1824. Sir William's propositions were greeted with enthusiasm and a further meeting was called for at the same venue three weeks later.

During that brief interim period, George IV had agreed to become Patron and the Prime Minister, Lord Liverpool, President. Those attending the second meeting, where the official title for the Institution was agreed, read like a large slice of the best parts of a copy of 'Who's Who' of the day. The Archbishop of Canterbury, Dr Manners Sutton, took the chair and such names as Sir William Wilberforce, Sir Robert Peel, the Chairman of Lloyds, the Governor of the Bank of England and a host of bishops and royal peers attended.

At a pace that was surprising in view of the slow communications systems of the time, The National Institution for the Preservation of Life from Shipwreck was formed on 4 March 1824. As is the case with the Royal National Lifeboat Institution today, it was to be supported by donations and subscriptions but it was another matter as to how the collection and distribution of funds might be managed.

The King's decision to become Patron helped the coffers of the new Institution to fill. Almost £10,000 were received within the first year of its existence, much from the City of London institutions such as Trinity House, who managed the lights and pilotage around the British coasts, and Lloyds, then and now, the world's leading marine insurance underwriters.

The Shipwreck Institution, as it quickly became known, perhaps unfortunately, became the catalyst for those far-flung places where some form of rescue service had been developed on a local level. Among these was the fortress town of Bamburgh on the coast of Northumberland.

The Bamburgh Connection, as it

might be called, began before the start of the nineteenth century. The Third Baron Crewe of Stene, Bishop of Durham, married the daughter of Sir William Forster of Bamburgh in 1700. The venerable gentleman was 67 years old and his bride 24. There were no children of this pacific union and because of this, great benefit was to fall upon the local people and particularly shipwrecked sailors and the orphans of those lost at sea in the environs of Bamburgh.

The life of the Bishop was as much one of trauma and excitement as that of Sir William Hillary. He was a Privy Councillor to Charles II and suffered exclusion from Court due to his apparent allegiance to King James II, but was later pardoned. Not so lucky his uncle by marriage, General Thomas Forster, who had forfeited his properties at Bamburgh to the Crown after his activities on behalf of the Jacobites.

They were taken from him, but the wily old Baron Crewe was no slouch and he with his new bride bought them from the Crown for £20,679 in 1704. He died in 1721, leaving his monies and estates to local charitable causes. There is no mention as to what happened to his young wife.

The trust was managed by Archdeacon John Sharp of Durham who had aspirations towards seafaring people and their wellbeing. Sharp soon realized the need for some type of lifesaving organization on the bleak wild north-east coast. There were already similar activities afoot at South Shields but this notwithstanding, Sharp acquired a coble,[1] a local type of fishing boat, and sent it overland to London for evaluation and conversion to a safety boat by coachbuilder Lionel Lukin. He did this at his own expense in 1786, a curious move when one considers the number of expert

Coble-type fishing boats on the beach at Cromer, Norfolk, home of the illustrious Henry Blogg.

boatbuilders on the coasts of Northumberland, Durham and North-east Yorkshire.

*****

[1] The coble is a traditional open boat of the area, still built in yards along the north-east coast, often by the old methods of adze and longsaw. Local people say that the design is still based on that of the old Viking ships of the Norsemen. This may well be so.

The coble has the high rounded prow of the traditional concept of the Viking ship but at the stern is a truncated version of the shape, cut flat with a steep transom — just as if someone had cut off the stern of a Viking vessel about three quarters of the way aft and filled the gap with planking. Many of these craft, of ancient design handed down from father to son, are used for in-shore fishing off the north-east coast. They are superb seaboats and many inshore fishermen would have no other. The coble became the basis of the design of various types of lifeboats right through to modern times, although the word 'design' in the early days of lifeboats is somewhat presumptive as the 'design' of the boats was passed down through generations by word of mouth and training. Even today many boats are built by shipwrights using measure of eye and in-built experience to cut planking and bend frames with not so much as a drawn sketch in sight.

Lukin converted the boat with the idea of saving life at the top of his list of priorities, and it was on station at Bamburgh in 1787. A signal system was evolved at Bamburgh Castle and look-outs rode the coast on horses in bad weather watching for shipwrecks. In the event of a ship in trouble being sighted, the castle would be alerted and a nine pounder gun fired from the ramparts to alert the villagers and

those from the local fishing fleet to prepare the lifeboat for sea.[2]

Once the boat left the harbour the women of the town would prepare special accommodation in the castle in which to shelter survivors and, if need be, see to their medical needs.

Apart from the work of Londoner Lionel Lukin at his southern coachworks and his efforts working successfully at Bamburgh, there were two inventors and designers at South Shields who had considerable influence on the future designs of lifeboats.

*****

[2] This tradition, a gun or maroon being fired, has been a tradition of the lifeboat service ever since, although in the 1990's this signalling system to summon the crew has been replaced in many instances by personal electronic pagers or 'bleepers', as used by doctors. However, the maroons are still fired at lifeboat stations on 'Open Days' to amuse the visitors and upset the local fraternity of seagulls.

Henry Greathead and William Wouldhave were based in the centre of what might be described as coble country and their designs were very much influenced by the shape of this craft. But in spite of their expertise, Greathead was bankrupt even before the new Institution was formed, although he had supplied boats for rescue stations being established by Trinity House and in August 1810 delivered a boat, to be powered by

Bamburgh Castle, Northumberland.

twenty oars, to Trinity House for use at Spurn Head, at the mouth of the Humber. The boat cost £200 but the same year Greathead was declared bankrupt, though he later regained solvency.

It was in 1838, fifty years after Lukin's work and fourteen years after the Institution had been founded that Grace Darling and her father, William, put out from the Longstone lighthouse on the Farne Islands close to Bamburgh when the coastal steamer *Forfarshire* ran onto the nearby Big Harcar rocks. The story of Grace Darling's heroism was built up to proportions that certainly embarrassed the girl and has become the subject of several books. While there is not the slightest doubt that she was indeed a heroine of her time, her father was equally, if not more, heroic. William Darling, employed by Trinity House as the keeper of the Longstone light, was married to the sister of Job Horsley, a gardener at Bamburgh Castle owned by the trust set up by Dr John Sharp on the part of Baron Crewe, while one of Grace's brothers, William Brooks Darling, was aboard a rescue boat that had put out from South Shields to join the rescue. In that corner of Britain, as in others at about the same time, the business of saving lives at sea was becoming a family affair.

The efforts of the Darling family, particularly young Grace, became folklore almost before the real story of the rescue had been told. Whatever else, it was a great boost to the aspirations of the founders of the Royal National Lifeboat Institution as we know it today.

The *Forfarshire*, a 360 ton topsail schooner, was on passage from Dundee to Hull with passengers and a cargo of freight. William Darling, his wife, Thomasin, and their daughter, Grace, were ready for bad weather at their remote outpost. At nightfall on 6 September 1838, William and his daughter secured their boat and equipment as best they could and prepared for the worst.

At first light next day, Grace saw through a telescope what appeared to be a wreck on the Big Harcar rocks with people apparently still alive aboard. Mother helped launch their coble, and father and daughter set out through fearsome seas towards the wreck. It was only 1,000 yards from the lighthouse, but they had to row the heavy boat much further. William Darling managed to scramble onto the Big Harcar rocks to survey the scene and organize those aboard the wreck. Grace, only 5 feet in height, was left to handle the boat.

William Darling decided that two trips back to the lighthouse would be needed to take off the survivors and dead. While Grace helped those rescued into the boat, Darling put two

Grace Darling and her father rowing to the wreck of the Forfarshire, *1838.*

or three others onto the oars to row back to Longstone.

Among those saved on the first attempt were a Mrs Dawson who lost two children, and several injured. William Darling left his daughter and wife at Longstone to tend the injured as best they could in the cramped conditions of the lighthouse and made his way back, helped by two survivors, where he picked up those remaining alive. The coble from North Sunderland, with William Robson as coxswain and William Brooks Darling in the crew, collected bodies offshore and returned to Longstone with their sad cargo. The master of the *Forfarshire*, Captain Humble, and his wife had been swept overboard during the stranding and drowned. In total there were nine survivors.

Four years later, possibly as a result of the effects of what might be called today 'media over-exposure', the quiet Northumbrian girl was dead from 'consumption'. Every artist, poet and romanticist had already written her epitaph.

Once the news of the efforts of the Darling family reached London and other populated areas of Britain euphoria was rife. Today William Darling might well have been awarded the George Cross. As it was, the young Queen Victoria, younger than Grace Darling, sent £50 in bounty money while the Royal Humane Society gave them gold medals and the Shipwreck Institution awarded them newly-established silver medals even though neither were part of the Institute's rescue organization. William Wordsworth, then poet laureate, wrote a verse which must have confused the straightforward Northumbrians and pleased the new Victorians:

Together they put forth, Father and Child.
Each grasps an oar and struggling on they go,
Rivals in effort, and alike intent.
Here to elude and there surmount, they watch
The billows lengthening, mutually crossed
And shattered, and regathering their might;
As if the tumult, by Almighty's will

Were, in the conscious sea, roused and prolonged.
That woman's fortitude, so tried, so proved
May brighten more and more.

The efforts to save those aboard *Forfarshire*, most of whom drowned or died on the rocks from cold and exposure, drew the attention of the local laird, the Duke of Northumberland, at his castle in nearby Alnwick, to the needs of the Institution.

During the mid-nineteenth century communications outside the larger areas of population were slow. A medal system of awards was instigated by Sir William Hillary, who won two for rescues he performed himself off the coast of the Isle of Man. Medals are even today a vital recognition of effort in the Royal National Lifeboat Institution and are often found hanging in pride of place in the homes of crew members, in local museums and even harbourside bars, but medals and awards of money have never been the reason that the lifeboatmen have put to sea.

A dour Scottish lifeboat crewman, who preferred to remain nameless, said it all: "One life saved is worth more than one hundred medals, gold or whatever."

It is often the case that charitable ideas are launched amid a wealth of enthusiasm which then falters once the initial concentrated energy is dispersed.

Funds were dwindling and not being recovered by subscriptions or donations. There were lean years between 1841 and 1850 during which time, in 1847, Sir William Hillary died, the holder of three gold medals for gallantry and the respect and affection of a wide and extremely varied cross section of the British population from royalty and peers of the realm to more humble fisherfolk.

In 1850 a young lawyer, Richard Lewis, was appointed secretary to the Shipwreck Institution at about the same time as the retirement as Chairman of Thomas Wilson who had been at the helm of the Institution since its conception.

A year after his appointment as secretary, Lewis decided to approach the Duke of Northumberland, who had served with distinction in the Royal Navy reaching flag rank, to ask him to take the position of President of the Institution. The Duke, known as the Sailor Duke because of his exploits against the French, accepted. A revival in enthusiasm ensued for the Institution, which was now being confused in some public minds with the recently-established Shipwrecked Fishermen and Mariners Royal Benevolent Society. Apart from providing help for the families of lost sailors, the Society also established several rescue boat stations, but while there was a conflict of identity there was no enmity between the two organizations. Indeed, in the years ahead the Institution was to take over the management and financing of the Society's boats.

The Sailor Duke set about a plan to rationalize the design of lifeboats by offering a prize of 100 guineas for the best model of a lifeboat design, to be judged by a special committee of marine experts, and a further prize of 100 guineas to the selected builder of the winning entry. An amazing 280 models were received at Somerset House, a section of the building having been loaned by the Admiralty for the purpose. The judging committee set about their task of evaluation which lasted six months.

James Beeching of Great Yarmouth, Norfolk, won the Duke's prize having obtained 84 out of a possible 100 points for his ideas. He was also the obvious choice to build a boat to the plans of his model and thus collected the second award.

When the Duke of Northumberland took over the active presidency of the Institution there were ninety-six rescue boats on the coast of Britain, many run by local organizations and more than half considered unsuited to their

intended task by the Institution. James Beeching completed the building of his prize-winning boat and it was put on station by the Institution at Ramsgate. She was the first ever self-righting boat and served her purpose well, the local crew saving many lives in the approaches to the Thames and the seas off the Forelands.

While Beeching's boat was a success other boats also made their mark. Among these were the designs from Henry Hinks of Appledore, North Devon, and Pellew Plenty of Newbury. The builders at T and J Whites' shipyard at Cowes also won acclaim but not quite at the top of the prize-winners list. We shall hear more of the famous Cowes yard later, as well as the association that developed between the town of Cowes and the subsequently-named Royal National Lifeboat Institution over a century later.

In spite of Beeching's success the committee of the Institute, particularly those involved in the selection of the winning design, thought that there was still scope for improvement. One of the competition judges, James Peake, was asked to take another look at the more successful models submitted in the competition and prepare plans for a boat incorporating the best attributes from each one. James Peake's final design was built at Woolwich in 1851-2 and sent for trials off Brighton in February 1852 where the spectators included the Duke of Northumberland and James Beeching.

The Duke of Northumberland must have been impressed because he ordered three of Peake's boats to be placed at stations on the coast of Northumberland, his home territory, in addition to the Beeching boat that he had already ordered. Whether the arrival of boats from the south was popular with the local people who manned them is not recorded, but some years earlier Lionel Lukin had observed that a boat suitable on one station might not be suitable on another where sea conditions and depths might be different.

In fact, the Duke advised the designers of lifeboats to visit the area for which the boat might be intended and see the type of craft used by local fishermen. Methods of launching would, of course vary from place to place which could influence the design of the boat, particularly in respect of weight and draft.

Curious as it might seem one of the most prolific builders of lifeboats for coastal use was the yard of J and E Pellew of Newbury, Berkshire, about as far from the coast as it is possible to be in southern England. Called the Pellew 'Plenty' class, it was a combination in design of inland river craft and lifeboats that the yard was commissioned to build for the Admiralty.

A number of 'Plenty' class boats were built at the cost of £160 each and two were very successfully operated out of ports as varied and far apart as Skegness and Appledore, the latter right on the doorstep of the Hinks yard.

Two army officers, Henry Richardson and his son Henry Thomas, had submitted designs from Bala in North Wales which were rejected in the competition but built anyway. One was sold to the Portuguese port of Oporto to replace an early Greathead boat, given to the port early in the century by the then Duke of Northumberland, grandfather of the Sailor Duke. This reflects the strong associations of the time between Britain and Portugal.

The Richardsons then built another boat in Manchester which they sailed round the coast from the port of Liverpool to Ramsgate, taking eight weeks in the early summer months. Two more boats were stationed at Rhyl and New Brighton but the design never drew much favour elsewhere although the Rhyl boat did good service on the station for forty years.

In 1852 the first issue of the journal 'Lifeboat' appeared at the cover price of $1\frac{1}{2}$d. Also in that year Captain John

Ross Ward was appointed Inspector of Lifeboats. He was to design the cork lifejackets that were to serve lifeboatmen so well for many years and be adapted and adopted by the merchant fleets.

During the 1850's the Institution had 70 lifeboats under its control around the coast including seven operated by the Norfolk Association. These were later signed over to the RNLI.

In 1854 the Government, through the Board of Trade, offered financial assistance with the payment of coxswains and the volunteer crews when they put to sea. This assistance continued until 1869 when the Institution became entirely self-financing through donations and appeals.

Although it was never announced publicly, there was a feeling in the Institution that government involvement gave the authorities an opportunity to dictate standards of design and construction of boats and equipment even though the Institution's own standards far exceeded the demands of either the Board of Trade or Lloyds of London. Among those wary of government involvement were the Elder Brethren of Trinity House whose organization had given staunch financial support to the Institution. Their services ran closely with those of the Institute and, indeed, they often depended upon each other. Many locally-managed lifeboat organizations had operated quite satisfactorily without government help and resented the fact that part of the offer of finance from the Board of Trade was coupled with an insistence that each local committee had a representative of the Board on it.

In 1854, the National Institution for the Preservation of Life from Shipwreck changed its name to the Royal National Lifeboat Institution, by which we know it today to avoid confusion with the Shipwrecked Fishermen and Mariners Royal Benevolent Society, which promptly handed over its nine boats and stations to the RNLI. Six years later Queen Victoria authorized the Charter of Incorporation which was published in full in the 'Lifeboat' journal.

By 1865 the RNLI was running 144 boats but there were still many locally-managed stations, particularly in Scotland, Ireland and the Isle of Man where the boats were in a sorry state of repair, some totally decayed and unfit for service. Gradually stations such as these were gathered under the RNLI wing but some held out independently until the 1890's.

Whitby had successfully run two lifeboat stations from its own resources from 1802 until 1861. In February 1861, a severe storm hit the East coast and the lifeboat was called out several times to attend to ships in distress outside the port. Coxswain James Storr took the boat out half a dozen times returning to port with survivors on each occasion but on his final return the boat was overwhelmed and the entire crew, save for Henry Freeman, lost.

Whitby, along with the rest of the nation, was stunned. Considering their situation the Whitby Lifeboat Association decided to become part of the RNLI, a move very much welcomed by the Institution's committee who, by the following April, only two months after the tragedy, had sent a new 32 foot self-righting boat to the port. Henry Freeman became coxswain.

Sadly, in the early days, it took tragedy to achieve unity as well as sudden surges of funds to the Institution's finances. This situation is the same in modern times; the public, who donate at a generous rate from year to year, increase in their giving when a lifeboat is lost. Until recently the RNLI was one of the few organizations that, without special appeals, received donations after accidents. Now almost every disaster seems to attract its appeal fund.

Captain John Ross Ward and lawyer Richard Lewis were a strong team, and it was the lawyer, rather than the

Henry Freeman, coxswain of the Whitby lifeboat and, prior to this appointment, sole survivor of the disaster in 1861 when the lifeboat was overwhelmed outside Whitby harbour after successfully completing a number of calls to fishing boats.

seafarer, who wrote an important work entitled, 'The History of the Lifeboat and its Work' which was published in 1874 to coincide with the fiftieth anniversary of the Royal National Lifeboat Institution. Many rescues and wrecks were described by written word and engravings, while in the appendices rules were laid down as to the formations of local committees, crews and helpers.

Committees were to consist, where possible, of five local people as well as the local area Coastguard Commander or even the local Coastguard Officer. Crews were to consist of a senior coxswain, an assistant coxswain, a bowman and, again if the local population of seafarers was large enough, at least twice as many oarsmen as were needed to pull the boats to ensure that there were always fully-manned boats in times of need.

The rules stipulated that the safety of the crew and those saved was the sole responsibility of the coxswain. There were also recommendations on the towing of lifeboats to the areas of a wreck. There was a period when on several stations where steam tugs were available, lifeboats would be towed out to sea when the seas were too severe for either oars or sail but this idea almost met disaster off Ramsgate when a towing tug was itself almost overcome. Liverpool was one port where tugs were often used, particularly when wrecks were well offshore and into prevailing westerly gales.

Salvage of life and property was also covered in the work of Richard Lewis. The proposals that he made still hold good today and it is the exception rather than the rule where the Royal National Lifeboat Institution crews claim salvage. They are paid a modest sum for putting to sea, but, if after effecting a rescue that saves not only life but also a vessel or vessel and cargo, the first job of a lifeboat crew was, and still is, to save life.

The era that was to see the end of the rowed and sailed boats was on the horizon. In 1883, the RNLI received a donation of £600 from the International Fisheries Exhibition which was to be used, as with the Sailor Duke's earlier prize, for the best lifeboat design that might replace the designs of Greathead, Beeching, Peake, the Richardsons and others.

Three judges appointed by the Committee of Management were Sir Frederick Bramwell, Sir Digby Murray from the Board of Trade and John Thornycroft. The name Thornycroft was to have long associations with the RNLI. Sadly, no design came up to the specifications demanded by the judges but in 1888, J and F Green of Blackwall, on the Thames, made proposals and a model of a

mechanically-propelled lifeboat incorporating the needs and ideas of the Committee of Management as well as those of their own experts. The design was accepted and in 1889 the first steam lifeboat was on station at Harwich. She was later moved to Holyhead, Anglesey, and then to New Brighton, on the north end of the Birkenhead peninsula at the entrance to the River Mersey. During operations the boat was launched more than forty times and fifty-six lives saved as well as five ships. Two more steam lifeboats were commissioned in 1894 following the successful evaluation and work of the prototype.

Most power-driven vessels had, until this time, been powered by paddle wheels but the propeller was now taking over and the internal combustion engine, as opposed to steam power, was not far away; though it would be some time before it could survive the demands and meet the requirements of the lifeboatmen.

The early boats were, of course, powered primarily by oars and used sail as a secondary method of propulsion. Though rigged fore and aft like a primitive version of the modern sailing boat, the sails were only efficient with the wind abeam or aft of the beam. Recommendations were that sail was not to be used when working close inshore, in breaking seas or when close to wrecks during the process of lifesaving. Mechanical power was obviously going to make the work of the lifeboatmen easier — if 'easy' is ever a word to be associated with their task.

The problems facing the early experimenters in power were those of transferring the steam into a driving force. Paddlewheels, already in use in many vessels in the late nineteenth century were not practical for a rescue boat as it was feared that the paddlewheels would be a hazard during rescues while a propeller would be at risk from floating debris. Thus, imaginatively, the first turbine drive

Launching the lifeboat from the beach at Cullercoats, north of Tynemouth during the 19th century. The station now operates a C class inflatable during summer months only while there is an Arun class lifeboat, George and Olive Turner, *based at Tynemouth two miles to the south.*

was invented and fitted to the first of the powered lifeboats from J and F Green's yard, named *Duke of Northumberland*. She was a hefty 50 foot steel vessel, could attain almost 10 knots under full power and was propelled by water being ejected through underwater ducts by powerful pumps. On trials at Harwich and later working off Holyhead and New Brighton it was shown how she could tow an older oar and sail-driven boat to the scene of a disaster and assist in operations. The engine was built by Thornycroft. The second steam lifeboat, *City of Glasgow*, also built at Blackwall, was slightly larger than the first and more powerful. The turbine pumping system doubled up as a bilge pump, using any water that entered the hull as a source of power while keeping the

boat dry within. This second boat could carry four tons of coal and half a ton of fresh water. These boats needed almost half an hour to raise sufficient steam to proceed from cold, although if bad weather threatened and the possibility of shipwreck was suggested then the boiler could be flashed-up in readiness for operations.

As a precaution against disaster at sea the RNLI had placed aneroid barometers at all lifeboat stations operated by them for some years. These, alongside up-to-date tidal information, made local seafarers more aware of forthcoming weather conditions. The next improvement to weather awareness of seamen was the issue by the RNLI of barometers to many coastal trading vessels and fishing boats. Even today, in spite of regularly-broadcast shipping forecasts on national, local and maritime radio programmes, lifeboat stations still display this information.

The third powered lifeboat, bigger than the first two and named *Queen* to commemorate the jubilee of Queen Victoria, was built by Thornycroft's yard. It replaced the *Duke of Northumberland* at the New Brighton station, the older boat being moved to Holyhead. It is an indication of the innovative qualities of the Committee of Management of the RNLI that the *Queen* was powered by both coal and oil.

Railway engineers from the Great Western Railway helped with trials of this new idea where the furnace was initially fired-up with coal and then oil, propelled by compressed air, was sprayed into the furnace. It worked, but for a number of varied reasons was not installed in other boats. Meanwhile, the RNLI was busy experimenting with propeller drive and in 1899 commissioned the yard of J Samuel White, at East Cowes, to build two prototype propeller-drive lifeboats. These boats, 56 foot 6 inches long, were twin screwed and like the turbine hydraulic driven boats, had two fore and aft tunnels not, in the case of the new boats, to direct the hydraulic water jets, but to protect the propellers from damage by wreckage and prevent injuries to people in the water who might be being rescued.

The boats, *James Stevens No. 3 and No. 4*, were sent to Grimsby and Padstow respectively, the former later being moved to Gorleston. Sadly, in 1900, the *No. 4* was capsized and wrecked off the Cornish coast during a storm and eight of her crew lost. The boat was replaced by a sailing lifeboat and a 200 ton twin screw tug was also placed at the Padstow station to take the lifeboat to sea off one of the least hospitable coasts of Britain. The RNLI committee released £1,000 to help the families of those lost. During the recent years, the funds of the Institution had

been steadily improving, just as the costs of building and maintaining boats and stations had been increasing.

The final twenty years of the nineteenth century saw changes. Richard Lewis died in 1883 after thirty-three years work with the RNLI as secretary. He was succeeded by Charles Dibdin, formerly employed by the Post Office and founder of the Civil Service Lifeboat Fund. John Ross Ward, now a retired Vice Admiral resigned his position as Inspector of Lifeboats. Dibdin's energy and enthusiasm that had driven the Civil Service Fund was to now directly benefit the RNLI while he continued the work of Lewis in the direction of the actual operations of the service. He laid down that the crews of boats should exercise fully manned at least four times a year and that one such exercise each year should be carried out at night.

While Dibdin was making his presence usefully felt at the Institution's headquarters in London, in the north a Scotsman, Charles Macara, was involving himself in the lifeboat service at his adopted home town of St Annes-on-Sea at the entrance of the River Ribble in Lancashire. He enjoyed the company of the local fishermen as a relaxing alternative to the people who he met through his business as a cotton trade industrialist and would occasionally put to sea with them on exercises aboard the local lifeboat, one of three stationed at the Ribble Estuary. He became Chairman of the local RNLI committee.

Early in December 1886, a coaster ran aground off the Ribble Estuary and the boat put out to rescue the crew of five watched by most of the small population from ashore. Later that evening the lifeboat crew, Charles Macara and those saved attended a musical evening.

A few days after the rescue of the coaster crew, a German merchant ship, the *Mexico*, went aground in very severe weather on shoals between Southport and the town of Formby, seven miles to the south towards the Mersey. Three boats were called out in darkness; the boat from Southport, which had to be manhandled for several miles along the coast before it was possible to launch her in a free wind, the St Anne's boat and a brand new boat, not used before, from nearby Lytham.

After four hours, the Southport boat reached the wreck but was overwhelmed and capsized with the loss of thirteen of her fifteen man crew. The St Anne's boat made for the wreck under oars and then sail. Nothing was seen of her again until next morning when the boat was found capsized and washed ashore with three bodies still attached to it. Eleven more bodies were later recovered from the south shore of the Ribble Estuary. The Lytham boat managed to rescue twelve of the merchant ship's crew and made the shore safely.

Macara immediately became Chairman of the St Anne's Lifeboat Disaster Committee and was galvanized into action by the enormity of the tragedy — as was the entire nation. The loss of the two lifeboats left sixteen widows and fifty orphaned children. Money and sympathy flooded in from every quarter including the Emperor of Germany and the City of Hamburg where the *Mexico* was registered. The RNLI immediately donated £2,000 while a donor from Rochdale gave the money to buy a new boat for St Anne's. Another donor paid for a new boat for Southport. This may have been Macara himself, but the donation was anonymous and remained so.

Chapter 2

THE ENQUIRY

During the latter half of the 1890s there had been reports in the press and words spoken elsewhere casting doubts on the integrity of the management committee of the RNLI. Generally, even generously, the press had been helpful and sympathetic towards the RNLI, particularly in the regions of fund-raising and reports on rescues performed.

Matters came to a head when a Mr E Bayley, a former London Member of Parliament who was also a coachbuilder who had tendered to build carriages for lifeboat transport at various beach stations, tried to bribe an RNLI inspector to pass his shoddy work as being to the required standards of the RNLI. The matter was reported back to the management committee who obviously rejected his work out of hand.

Thick-skinned and verbose, Bayley set out on a campaign of malice towards every aspect of the RNLI from the honesty of the management committee to the standards of crew expertise and the suitability and standards of boats. He accused crewmen of being guilty of plundering wrecks (which was found to be the case, but not by Bayley) and said money from disaster funds was being misplaced and mis-spent. He submitted articles to the press and various journals, gave lectures and generally spread a trail of unpleasant and inaccurate accusations among the minds of those who may not have known as much about the RNLI as those who were directly involved in it.

Alarmed by the effect Bayley's rantings might have on the fund-raising and running of the RNLI, the management committee requested a Parliamentary inquiry into their entire activities. In March 1897 a select committee comprising fifteen specially chosen members, and headed by C J Darling QC, was approved. Twenty-five sittings were held, fifty witnesses called and an incredible 11,864 questions asked of the witnesses.

Certainly there were other critics apart from Bayley. Among them was a reluctant Colonel H M Hozier, secretary of the committee of Lloyds who had some differing thoughts on matters to do with salvage. The RNLI's own rules on the matter were found to be completely adequate. Where crews had, on few occasions, broken them or helped themselves to salvage they had been adequately reprimanded. One or two had been dismissed.

Surprisingly, perhaps, one critical witness was Charles Macara, but his complaint was based on the fact that many of his ideas, born in the north-west, had been taken over by the London-based administration on a national basis thus wresting the management of these activities out of his control.

Mr Bayley's suggestion that the work of the RNLI should be handed over completely to government management was rejected as was almost every other criticism. A massive report on the hearing, running to over a thousand pages giving every smallest detail, was written, edited and printed for distribution to those concerned within a month of the select committee ending their work. The RNLI was totally vindicated.

Bayley was extremely lucky not to have ended the proceedings with a number of libel writs being handed to him, but the RNLI was satisfied enough to have their work clear of accusation and recrimination without dragging matters further through the courts and thus the media. Given a clean bill of health by independent investigators, the job in hand of raising funds to support those who risked their lives to save lives at sea was set about with renewed vigour and enthusiasm.

The public were greatly reassured by the very positive outcome of the inquiry. More local committees were formed, more boats put on new stations and old boats powered by oars and sail replaced by more modern designs powered by motors, almost all self-righting.

Chapter 3

TOWARDS WAR

The RNLI entered the twentieth century in good health financially, its reputation and that of its management completely acceptable to the British public at all social levels and development proceeding apace. The years between 1900 and the beginning of the First World War, in 1914, were to be busy times.

The Duke of Northumberland, President since 1866, died early in 1899 and the Prince of Wales took over the Presidency having been involved with the running of the RNLI for thirty years. However, in 1901 he succeeded Queen Victoria, so once more a change occurred at the top, this time the Duke of York, who, on the succession of Edward VII, became Prince of Wales and also RNLI President, a popular appointment as he was a professional officer in the Royal Navy.

Earlier, in 1887, a lifeboat designed by the Scottish architect G L Watson, had entered service and later Mr Watson was appointed Consulting Naval Architect to the RNLI. The name of G L Watson is well known for his designs of private yachts, many of which still survive. Sadly, Watson died in 1904 at the age of fifty-three, but his work for the RNLI was to survive and his honorary post passed to his partner, Mr J R Barnett. Barnett took up the business of providing an engine, an alternative to steam, that might at least work as an auxiliary to oar and sail power.

The internal combustion engine was developing rapidly, though there were thoughts at the RNLI that while these engines were safe enough on land where failure simply lead to a dead stop, the same could not be said for an engine at use at sea, especially in the severe conditions that lifeboats, in particular, had to face. Many early engines were supplied with petrol by gravity. Efficient fuel pumps were available but cars were still having to be driven backwards up steep hills in order to allow fuel to flow from the tank at the back to the engine in the front. Electric ignition systems were also fairly primitive while starting by crank handle was the rule rather than the exception.

Experts in the waterproofing of machinery and engine designers were consulted to provide a new lifeboat engine. Specifications were severe and taxed the experts. The engine had to be waterproof, be able to run without supervision, not affect the self-righting abilities of the boat and be self-lubricating. Several engines were submitted for test. The lifeboat *J McConnel Hussy* was fitted with a two stroke engine from Fay and Bowen and trials were carried out at Folkestone.

The trials were successful, including self-righting, and the boat was despatched to Tynemouth, Northumberland, but local boatmen wanted nothing to do with the new powered boat. Captain H E Burton, who was head of the local RNLI committee, took over the boat and, with a crew formed by local militia, took her to sea to effect a successful rescue while the local seamen stayed ashore.

There were several engine manufacturers involved in the trials, some engine names surviving, some not. A Thornycroft engine was fitted to the Newhaven boat, a Blake engine fitted to the Walton-on-the-Naze boat and a Tylor engine powered the Ramsgate lifeboat. Sail and oars were still carried in the boats and still used. As a result of trials between 1905 and 1906 a boat was being specially planned for the Stromness station in the Orkneys. She was a 42 foot self-righting boat with a Tylor engine. A second boat, to the Watson design, was ordered for another Orkney station, Stronsay, while a third lifeboat, not powered by engine but reliant on oars and sail, was to be stationed at Thurso on Scotland's north mainland coast. All arrived safely, having made the voyage in company, but not without incident during the seventeen days it took for the journey. The voyage, where the powered boats helped one another and often towed the sailing vessel, was interrupted by harbour stops and headwinds.

This delivery of boats to stations by the crews who would serve in them started a precedent that operates today. In the earlier years lifeboats were transported. free by railways. As boats became larger and heavier this became less practical.

By the end of 1912 there were seventeen motorized lifeboats on station. The boats were mainly of the Watson type powered by Tylor engines of varying power depending upon the size of boat. At about this time the Thomas Ironworks Yard, on the Thames, closed because of financial problems. The Thomas Yard had built most of the new boats so the management committee now had to look elsewhere for an alternative yard. It was a sad blow because the Thames boatbuilders had been dedicated in their work for the RNLI.

The committee selected the yard of S E Saunders at Cowes for future boatbuildings, the yard being the forerunner of Saunders Roe, the aircraft and hovercraft builders. The change was to strengthen links between Cowes and the RNLI which have lasted to this day. It was at Cowes that in 1913 King George V put to sea in a newly-built boat, the *Frederick Kitchen* destined for the Beaumaris station on the Isle of Anglesey.

The First World War began on 4 August 1914. On the same day a new self-righting lifeboat was put on station at Fraserburgh, powered by a Tylor engine and financed by the Countess Rothes, who named the boat *Lady Rothes* after her daughter who survived the sinking of the liner *Titanic* two years earlier. In fact the Countess had been a passenger in the liner and after the sinking had taken command of a lifeboat. She was at the helm for eight hours before being rescued by the ship *Carpathia* which had been in the area at the time of the disaster. Within days of the boat being handed over to the RNLI at Fraserburgh, on the coast of Aberdeenshire, the boat was at work rescuing the crew of a Belfast coaster sunk by enemy submarine fifteen miles offshore in the North Sea.

The war was to produce difficult times for the RNLI in many ways ranging from a drain on financial resources to crews required to man lifeboats. Fund-raising for anything other than matters directly connected with the war effort was abandoned. Many local committee members, coxswains and crews were called-up into the armed forces. The Coastguard service was virtually withdrawn and their work, particularly as coastal lookouts, was taken over by the Boy Scouts.

On a purely practical front, the coasts were rendered even more dangerous than before when all navigational aids were removed where possible and lights extinguished, whilst coastal channels were sown with defensive minefields.

Chapter 4

RESCUE AT WAR

Fortunately the financial coffers were in a healthy state when war began, most of the lifeboats and stations in full operational condition and a majority of the lifeboats reasonably modern. As the younger members of the lifeboat crews were enlisted in the armed forces older people from local coastal communities replaced them, often being trained to their tasks by those of the crews who were able to stay. The recruitment of non-seafaring men in the lifeboat service was a gradual business, but has continued to this day. While at most stations the crews are made up from local boatmen there are often people to be found among them who come from other walks of life. Office workers, policemen and others, who may have experience of the sea from time spent sailing their own private yachts, dinghies and powerboats, are to be found among the crews.

In 1914 one of the first rescues of the First World War took place at Whitby, Yorkshire, when a 7,400 ton ship with 299 passengers and crew aboard ran onto rocks near the town. The ship, struck by a tremendous gale from the south-east, was on passage from the River Forth to Dunkirk. Among the passengers were five nurses on their way to the Western front.

There were two lifeboats at Whitby, the senior coxswain being Thomas Langlands who had originally come from Bamburgh. It was soon realized that it would be impossible to launch the first lifeboat, powered by oars and sails, into the ferocious winds and seas but the second boat was moored in Whitby Lower Harbour.

The wreck of the Rohilla *at Whitby October 1914.*

The stranded ship, the *Rohilla*, was stuck fast on the off-lying rocks and directly to windward of Whitby. Langlands decided that the only way to reach the ship was to take the workable lifeboat on a sledge of skids to the cliff top.

A mass of local people turned out to help and the lifeboat was hauled along the cliff tops and then lowered down the cliff to the sea. The lifeboat was damaged during this effort but Langlands decided to attempt a rescue. He and his brave crew, watched by most of the local population, battled their way out to the ship not once, but twice.

On the first rescue attempt they took off seventeen people including the nursing sisters. Eighteen more were saved on the second attempt but the lifeboat was by now too badly damaged to make any more bids for survivors. Another lifeboat, from Upgang along the coast to the north-west of Whitby, was by now being brought by horse-drawn trailer to the cliff top and this too was lowered down the cliff face but the weather was by now too rough for the crew to be able to reach the ship. Next morning they launched the boat but were driven back by the seas while a number of those on board jumped into the sea. Some drowned and others managed to be plucked from the breaking seas by those ashore who ran through the surf to their aid.

Another lifeboat had put out from Teesmouth to the north-west and one from Scarborough to the south. They reached the scene that evening but were not able to reach the wreck. In fact the Teesmouth boat, towed by a tug, was holed and almost sank during the passage to Whitby but made it safely back to Teesmouth half-submerged.

Thomas Langlands had managed to put to sea in Whitby's number one boat but not even he, with his knowledge, was able to reach the *Rohilla*. A request for help had been sent by telegram to the Tynemouth station where a motor-powered lifeboat was based. Her crew put to sea under the command of Coxswain Robert Smith with Captain H E Burton, the believer in the powered lifeboat that first went to the area, aboard.

The boat arrived at Whitby in darkness early in the morning of Sunday 1 November after a terrible passage, with no lights ashore to guide her. The whole community turned out to watch as the visiting boat charged towards the wreck having dropped oil into the sea in an attempt to calm it. She was rushing towards the ship from windward amid terrifying seas but was able to put alongside to take off forty of the fifty people still alive aboard the ship. A second run was made and the rest taken aboard, the last person saved being the master, wearing a greatcoat, cap and monocle.

Gold medals were later awarded to the coxswains Langlands and Smith as well as Burton, the army officer who was at the time Honorary Superintendent of the Tynemouth station. Silver medals were given to Richard Eglon, number two to Langlands in both Whitby boats, to James Brownlea, number two in the Tynemouth boat and to local Whitby man George Peart, who had led attempts to save those who had leapt from the *Rohilla* and tried to swim for the shore.

The north-east coast claimed another victim in the winter of 1914 that involved the RNLI in rescue activities. The destroyer *HMS Success* ran ashore in bad weather on a night in December. The ship came ashore just inside Fife Ness, the headland that juts out to the south-east of the Tay Estuary. Andrew Cunningham put to sea in the lifeboat based at Crail, just round the headland to the south. The seas were massive and the boat was soon damaged. Coxswain Cunningham, with a crewman, was washed overboard but recovered. In spite of these problems Cunningham made two rescue runs to the warship saving twenty men at the first attempt and a further thirty-four on the second. He then put back to Crail leaving the St Andrews lifeboat, which had reached the scene, to complete the task, saving thirteen more men.

It was at about this time that the name of Henry Blogg appeared in the lifeboat annals. Blogg had joined the Cromer lifeboat crew in 1899 and by 1909 was appointed coxswain. Cromer, on the Norfolk coast, faces one of the most dangerous areas of the North Sea, the Haisborough Sands. These are shoals as dangerous as the famous Goodwin Sands in the Straits of Dover and lie some ten miles from the shore.

The Cromer boat was an oar and sail-powered Liverpool type, launched from the beach, a difficult operation when the wind was blowing onshore, a time when most wrecks seemed to occur and when the seas are at their most treacherous.

Coxswain Blogg's notable wartime rescues included those of the crews of

Coxswain Henry Blogg of Cromer – painting by T C Dugdale.

The Cromer lifeboat Louisa Heartwell *rescuing the crew of the Swedish steamer* The Fernebo *on 9 January 1917. For this service coxswain Henry Blogg was awarded the RNLI gold medal.*

the ships *Pyrin* and the Swedish ship *Fernebo* on the same day, 9 January 1917. The *Pyrin*, a Greek vessel, was stranded on the Sands directly into the wind from Cromer. Blogg, helped by soldiers stationed in Cromer, launched the boat through breaking surf and eventually reached the coaster, saving her crew of sixteen but exhausting the lifeboatmen, many of whom were of older years due to the recruitment of the younger men of the town into the armed forces.

No sooner had the crew successfully beached their boat and safely landed the survivors than the engineroom of the Swedish ship exploded while she was off Cromer and she split in two. The exhausted lifeboat crew set out once more but were unable to row through the breaking seas towards the broken ship which had launched a small boat. This was promptly capsized but the soldiers once more rushed to help, dragging survivors from the water as they neared the beach. A Scottish soldier, Stewart Holmes, was later given the RNLI silver medal for his bravery.

Commander Basil Hall, now serving in the Royal Navy, who had taken such a gallant part in the *Rohilla* rescue, was in Cromer at the time. In the evening he gave Blogg permission to launch the lifeboat one more time in a final effort to reach the stricken ship. After oars were smashed by the seas and others swept away Blogg conceded temporary defeat, but he launched his boat once more in a final effort.

Blogg's leadership, determination and the fortitude of his exhausted crew were rewarded. They finally reached the wreck and managed to save the eleven crew who were still aboard. This was a rescue that earned the indefatigable Blogg his first gold medal. This occurred in 1916 when the pressures of war were troubling the RNLI in terms of manpower, maintenance and money. During that year their crews saved 1,300 people.

The following year the Salcombe lifeboat was called out to assist the sailing schooner *Western Lass* in

A view of the wrecks on the Haisborough Sands on the morning of 6 August 1941, showing destroyers patrolling before the arrival of the lifeboats from Cromer, Great Yarmouth and Gorleston, Lowestoft and Sheringham. The two Cromer lifeboats and the Great Yarmouth and Gorleston lifeboat rescued between them 119 lives from six shipwrecked steamers. The painting is by Dr K F Lund.

trouble off Prawle Point, the most southern headland of Devon. A crew of fifteen local men took the boat out, crossing the notorious sand bar that lies in the harbour entrance. The boat capsized while crossing the rough waters. All but two of her crew were lost.

At the end of the war, in November 1918, crewmen and other employees of the RNLI began to return to their stations, workshops and offices but many were never to return. During the war lifeboats had been launched 1,808 times, 549 times to assist vessels on service connected with the war. During the war years a total of 5,332 lives were saved from several different nations. Apart from survivors from British ships there were also Scandinavians, French and Italian seafarers rescued. During one storm alone, in November 1916, the lifeboats from Deal, Ramsgate and Kingsdown, just south of Deal, saved a total of 82 lives.

Sadly disaster befell the lifeboat *Lady Rothes* just as the war was over and Europe settling down to peace. It will be remembered that the boat had been launched and handed over to the RNLI at the Fraserburgh station on the outbreak of war. An Admiralty vessel, the *Eminent*, was seeking shelter off the north-east coast of Scotland after engine failure. Her captain anchored but the ship was swept shorewards as the anchors dragged. Answering distress signals, Coxswain Andrew Noble and his crew put to sea. The lifeboat was soon in trouble and most of the crew swept overboard but the boat self-righted, as it was designed to do. Most of the crew managed to scramble back aboard and those who could not made it ashore supported by their lifejackets. Neither the coxswain, Andrew Noble, nor the second coxswain a Mr Farquher, both men in their fifties, survived the cold and died from exposure. It was a severe blow both to the RNLI and Fraserburgh where Andrew Noble had served as senior Trinity House Pilot and senior Scottish lifeboat coxswain.

Chapter 5

100 YEARS ON

The First World War had taken its toll of the lifeboat service, as has been said, but it also produced improvements to equipment. Marine engines of the size suitable for use in lifeboats had been developed considerably during the war years to meet the demands of the Royal Navy and auxiliary services. The tank, with its caterpillar tracks, was the forerunner of the tracked launching vehicle (tractor) used to transport lifeboats from lifeboat sheds to the sea across beaches and even sand bars. The Birmingham Small Arms Company (best known, perhaps, as BSA) had perfected a gun launcher for firing lines over considerable distances.

The Chief Inspector of the RNLI, Captain Rowley, carried out trials with the first of these tractors on the Norfolk coast. The result was a near disaster. The three ton transporter carried the five ton lifeboat to the sea where the Captain gave the coxswain the order to launch. The tractor was only in two feet of water and the coxswain decided against the idea. The tide rose, floating the lifeboat off the tractor while completely covering it. Captain Rowley and his assistant were then rescued and taken ashore by the lifeboat crew aboard the lifeboat! Tractor and Inspector survived. Tractors are still in use in several beach stations today, developed from this early model.

Engines were improving in efficiency all the time. The Tylor Company, which had supplied many engines to the RNLI in the early years of powered boats, ceased to make marine engines so a new designer and builder was sought.

The company chosen was Weyburn Engineering of Godalming, which still exists in the area today. The initial engine was delayed in production when the workshops burned down, but in its centenary year the RNLI announced that Mr J Barnett, a Consultant Naval Architect, had proposed a 60 foot twin screw lifeboat to be powered by two Weyburn engines.

The prototype 76 hp engine was completed and installed in a new lifeboat bound for service at Penlee, Cornwall, where it was successfully tested and proved itself both powerful and reliable. The larger new boat was by now under construction and the two Weyburn engines installed. Sail had been reduced to just a single steadying sail on one mast. The vessel carried life nets, the new line-throwing equipment, had separate engine compartments and two covered cabins. It was completed in 1924 and stationed at New Brighton.

One reason that funds of the RNLI were dangerously low at the beginning of the 1920's, apart from the effects of war, was the lack of support from the owners of British merchant shipping companies. This may seem extraordinary in view of the fact that the merchant fleet so often depended on the efforts of the RNLI crews when their ships ran into difficulties in home waters. The RNLI Committee discussed the matter and decided to elect a Merchant Navy Master to join them. Captain G C Holloway was invited and was soon to stir up interest in the RNLI among the shipping companies.

Another inspired idea was to invite world-renowned seafarer and writer Joseph Conrad to address the 1923 annual general meeting which was chaired by Admiral of the Fleet Earl Beatty. Conrad made an inspired speech elevating the RNLI in the eyes of the ship owners. It was well publicized.

That same year included a special fund-raising day, called Prince of Wales Day after the Institute's President who was himself very active on the day, visiting many of the London collecting points where all records were broken. The collecting was organized by the newly-formed Ladies Lifeboat Guild which, in 1923, had Princess Louise, Duchess of Argyll, as its President.

Plans were well in hand for the 1924 centenary. Sir Godfrey Baring, of the banking family, had taken over the chairmanship from Lord Waldergrave whose failing health would probably not have enabled him to handle the centenary celebrations. Sir William Hillary's grave, at Douglas, on the Isle of Man, had been neglected. A local craftsman was commissioned to restore it, incorporating the RNLI badge on the renewed tombstone.

The annual general meeting was planned for 3 March 1924 at the Mansion House, not far from the site of the first meeting one hundred years earlier. The Lord Mayor of London hosted this event. A Lifeboat Ball was arranged in the summer. The Empire Exhibition, held at Wembley that year, gave the RNLI the opportunity to show the world its work at a special feature in the exhibition which included a modern lifeboat and a pictorial

description of the rescue of the crew of the *Rohilla*.

The celebrations continued throughout the year with an official dinner in London to which delegates from lifeboat services in other countries were invited. King George V invested the holders of gold gallantry medals with the Empire Gallantry Medal at Buckingham Palace. These were Captain Thomas McCombie, of Kingstown, Ireland, who had rescued the crew of a ship with his own boat after the entire crew of the Kingstown, later Dun Laoghaire, lifeboat had been lost; Major Burton and Robert Smith, of Tynemouth, Coxswain Howells of Fishguard, Coxswain Blogg of Cromer, Coxswain Fleming of Gorleston and Coxswain Swan of Lowestoft. The youngest man there was Henry Blogg, who, with William Fleming, survived into the Second World War when his Empire Gallantry Medal was changed for the George Cross by King George VI. The oldest was Robert Smith, from the Tyne. These two men were to share the attempts to save the tanker *Georgia* in the months ahead.

A flotilla of lifeboats assembled in the Thames including a new 60 foot Barnett lifeboat and a new Watson, 45 foot and powered by a single 76 hp Weyburn engine. There were also boats from Holland, Denmark, Norway, Sweden, Japan and the United States Coast Guard Service. The discussions proved invaluable to all who attended. Finally a service of thanksgiving was held at the Central Hall, Westminster, in December which was attended by the Prince of Wales.

It was in the year after the centenary that one of the most important independent lifeboat stations joined the RNLI fold. The Aberdeen harbour commissioners had operated their own lifeboat, with local seamen as crew, since the beginning of the nineteenth century. The Aberdeen commissioners had been approached by the RNLI on several occasions but remained independent until 1925 when, seeing the success of the new motor lifeboats and, perhaps worried about the cost of acquiring one, they approached the RNLI for help.

Two pulling and sailing lifeboats were despatched to Aberdeen at once and an order placed for a new Barnett boat, which was delivered and collected by her crew the following year at a cost of £14,000. The harbour master at Aberdeen became honorary local superintendent. The lifeboat was soon at sea after arriving at Aberdeen, attending to the rescue of a steam trawler crew whose vessel had run aground.

Scotland had some of the best boats along its coast and the upkeep of these and the RNLI stations where they were based was costing almost £20,000 per year, but fund-raising in Scotland was not matching the money being spent by the RNLI. During the special fund-raising efforts of the centenary year Scotland only managed to raise about £13,000. In 1927 a special Scottish Council was proposed at a meeting in Edinburgh which seventy Scottish representatives attended. At the inaugural meeting in February of that year the Duke of Montrose accepted the Chair. The Scottish Council and its helpers have successfully raised funds to support Scottish operations ever since.

Two years after the centenary celebrations, Britain was brought to a standstill by the General Strike of May 1926. There was one section of people that did not strike; by nature of their work they could not. They were the lifeboatmen and their permanent workers at the London head office and elsewhere.

There were four calls on the lifeboat service during the ten days of the Strike and all were answered. Two French ships ran aground on the Goodwin Sands and were attended by the lifeboats from Deal and Kingsdown. Three days later the New

Brighton Barnett type motorboat attended a drifting yacht which had been abandoned by her crew. The crew were drowned before the lifeboat was alerted but the yacht was saved. Off the North Devon coast the Clovelly boat was launched to assist the trading cutter *Curlew*, out of Bideford. The vessel and crew of three were saved and escorted to a safe harbour.

Two notable gold medal awards were made to the coxswains of lifeboats based on the western shores during severe storms in October 1927. Under the command of Second Coxswain William Roberts, the rowing-sailing lifeboat, now with auxiliary power, put to sea from Moelfre, Anglesey, to assist a ketch in trouble off Point Lynas, the north-east corner of the island. They found the ketch alongside a German ship which then left as the lifeboat approached. Roberts drove the boat, under sail, aboard the sinking vessel and saved three crew. His boat damaged and sails torn he beat south-east to shelter, being found by the motorized Beaumaris lifeboat which towed him and his exhausted crew into the Menai Strait.

After a continuous fifteen hours at the helm Roberts was taken ashore blinded by the effect of the salt spray. He was awarded the gold medal while his crew all received bronze awards, including one, a namesake of the gallant coxswain, William Roberts, who had died of exposure and exhaustion during the rescue. Captain Owen Jones, also aboard the lifeboat, was awarded the gold medal. He was at Moelfre at the time and an expert on local waters.

During the same storm, and at about the same time, the St Mary's lifeboat, from the Scilly Isles, put to sea under the command of Coxswain Matt Lethbridge to attend an Italian cargo ship, the *Isabo*, aground on the Scilly Rock, due west of the island of Bryher, the most western of the inhabited Isles. Local Bryher men heard the siren of the ship and put to sea in their own boats to rescue many of the crew while Lethbridge and his men arrived through fog and rough seas to gather the remaining survivors, one of whom had swum to nearby rocks and was lying naked, asleep, when found by the lifeboat crew. Lethbridge was awarded the silver medal, his brother James aboard as second coxswain, the bronze. Silver and bronze medals were also awarded to the men of Bryher.

A month later it was the turn of the east coast crews to be busy. The legendary Henry Blogg was involved, but not until the Gorleston boat, commanded by Coxswain William Fleming, had unsuccessfully attempted to rescue the crew of the Dutch oil tanker *Georgia* that had broken in two in a storm on the Haisborough Sands. The British merchant ship *Trent* had sent the radio distress signal and later managed to rescue half of the thirty-one man crew. The British destroyer, *HMS Thanet*, was also at the scene providing light as well as emergency sustenance to the lifeboat crew, but the seas were too rough for the lifeboatmen to close with the divided wreck once it had broken into two parts.

The Gorleston lifeboat had been at sea for almost twenty-four hours when her crew had to retire from the struggle. The Southwold lifeboat also put to sea with no better luck in spite of courageous efforts. Henry Blogg had put to sea from Cromer and, after a ferocious battle in tumultuous seas, managed to reach the remains of the wreck of the *Georgia* and take off the remaining crew. For this he was awarded his second gold medal while his crew all received bronze awards. Coxswain Fleming received a bronze as did Coxswain Albert Spurgeon, from Southwold, who had damaged his boat badly in an earlier rescue of a fishing boat crew which prevented him from assisting the *Georgia*.

The Prince of Wales was able to use

these rescues to encourage funds from the shipping companies when he attended the 1928 annual general meeting of the RNLI as President. Guided by the secretary he later made a direct approach to the leading British shipping companies, Cunard, P&O and the Royal Mail Steam Packet Company among them, with success. The following year he attended the Scottish Society annual general meeting, praising their efforts while several years later he made a thrust at the owners of the trawler fleets, encouraging them to give more support to the RNLI. Wherever he went, whatever he did for the RNLI, similar success followed, a fact recorded in obituaries accorded him when he died as the Duke of Windsor in 1972.

In June 1928 the second International Lifeboat Conference was held in Paris. Britain's representation was an interesting and powerful one. Led by Sir Godfrey Baring it included the Honourable George Colville, Deputy Chairman of the management committee, Captain Rowley, by now Chief Inspector of Lifeboats and Mr Barnett, whose large motor-driven boats were proving themselves time and again.

The heavy oil engine was on its way. During the Conference, when delegates from seventeen nations from as far apart as the USSR, the United States and Japan, saw a special French design of a twin screw lifeboat, Germany offered a paper on the use of the diesel engine. Germany, the Dutch and the Scandinavians were well ahead of Britain in this development in 1928.

Hardly was the Conference over than a horrendous tragedy overtook one of the RNLI's older boats. The Rye lifeboat, powered by oars and sail, put out in a storm to assist the Baltic steamer *Alice*, from Latvia. Even as the lifeboat left harbour the coastguards received a radio message that the ship's crew had been taken off by another vessel.

There was no radio link between lifeboats and the shore, although the matter of radios had been discussed earlier in Paris. Recall signals were fired but not seen by the lifeboat crew because of the weather. The lifeboat eventually returned towards harbour under sail but was capsized near the entrance. The seventeen man crew were thrown out of the boat but, although near the shore and wearing lifejackets, all were beaten to death by the enormous breaking surf.

Typical of these lifeboat tragedies there were terrible losses to local families. The coxswain, Herbert Head, was in the boat with two of his sons. There were three brothers from the Pope family in the boat, two brothers from the Clark family, while bowman Henry Cutting and his two brothers were also lost. Two cousins from the Downing family also drowned.

A memorial service is still held annually in Rye, a small community devastated by the loss.

The end of the 1920s saw more and more fully-powered lifeboats replacing the old oar and sail and oar-sail and auxiliary powered boats, as well as the withdrawal of the steam tugs on stations where the lifeboats were towed out to sea. The RNLI headquarters moved from Charing Cross to Grosvenor Gardens, Victoria, in the summer of 1931 while Captain Rowley retired as Chief Inspector and George Shee retired as secretary. During his twenty-eight years with the RNLI, interspersed with war service, Captain Rowley had seen the powered lifeboat fleet grow from 19 to 88. George Shee had seen revenue grow

from £97,000 per year when he joined in 1910 to £264,000 when he left. He received a knighthood in the honours list in 1932.

George Shee's position was taken up by Lieutenant Colonel C R Satterthwaite, a veteran of Gallipoli, who had worked as Shee's assistant since leaving the Army six years earlier. Captain Rowley was replaced by Commander E D Drury while Charles Vince, who had been an assistant secretary for publicity, became head of public relations for the RNLI and editor of the magazine 'Lifeboat'.

The third International Conference was held in Rotterdam during the summer of 1932. Sir George Shee came out of his retirement to attend while the British delegation included Sir Godfrey Baring, Commander Drury, Mr Barnett, and the superintendent engineer, Captain A G Bremner. Several regional directors also attended, as did the Chief Inspector of Coastguards.

This third Conference was a friendly business. Many of the delegates had come to know one another at the first two. One important matter discussed at length was the use of radio telephony between lifeboats and shore stations, a matter still in experimental stages in most delegate countries. The Dutch hosts were leaders in the field of motive power and electronics in lifeboats. They specialized in light displacement boats for beach and transporter launching, necessary when one considers the nature of the coast of Holland, low and flat with large expanses of sandbanks and dunes.

Chapter 6

CHANGING TIMES

A new boat appeared at Dover at about this time specifically designed for fast rescue. At 64 foot in length she was four feet longer than the Barnett boat, powered by two 12 cylinder Thornycroft 375 hp engines driving twin screws and could make 18 knots. Aircraft rescue was behind the planning, with flights from England to France and back, via the Straits of Dover, now a daily occurrence. The new boat had a range of 78 miles at full speed and she could accommodate 100 survivors. Meanwhile Thornycroft were experimenting with a six cylinder diesel, producing 80 hp at 1,600 rpm. The engine was fitted to a Watson boat which was tested along the south coast at Weymouth and Falmouth before the boat was placed on station at Yarmouth, on the Isle of Wight near the dangerous Needles Channel and Hurst Narrows.

Weight was the main problem with the newly-designed diesel engines, particularly the six cylinder type. Thornycroft continued their experiments, testing a smaller four cylinder engine that produced 40 hp at 1,200 rpm and which was only marginally heavier than the equivalent petrol engines. This engine was put into production after extensive testing and eleven were ordered by the RNLI to be installed in the Watson covered boats.

There were several advantages of engines fuelled by diesel oil over those using petrol. The fire risk was considerably less; the elimination of electric ignition meant that there was less to go wrong and they were more economical. Because of this they had a wider operating range which, in turn would eventually mean that there would be a reduction in the number of lifeboat stations as the diesel powered boats covered larger areas of the coast.

At the same time as these changes in engines were taking place experiments were also progressing in the use of radio electronics that could operate under the severe conditions demanded. In the early 1930s half the 53 cabin Watson boats were fitted with radios enabling lifeboat crews to communicate with ships, their bases ashore and the Coastguard service. It was a pity that this extra facility was not available to the men of Rye back in 1928, but they did not even have an auxiliary engine.

Radio was helping the RNLI in other ways in the 1930s. The BBC had started its weekly charity appeals and offered the RNLI three opportunities to use the service. During the final one, made by Lord Mottistone in 1934, a sum in excess of £2,400 was raised, probably because he used the story of a rescue made by the lifeboat station of Runswick, on the Yorkshire coast north-west of Whitby. A steamer, in the tow of a tug, was sinking. The tug managed to take all but one of the steamer's crew off but one man, with an injured leg, would not jump from the tug's deck.

Under the command of Coxswain Robert Patton, the Runswick lifeboat went alongside the steamer in heavy seas. Patton grabbed the man by the legs as the lifeboat passed, the injured man having hung over the rails, his legs dangling towards the sea. The frightened man refused to release his grip on the rail. Coxswain Patton held on, both men falling into the sea between the lifeboat and the ship where they were crushed several times, Coxswain Patton taking almost the entire force of the lifeboat as it surged against him. He and the survivor were eventually pulled aboard the lifeboat.

Robert Patton was badly injured but later, in hospital, told a representative of the RNLI that he could not have let the man go as he might have drowned, although had he done so he would probably not have been injured. He died from his injuries some days

Patrick Sliney of Ballycotton.

after the rescue and was awarded a posthumous gold medal for his gallantry.

War drums were rumbling again when one of the most famous rescues in the history of the RNLI took place off the coast of Ireland. During February 1936, a severe storm, with winds sometimes reaching hurricane strength, was raging in the western approaches and along Ireland's south and south-west coast. Lifeboat crews were on stand-by but falling trees had cut communications between those manning Coastguard lookout posts, lighthouses and the lifeboat stations.

At the height of the storm, with the wind in the south-east and blowing with considerable force straight onto the south-facing shores, the Daunt light vessel, lying off the entrance of Cork Harbour and a short distance from the shore, broke her moorings and began drifting towards the coast. The eight man crew of the lightship managed to drop an emergency anchor, which held. A messenger arrived at the village of Ballycotton with the news. It was decided not to attempt to launch the lifeboat straight into the direction of the storm. The lifeboat was powered by a petrol engine and sail.

The coxswain, Patrick Sliney, heard the news and summoned his crew who, as in so many small coastal communities, was very much a family affair. Second coxswain was John Walsh, two other crewmen were Thomas and Michael Walsh while the mechanic was Thomas Sliney, Patrick Sliney's brother. John and William Sliney made up the crew of seven who, in spite of winds that were lifting spray over the 190 foot local lighthouse, put to sea. Prayers were said in the local church.

The lifeboat crew made a search downwind of the official position of the lightship which was there to give warning of the Daunt Rock. They found nothing. Exhausted they put into Cork Harbour where they managed to obtain a known position of the vessel. They put back out to sea and found her only half a mile from the lee shore. Two ships, a warship and a merchant steamer, were standing by the stricken lightship whose crew were at that time reluctant to leave their ship. However they asked the lifeboat crew to stay by them until the storm abated. It did not. The merchant ship left but the warship, *HMS Tenedos*, stayed.

Efforts were made by both the warship crew and the lifeboatmen to pass a line to the lightship but without success in the terrible seas. It was decided that the warship would stay there all night while the lifeboat returned to Cork Harbour for fuel, food for the crew and dry clothing. Early next day the lifeboat returned and stayed there, although the warship left to be replaced on guard by the *Isolda*, a lightship tender operated by the Commissioners of Irish Lights. The Slineys and the Walshes stayed out there all the next night but had to return to Cork Harbour next morning for petrol. The crew were hungry, cold, exhausted and one or two seasick, but they returned that evening for another night vigil. That evening the wind changed, the anchor was torn from the seabed and the lightship began drifting back towards the rock which it was intended to guard.

The lifeboat, a 52 foot Barnett type, made five runs alongside the lightship which was rolling through forty degrees.

Six of the eight lightship crew were taken off during these runs, but two remained aboard clinging to the guard rails. Sliney decided to make one more run alongside and ordered his crew to grab the two final survivors as they passed. The lightship had extensive bilge keels that were swinging up out of the water as it rolled violently from side to side. The risk to the lifeboat and her crew was considerable but the Irishmen managed to grab the last

two men on their final pass and headed for the shelter of Cork Harbour.

The men of Ballycotton had been away on duty for more than three days of which 63 hours had been on service and over two days at sea without hot food and rest. They had ended their epic struggle with a total success having carried out an operation in the last moments that would have troubled a crew of fresh men. Patrick Sliney was awarded a gold medal, silver medals were awarded to his brother Thomas and John Walsh while the remainder of the crew received bronze medals.

At about this time a rapid change took place in the holder of the position of President of the RNLI. The Prince of Wales succeeded to the throne as Edward VIII and his brother, the Duke of York, took the Presidency, but this situation was short-lived when Edward VIII abdicated and the Duke of York became George VI. As it was, the preoccupations of the Duke of York had prevented him from attending many RNLI functions and meetings, but the Duke of Kent stood in for him on several such occasions.

When the Duke of York became King the Duke of Kent agreed to accept the Presidency while the new King became Patron. This connection with the Royal Family has remained the same ever since then with the present Duke of Kent holding the post of President and Her Majesty the Queen, Patron. The Queen Mother, then Queen Elizabeth, also became a Patron with her husband the King in 1937. When the Duke of Kent was tragically killed in a flying accident in World War II his wife, Princess Marina, Duchess of Kent, succeeded him as President.

The next International Lifeboat Conference was held in Gothenburg, Sweden, in 1936 and was attended by the Swedish Crown Prince Gustav. Britain sent a strong delegation which included, as ever, Mr Barnett. Sixteen nations were represented and discussion papers included the subject of diesel power, radio-telephony and designs of boats. The incorporation of tunnels to protect propellers was also raised.

There were two tragedies on the horizon at this time. The first was the Second World War. The second a double disaster that struck a Cornish lifeboat crew within the space of a little over a year.

In January 1938 the crew of the St Ives boat were called out to attend a collier in trouble close to the shore. Coxswain Thomas Cocking, with a crew of eight, manned the 35 foot self-righting boat and went alongside the collier, taking off her crew of twenty-three who were, it seemed, unaware of the peril that they were in and were not only reluctant to leave but took their belongings with them.

Because of delays in embarking the survivors the tide and winds were against Coxswain Cocking. The boat capsized before reaching harbour. Those waiting ashore managed to rescue the entire lifeboat crew and all but a few of the collier's people. The lifeboat was totally destroyed and later burnt. The following January another coaster was in trouble off St Ives and, in fact, sank before she could be reached by the lifeboat, which had put out with a crew of eight again led by Coxswain Cocking. As usual the small community had formed their crew from several men from the same families. Coxswain Cocking was accompanied by his son John and his son-in-law. There were two brothers from the Barber family, William and John.

As with the previous rescue, the replacement boat was of the self-righting type. She capsized while seaching the area where the ship in distress had been thought to be. Coxswain Cocking was swept away before the boat righted, as were William Barber, Edgar Bassett and John Thomas. They were never seen again. The four survivors struggled towards the coast but the boat capsized again, this time carrying away three more of the crew and leaving only William Freeman aboard on his first lifeboat call-out. The boat came ashore near Godrevy Point, to the north-east of St Ives. It was a considerable time before the people of St Ives had even started to recover from the tragedy. Some never did.

Chapter 7

TO WAR AGAIN

The start of the Second World War saw the RNLI move its maintenance workshops and boatyard from Poplar, in east London, to Boreham Wood, in Hertfordshire. The move was obviously carefully planned but was also fortuitous because the London depot was in an area of the docklands that was reduced to rubble during the 1940 bombing raids on London.

When the war began in the autumn of 1939 it was the east coast of England that was to take the initial strain. Mines were laid by both Britain and Germany in the North Sea and the Straits of Dover. Among these mines were the magnetic type, dropped from the air by the Germans. These took an early toll of shipping until a method of sweeping them was devised. Twenty-seven merchant ships were sunk by these mines in a single month in the early days of the war. The sinking of the steamer *Magdapur* off Aldeburgh was typical. The ship's back was broken and several of her crew killed by the explosion while others were wounded, but the Aldeburgh lifeboat reached the ship and rescued over seventy people, many blackened with oil and covered in blood. Among the older coxswains who were to establish their reputations even further on the east coast were the redoubtable Henry Blogg of Cromer and Robert Cross of Humber. Both men had, of course, seen service in the lifeboats during the First World War.

Once more recruitment to the armed forces depleted crews of their regular volunteers and older men were taken in to replace them. Among these, and typical of many, were John Dryden and Christopher Wale, of the Whitby boat. Sadly they were both lost at sea during a rescue close to the spot where the *Rohilla* had been lost twenty-six years earlier.

Robert Cross, a veteran coxswain with thirty-seven years service with the RNLI, was in charge at the remote station at Spurn Head, at the entrance of the Humber River, a breeding ground for lifeboat heroes, if ever there was one. Cross and his crew put to sea in wild weather in February 1940, during one of the worst winters on record, to aid a trawler aground. The area is well known by sailors for its strong tides, shoals and steep seas. The boat was a twin screw Barnett type. In spite of driving snow the lifeboatmen found the trawler sinking with her crew of nine clinging to the bows. Cross closed the ship, near to the shore, and anchored to windward and seaward of her, dropping astern on the anchor until his men could grab six of the trawler crew. They then went ahead again and then repeated the whole operation, saving the remaining three. At every moment they were at considerable risk of being swept by the seas onto the shore. A rope fouled one screw, but this was cleared and they headed for the shelter of Grimsby ten miles away, the harbour entrance, unlit in the wartime conditions and the use of the lifeboat searchlight prohibited.

After eleven hours at sea their boat was a sorry sight. Guard rails and stanchions were flattened, fendering torn away and the boat partly flooded. King George VI had instituted the George Cross and George Medal as civilian gallantry medals comparable to the Victoria Cross and the Military Medal awarded to servicemen and women. Robert Cross received the George Medal and the RNLI gold medal for this rescue.

After the terrible weather of the winter of 1939 there followed a contrasting summer that probably saved many a life at the evacuation of Dunkirk in May 1940. As the armies of Britain, France, as well as soldiers who managed to escape capture in Holland and Belgium, made for the French port a fleet of small craft was assembled along England's south coast. Lifeboats from as far west as Shoreham and as far north as Gorleston were alerted and put to sea. Lifeboats came voluntarily from further away, including one from Poole, Dorset.

The first lifeboatman to reach Dunkirk beaches was Coxswain Harold Knight, skippering the Ramsgate boat. He was closely followed by Edward Parker from Margate. Both spent considerable time with their crews off the beaches ferrying troops from the shore to larger ships in deeper water before finally loading with all the men they could carry and sailing for Dover, but trouble lay ahead for the crews of the seventeen other boats that sailed for Dover for orders to proceed across the Channel. The coxswain of the Hythe lifeboat asked that a written agreement should be given by the authorities assuring that any lifeboatman losing his life during the operation could expect that a pension would be paid to his family. He also considered that orders to go to the beach were unwise due to the draught

of his lifeboat, a point later proved correct under Royal Naval command.

The reaction of the overstretched officers in charge of evacuation operations was to send the entire Hythe crew home and man the lifeboat with Royal Navy personnel. The Hythe coxswain, a man of twenty years service with the RNLI and his mechanic, were dismissed from service by the Institution but not before the crews of the Walmer and Dungeness boats had been persuaded not to go to Dunkirk. The reaction of the naval authorities masterminding the Dunkirk rescue was spontaneous. All lifeboat crews were sent home and their boats commandeered by the Navy to be manned by naval personnel.

Many lifeboatmen stayed at Dover in spite of having been told they could leave. They set up workshops to service and repair the many small craft working between Kent and the French coast, working round the clock, while others did go home and put to sea in their own boats for Dunkirk. It was all a sad business, but while the lifeboat crews said they would have gone without hesitation if the order had come from the RNLI, it seems they over-reacted to the authoritarian ways of the Royal Navy and others. There were those who felt that a situation such as that at Dunkirk was hardly a time to quibble about the written and unwritten rules that applied to the job. Meanwhile across the water Coxswains Parker and Knight were busy earning themselves the Distinguished Service Medal.

The seventeen lifeboats that went to Dunkirk with their temporary naval crews performed many dangerous tasks but only one was lost. This was the Hythe boat, which, as predicted by her coxswain, had been beached while trying to take troops from the shore. Apart from his demand for a guarantee of pensions for the dependants of the crew if they had been lost, he had stated that the boat, one of the larger type, was too deep draughted for work close inshore, the task allocated to him by the Navy. Many of the boats were damaged by attacks from aircraft, gunfire from ashore and even, in one case, collision with a French patrol boat. The Eastbourne boat, commandeered by the Navy, met every sort of trouble while off the French coast and was abandoned. Two days later the boat was found out in the Channel still just afloat and was towed home where she was successfully repaired.

Following the evacuation of Dunkirk came the anxious time of waiting. Everyone in Britain expected that once the Germans had consolidated their position in France, invasion would surely follow. Nothing happened until August 1940 when the Battle of Britain began in the air, reaching its climax in mid-September. The Royal Air Force and the Royal Navy both operated high speed rescue launches specifically designed to recover aircrew but, while faster than the lifeboats, they had their limitations in rough weather.

During the period of the Battle of Britain lifeboats were launched 264 times, 131 times on operations connected with 'downed' aircraft. Lifeboatmen rescued ten British airmen and eight of the enemy during the battle. This might not seem a vast number when compared with the number who ditched or parachuted into the sea, but other rescue facilities that were also available must be taken into consideration.

One pilot saved by lifeboat was Richard Hillary, a descendant of Sir William. He was shot down over the Channel and bailed out severely burnt. He was found by the Margate crew, one of the busiest during the Battle of Britain, and taken ashore in considerable pain. Once in hospital the lifeboat crew visited regularly. His hands were so severely burnt that there was doubt he would ever be able to fly again, but he did. Sadly he

was killed while training as a night flier in 1943 and his ashes dropped from the air into the sea near where he had been rescued back in 1940. He had meanwhile written his memoirs entitled 'The Last Enemy' which included a graphic description of his rescue by the men of Margate and their subsequent care for him.

The lifeboats on the islands of Jersey and Guernsey were lost in the German occupation of the Channel Islands and others damaged by bombing. Several were straffed by German aircraft while on service both at Dunkirk and subsequently.

The office headquarters of the RNLI at Grosvenor Gardens, Victoria, were damaged by bombing in 1940. Issues of the magazine 'Lifeboat' were reduced to a news sheet by economies imposed on newsprint by the war. In spite of this fund-raising continued and the lifeboat service maintained as near to full strength as shortages of men and materials allowed.

One of the most dramatic rescues of the war occurred on the Haisborough Sands when a convoy of six merchant ships ran aground one after another in severe weather, during the night and while steaming through an unlit channel cleared of mines. The leading ship steered the incorrect course and the five astern followed. All ran aground on the fateful Sands.

Some hours after the disaster the lifeboats were alerted by the Navy. Boats put out from Lowestoft, Sheringham, Great Yarmouth and, under the command of the aforementioned Henry Blogg, from Cromer.

Naval escort vessels had managed to save some of the stranded crews, but others had drowned trying to reach the naval ships by swimming as their ships broke up on the Sands. Henry Blogg and his men aboard the larger of the two Cromer lifeboats arrived on the scene mid-morning, making for a sunken ship whose crew were clinging to what little remained above water as their ship broke up beneath them. Blogg closed with the ship and time and again rammed the lifeboat into a split in the superstructure in raging seas, eventually saving sixteen men. He then went alongside another sunken ship and took off thirty-one men before putting alongside a destroyer to unload the survivors. The second Cromer boat then arrived with the boat from Great Yarmouth as Blogg, transferring his second coxswain to the second Cromer boat, set off for his third stricken ship. Again he sailed the lifeboat over the superstructure, rescuing nineteen men huddled on the ship's bridge.

The other two lifeboats from Cromer and Great Yarmouth attended to the fourth and fifth ships while Blogg tackled the sixth in the convoy saving twenty-two men before running aground on the Sands, but mercifully being swept off again by a breaking· sea which swept across the Sands. One hundred and nineteen men had been saved of which Henry Blogg was responsible for the majority, eighty-eight in all. His boat was badly damaged, but this was a small price to pay for the success of the work. Henry Blogg received his third gold medal from the RNLI as well as the British Empire Medal which he added to the George Cross which the King had awarded him earlier.

Two months later, in October 1941, Coxswain Blogg was out again, this time to the rescue of the crew of a British coaster that had sunk on the Hammond Knoll, a sandbank some twenty-five miles from Cromer. As ever, strong north-easterly winds swept the North Sea as Blogg approached the wreck which was showing only the mast, the funnel and the chart house where the surviving crew were huddled. He waited for slack tide in order to approach the ship but his patience ebbed while it seemed the

strength of those aboard the ship was going the same way. He approached the ship only to have the lifeboat almost capsized by an enormous wave. Those aboard the wrecked ship could see the keel of the lifeboat which was not of the self-righting type, but she came back upright. Blogg, the second coxswain and two others were overboard. The crew threw Blogg and the second coxswain an aircraft life raft which they managed to grab before being hauled aboard. The search was then mounted for the other two crewmen, Henry Blogg back in charge. They found the first within reasonable time but the second, the signalman, had been in the water and was unconscious when they recovered him. He revived in the shelter of the cabin but then relapsed and later died ashore.

The lifeboat made for the shelter of Great Yarmouth, passing, unbeknown to either crew, the Great Yarmouth boat as she went out to the wrecked ship. The Great Yarmouth crew managed to fire a line aboard the wreck after five attempts to go alongside, but the line broke. Several times the lifeboat was almost capsized.

Henry Blogg and his men reached Great Yarmouth that evening and were forbidden to put to sea until later. They refuelled the boat, rested briefly and discussed plans with the Great Yarmouth crew which had returned the same evening having had no more success at rescuing the steamer's crew than the men of Cromer. The Cromer boat sailed three hours before dawn and reached the wreck in moderating weather. It was able to go alongside the ship and take off forty-four exhausted men. In spite of the fact Henry Blogg's efforts seemed to have earned him his fourth gold medal he was, instead, awarded his fourth silver medal.

Chapter 8

PEACE AND PROGRESS

The first International Lifeboat Conference after the war was held in Oslo in 1947 chaired by Dagfinn Paust, President of the Norwegian Lifeboat Service. Ten nations attended including Turkey and the United States of America. The proceedings lasted a week, meetings interspersed with social functions which were attended by King Haakon and Crown Prince Olaf. It was a time for reunions and the meeting of old friends again who had been separated by war. Another event, less of a cause for celebration by the RNLI, was the retirement of Coxswain Henry Blogg of Cromer.

Henry Blogg had joined the Cromer lifeboat as a crewman in 1894 and was appointed coxswain in 1909. During his thirty-eight years as a coxswain of the Cromer station he had saved 448 lives as a result of 155 launches. He had been awarded the George Cross, three RNLI gold medals, four silver medals and a medal from the Canine Defence League for the rescue of a dog from a merchant ship. He accepted the medal and kept the dog.

Also retiring in 1947 was J R Barnett, the designer of some of the most successful types of lifeboat. By that year all but two of the RNLI lifeboats were motorized, a total of 158 in all. There was still a rowing lifeboat based at Whitby which was stationed there to cope with special conditions at the port. A sailing lifeboat, built in 1907, was still on station at New Quay, on the north coast of Cardiganshire, which is now Dyfed. This boat was replaced by a Liverpool-type twin screw boat although those who inherited the old boat pronounced it to be in first class order, a tribute to her builders and those who looked after her.

Coxswain Thomas King, of St Helier, Jersey, who, in September 1949 won a gold medal for gallantry while saving the crew of the cutter Maurice Georges *as well as the vessel. His crew were all awarded bronze medals.*

The first gold medal awarded after the war was given to Thomas King, of the St Helier station in Jersey. In September 1949 he and his crew were called out in their single screw boat to search for a French aircraft reported to have ditched in the sea to the south-east of the island. They failed to find it as it had, in fact, sunk with the loss of six lives while three survivors came ashore on the French island of Chausey about 25 miles south-east of Jersey. When returning to St Helier low on fuel after eight hours at sea, Coxswain King was asked to investigate a light seen offshore to the east of Jersey.

A strong north-east wind was blowing against the north running ebb tide. The lifeboat crew found a yacht, the *Maurice Georges*, anchored close to the shore among rocks and in danger of breaking her cable. Coxswain King drove his boat, a reserve vessel that was replacing the regular boat during refit, straight to the yacht, managing to pass a towline to the crew at the third attempt. He decided to try and tow the yacht out of danger, this being safer than trying to take off the crew, and return to St Helier. Lifeboat and yacht were in safe waters less than twenty minutes later. Sometime later, in calm weather and daylight, Coxswain King returned to the scene of the rescue with the local inspector but refused to take the lifeboat within a mile of the place where he had found the yacht as he considered it far too dangerous!

The flooding of the land bordering the southern North Sea at the end of January 1953 caused considerable damage and loss of life along the coasts. The low lying lands around the Thames Estuary, notably Canvey Island on the Essex coast and the land around the Medway Estuary in Kent, were badly flooded, with heavy loss of life. The problems were even worse across the North Sea in Holland.

Lifeboats were busy rescuing people stranded as well as standing by ships in distress. More than a dozen lifeboat stations were damaged by the storms which swept Britain from the west coast of Scotland to the southern east coast. The biggest single disaster during the storms was the loss of the ferry *Princess Victoria* on the Stranraer to Larne route. The ship's master was well used to extreme weather on the route and was not deterred by winds gusting at over 70 knots and driving snow squalls.

Once out of Loch Larne and past Milleur Point the ship was steaming in confused seas predominately running from astern driven by strong north-east winds. One of these seas struck the loading doors of the car deck aft stoving them in and flooding the car deck. The ship began to list. A tug was requested and, as the list to starboard increased, an SOS message was sent as preparations were made to abandon ship. Shortly after this the ship was overwhelmed, capsized and sank. The lifeboat from Portpatrick had been launched and made for the known position. Meanwhile the boat from Donaghadee, on the coast of Ulster, put to sea after the search by the Scottish boat had found nothing.

Coxswain Hugh Nelson, from Donaghadee, decided to follow the warship *HMS Contest* which was searching the North Channel between the Stranraer peninsula and Belfast Lough. There had been 127 passengers and 49 crew aboard the ferry. It was soon apparent to the lifeboatmen that there would be few survivors in the terrible conditions. One lifeboat from the ship had been successfully launched with 29 people aboard while another was found with one survivor aboard. The lifeboat from Cloughey, on the Ards peninsula, joined the others in the search, but only bodies were found. The three lifeboats then returned to Donaghadee, motoring together before the gale. It was a sad business. A total of 133 people had drowned and only 43 saved. The coxswain of the Donaghadee boat was awarded the British Empire Medal for his efforts as was Coxswain William McConnel, of the Portpatrick station.

A week later disaster struck the RNLI at Fraserburgh in an incident that was very much akin to that when the lifeboat *Lady Rothes* was lost after the First World War. The Fraserburgh lifeboat, the *John and Charles Kennedy*, had put to sea in strong easterly winds with Coxswain Andrew Ritchie in command. Their task was to escort several fishing boats, thought to be in difficulty in the heavy seas, into the harbour. When approaching the harbour entrance a massive wave from astern lifted the lifeboat clear of the water and capsized her. Coxswain Ritchie was thrown out of the boat but was killed by wreckage while six of the crew were trapped and drowned in the hull which did not right but was virtually destroyed when it struck rocks. There was one survivor, the second coxswain, C F Tait, whose 61 year-old father Charles Tait was lost with the boat. The young survivor immediately volunteered for further service with the RNLI once the Fraserburgh boat could be replaced.

Disaster struck Scotland later in the same year when the lifeboats from Anstruther and Arbroath were called out after the coastguards on the Fife Ness had seen flares out to sea. The area was searched in heavy seas and a gale from the south-east. Nothing was found and because of the weather the Arbroath lifeboat coxswain, David Bruce, was advised to make for Anstruther. In fact he waited at sea until daybreak and made for his own port. As both ports were described as dangerous to enter in south-easterly winds there was little to choose between them so Coxswain Bruce made for the place he knew best. Coastguards manned the harbour entrance and prepared rocket lines in case of problems. As the lifeboat neared the entrance it was struck by a massive following sea and capsized. Lines were fired and one man of the

seven man crew, Second Coxswain Archibald Smith, was hauled ashore. The remainder were drowned.

A similar disaster befell the Scarborough lifeboat the following year where the coxswain, second coxswain and radio operator were lost as the boat returned to harbour after assisting fishing boats.

During the winter of 1954 lifeboats from Wales and Ireland attended the wreck of the 20,000 ton oil tanker *World Concord* which had broken in two in the Irish Sea in a storm of hurricane strength. The forward part had drifted into Wexford bay on the Eire coast. The ship's master and six of the crew were aboard this section while there were 35 people, mostly Greek, aboard the aft part which was being shadowed by the aircraft carrier *HMS Illustrious* as it drifted 16 miles north-west of St David's Head, on the south-west coast of Wales.

Coxswain Richard Walsh and his crew put out from Rosslare to attempt to save those on the forward part while Coxswain William Watts-Williams and his men launched from St David's station. Guided by those aboard the aircraft carrier they found the wreck. After over thirty passes alongside the high-sided stern section they took off all the crew, returning to their station after many hours at sea in terrible conditions. The Rosslare crew, unable to return to their station because of the winds and high seas, made for Holyhead which they reached after being at sea for over 36 hours. Both coxswains were awarded silver medals while various crew members of both boats received bronze awards.

At about the same time and probably because of the same storm, the light of the South Goodwin lightship disappeared from the view of the Deal coastguards. Lifeboats were launched from Walmer and Dover while the crew at Ramsgate had to work to remove a high sand bar that had been formed by the storm before being able to put to sea.

The Dover crew reached the Goodwin Sands to find the lightship lying on her side without any sign of survivors. A helicopter arrived on the scene at daybreak, from an American rescue squadron based at nearby Manston, flown by Captain Howard Richard. He was not quite so sure that there were no survivors so a second helicopter was sent to the scene. The lifeboat from Dover, now joined by those from Ramsgate and Walmer, was unable to approach the wreck because of the shallowness of the water on the quicksands. The captain of the second aircraft, Captain Curtis Parkins, then sighted someone clinging to the upper side of the lightship hull. It was Ronald Murton, an ornithologist working for the Ministry of Agriculture and Fisheries. Captain Parkins descended to about 30 feet. One of the helicopter crew then lowered a winch wire to the survivor who was successfully lifted off the lightship. This was the first rescue by helicopter on an occasion when lifeboats could not approach a wreck. Bravery awards were given to the American airmen who saved the single survivor.

This combining of sea and air rescue was discussed at the International Lifeboat Conference, held in Portugal in 1955, which was attended by delegates from twenty-two nations. In Britain limited training of lifeboat crews in the skills of being winched to a helicopter were being organized with the embryos of what are now the Search and Rescue helicopter squadrons of the Royal Navy and Royal Air Force and HM Coastguard.

During 1956, when Samuel White's shipyard at Cowes completed its 100th lifeboat for the RNLI, Sir Godfrey Baring retired as Chairman of the Institution to be succeeded in the post by the Earl Howe. The Earl had held the position of Deputy Chairman since 1946. He was a Commodore in the Royal Naval Volunteer Reserve while his wife was Chairman of the Central London Women's Committee.

It had been suggested in some quarters that the helicopters might make the lifeboats redundant, but this was quickly refuted by experts who pointed out the very limited operating abilities of the petrol-powered helicopters of the 1950s as well as their limited capacity in terms of carrying survivors. They could not fly at night or in severe weather and could only carry two or three people in the small Sycamore and Dragonflies and no more than seven in the larger Westland Whirlwind. The helicopters were used to assist lifeboats in rescues as well as take medical help to people aboard ships with injuries or other troubles.

In 1956 the first of the Richard Oakley designed class of self-righting twin screw lifeboats was built at William Osborne's shipyard at Littlehampton. Tank testing of a model by Saunders Roe at Cowes had preceded the construction of the prototype which was powered by two Perkins diesel engines. The design proved very successful and the Oakley class became established as a popular workhorse of the lifeboat fleet. Many more were built over the years ahead, some being still in service in 1989.

Seventeen countries sent delegates to the 1959 International Lifeboat Conference, which was held at Bremen, West Germany. The Dutch, who had always been extremely innovative since the early days of lifesaving at sea, enthused about the co-operation between helicopters and lifeboats. It was towards the end of the same year that disaster struck at Dundee. The keeper of the North Carr lightship reported that the lightship was dragging its cable. The Dundee lifeboat, based at Broughty Ferry, was launched under the command of Coxswain Robert Grant. Though an old boat, built before World War II, the Watson lifeboat was in first class condition. After some time at sea in a full south-easterly gale all radio communication with Coxswain Grant and his crew was lost. The lifeboat had capsized and all her crew were drowned.

As if to prove the point of the Dutch delegation at the conference earlier in the year the Royal Air Force sent a helicopter from 228 Squadron to the lightship where Flight Sergeant Breach and his crew managed to take off the lightship crew. The lightship is now replaced by a buoy. The people of Dundee were stunned by the loss. The Lord Provost immediately set up a fund as a memorial to the lost men. Within days the fund had reached over £90,000.

Chapter 9

THE PROSPEROUS SIXTIES

During 1959 the RNLI Chairman, Lord Howe, announced that revenue from fund-raising had exceeded £1 million during the previous twelve months for the first time. Another 'first' was achieved during the early part of 1960. The lifeboat from Barra, an island at the southern end of the Outer Hebrides, was taking an expectant mother to hospital on the island of South Uist, further north. The baby was safely delivered during the voyage, the first time that this happy event had occurred aboard a British lifeboat. It was not the first time that such an event had occurred elsewhere. The French recorded a similar story between the Ile de Molene off the Brittany coast at Ushant and the French mainland.

During the 1960s engine changes were ordered by the technical committee, replacing petrol engines that had, in some cases, been in use for many years, with diesel. The Perkins diesel engines had proved popular and reliable. Meanwhile trials had taken place with engines from Gardners which proved very successful, especially as they could now be controlled directly from the bridge. They were more expensive than the Perkins engines but expense has never been spared by the RNLI where the pursuit of total excellence has always been the prime criterion.

The Watson class lifeboat RA Colby Cubbin No 3. It was on this boat, in 1960, that a baby was born aboard a vessel operated by the RNLI for the first time.

Towards the end of 1961 the lifeboat from Seaham, Northumberland, was lost with all her crew as well as the crew of a fishing coble that the boat had put out to save. A local memorial fund raised almost £50,000. It was at about this time that the RNLI agreed that dependants of those lost at sea in the service of the RNLI should receive pensions equivalent to those awarded to Chief Petty Officers in the Royal Navy.

Two important innovations appeared during the opening years of the 1960s. The first was the appearance of inshore rescue boats. The second was the compilation of a list of owners of small craft based along the south coast of England between Sussex and Dorset who would be ready to go to sea on rescue operations.

Inflatable boats had come a long way since the war when rubber Carley Floats were carried aboard aircraft capable of carrying one or two men and ships carried primitive life rafts. The use of man-made fabrics such as nylon and neoprene produced strong hard hulls and floors for inflatables. Outboards were increasing in power, improving in reliability and the power to weight ratios of outboard engines, particularly of American design, was becoming better and better. Rigid flooring added to the strength and speed capability of these craft. Powered by a 40 hp outboard and nearly 16 feet in length they could travel at 20 knots in shallow waters where the conventional lifeboat could not go because of its draught. From the beginning the inshore boats were stationed in areas where inshore rescues were likely to be needed, such as sailing centres and holiday resorts.

Sailing for pleasure was growing apace in the 1960s. More and more people were putting out to sea in everything from offshore racing and cruising yachts to power cruisers and smaller dayboats and dinghies. Today, in the 1990s, the largest proportion of

RNLI rescues both by all-weather and inshore lifeboats is of people from pleasure craft.

During 1963 a new design of lifeboat from the drawing board of Richard Oakley was launched from the yard of William Osborne at Littlehampton. The boat was 48.5 feet in length, weighed 27 tons and had a best speed of 9 knots. Named *Earl and Countess of Howe* after the RNLI Chairman and his wife, the lifeboat, now retired from the fleet, stands proudly on display at the RNLI depot at Poole, Dorset. The first task allocated to the new boat in 1963 was attendance at the International Lifeboat Conference being held that year in Edinburgh. The boat was moored at nearby Leith harbour and inspected by delegates attending the conference before being put on station at Yarmouth, Isle of Wight. Sadly at the age of 80, Lord Howe died the following year, having handed the Chairmanship of the RNLI over to his deputy, Captain the Honourable V Wyndham-Quin.

The Duke of Kent opened the 1963 conference, attended by seventeen nations. Papers were read from several nations covering the work of inshore rescue craft while the delegation from the United States Coast Guard gave details of a lifeboat of steel construction. This information led to a visit to the United States by the new RNLI Chairman and his deputy which, in turn, led to the ordering of an American steel boat for evaluation trials in British waters. While in the United States Captain Wyndham-Quin announced RNLI plans to name a new lifeboat after the late President Kennedy. The boat would be sent to an Irish station.

There was one rescue in 1963 which earned the coxswain in charge a gold medal. In fact he earned two because Norway, the country from which the casualty came, awarded him one from their lifeboat society. The cargo ship *Johan Collett* was 15 miles north-west of Guernsey carrying a cargo of zinc which had shifted in gale force winds. Coxswain Hubert Petit, with his son John aboard among the crew, put out from St Peter Port into mountainous seas and made towards the heavily listing vessel some 25 miles from their station. The lifeboat, the *Euphrosyne Kendal*, a 52 foot Barnett boat, arrived at the scene in the early evening. It was already dark. A merchant ship had managed to take off some of the Norwegian ship's crew while a small group were rescued from a rubber dinghy by another ship. A tug had been requested and was on its way from the French port of Cherbourg.

Also at the scene was the South African warship *President Kruger* and later the British aircraft carrier *HMS Ark Royal*. The master and five crew remained aboard the *Johan Collett* which was being illuminated by lights from the South African ship. Heavy snow added to the visibility problems and at around midnight, after the tug had managed to pass a tow with considerable difficulty and risk to all involved, the Norwegian master decided, as the storm increased, to abandon his ship. Coxswain Petit, helped by light from *President Kruger*, made seven runs alongside the listing ship, taking a man off each time on all but one attempt. The task was completed in the early hours of 6 February 1963 when the lifeboat began a long and difficult five hour journey back to the safety of St Peter Port. Coxswain Petit received an RNLI gold medal for this rescue while his son and the motor mechanic each received the bronze award.

Following the tests with the American boat, plans were in hand to build two large steel lifeboats, while the construction of six smaller steel boats had been put in hand at the yard of Brooke Marine, in Lowestoft. These were named the Waveney class and were 44 feet in length. The two 70 foot steel boats, the Clyde class,

were built at the Jarrow Shipyard, near Glasgow, one to the design of Richard Oakley and the second to the design of Irish marine architect John Tyrrell who owned a boatyard at Arklow on the east coast of Eire. The first boat, costing £57,000 from funds provided by the Civil Service supporters of the RNLI, was powered by twin Gardner diesels and was able to carry two inflatable boats aboard. The Civil Service organization provided a constant flow of money each year and many lifeboats of every class were provided from this source of finance. This happy situation remains the same up to this time.

Towards the end of 1966 a sensational rescue took place off Anglesey. A Greek merchant ship had suffered engine failure to the north of the island in winds of up to 100 miles an hour. The Holyhead and Moelfre lifeboats were alerted and launched, the Moelfre boat having already been at sea on an abortive mission. Coxswain Thomas Alcock put to sea from Holyhead with their divisional inspector, Lieutenant Commander Harold Harvey aboard, who happened to be at the port at the time of the emergency.

The Holyhead lifeboat was a 52 foot Barnett type, the *St Cybi* (Civil Service No 9), while the Moelfre boat was a 42 foot Watson, the *Watkins Williams*. Her coxswain was Richard Evans, a veteran of a previous gold medal-winning rescue seven years earlier. The two crews located the Greek ship which had a Russian vessel standing by. The Russians had managed to put a towline aboard but this had later broken. First the Holyhead boat approached the wildly rolling ship in waves of 35 feet from trough to crest. They made several approaches and rescued five men. The Moelfre boat then made several runs, taking off a further ten people while the ship's master and three other men stayed aboard. The Dutch salvage tug *Utrecht* arrived shortly after these rescues and

The Torrey Canyon aground on rocks between the Isles of Scilly and Lands End, 1967.

took the ship in tow to a sheltered shore.

Coxswain Evans collected his second gold medal, while a second gold medal was awarded to Lieutenant Commander Harold Harvey who had helmed the Holyhead boat while the crew grabbed the Greeks from their ship. He was the first Inspector of lifeboats ever to receive the gold award. Coxswain Thomas Alcock received the silver medal as did the motor mechanics of both boats.

It was hardly coincidental that the Dutch salvage tug *Utrecht* was involved with one of the most serious disasters at sea the following year when the oil tanker *Torrey Canyon* ran on rocks off Land's End, Cornwall. The Dutch place salvage tugs at strategic points around the world to await disaster and claim the salvage due if able to save the ship.

The *Torrey Canyon* disaster, as it soon became known, was a lesson to the world in the potential problems of oil spillage from tankers that were becoming larger and less manageable each year. On a clear spring morning

of 1967 the *Torrey Canyon* ran on to the Seven Stones rocks in spite of having received a navigational warning from coastguards. The 61,000 ton ship soon began to spill heavy crude oil into the sea which eventually reached the coasts of Ireland, north-west France and Wales. Coxswain Matt Lethbridge put to sea in the St Mary's lifeboat from the Isles of Scilly not to save a life at that point but to liaise between the salvage tug *Utrecht* and the stranded ship and to advise other shipping of the wreck. The weather then deteriorated. It was decided to take off some of the crew by lifeboat, nine in all, while others were winched off by helicopters from the Royal Naval Air Station, Culdrose.

The Penlee lifeboat then came to the scene with her crew of men from the small fishing village of Mousehole, on the Cornish mainland, to relieve the St Mary's crew. After two days and the loss of considerable quantities of oil into the sea the authorities decided to bomb the ship. The Royal Air Force made the first attempt but failed to set her alight. The Royal

Navy sent Sea Vixen aircraft from RNAS Yeovilton. Their crews had the ship burning after their first strike. Much of the remaining oil was burned off but it was too late to prevent ecological damage to fish, seabirds and plant life over a considerable area. The two lifeboats returned to their respective station, the St Mary's boat having been at sea for well over two days and the Penlee boat for a total of 30 hours. The crew of the oil tanker saved by lifeboat presented a commemorative plaque to the people of the Isles of Scilly.

Matthew Lethbridge was to earn a silver medal during the May of the same year when the motor yacht *Braemar* reported engineroom trouble when 30 miles west of the Isles of Scilly. The weather was bad and the seas running high. A towline passed by a merchant ship standing by broke. The St Mary's lifeboat then took off most of the crew of the yacht with some difficulty when the yacht's captain feared that his vessel might soon sink. A line was passed from the lifeboat to the yacht in winds of force 10 and towing commenced. Eventually the safety of Mount's Bay, Cornwall, was reached and the yacht saved, but it had been a close thing.

It was the turn of France to host the 1967 International Lifeboat Conference which they did with considerable success at St Malo and Dinard. Sixteen nations sent delegates including, for the first time, New Zealand. A few weeks later HRH Princess Marina of Kent, President of the RNLI for twenty-five years, was given the gold award at a special reception organized to commemorate her long service during which time she had taken an active interest in the affairs of the Institution.

The following year Captain Wyndham-Quin relinquished the Chairmanship of the RNLI, his place being taken by Admiral Sir Wilfred Woods, the first Royal Naval Flag Officer to hold the position. Shortly after the annual general meeting of 1968, when the Admiral made a pointed speech on matters concerning salvage and lifeboat crews, the Longhope lifeboat, based on the island of Hoy, in the Orkneys, under Coxswain Daniel Kirkpatrick rescued fifteen trawlermen from a stranded fishing boat in severe weather at night. This earned him a third silver medal, but the next year, 1969, disaster was to strike the same boat and crew.

On the night of 17 March 1969 the cargo ship *Irene* had run aground on rocks off the coast of South Ronaldsay during a severe storm. South Ronaldsay lay dead to windward, south-east of the island of Hoy. The Longhope lifeboat was called out.

The Longhope men were again led by Coxswain Daniel Kirkpatrick who had two of his sons in the boat with him, Raymond and John. Robert Johnston, the oldest man in the boat at 62 years, also shared the voyage with his two sons, Second Coxswain James and Motor Mechanic Robert, named after his father. Also aboard were second mechanic John James Swanson and crew member Eric Macfayden. The coxswain was already the holder of three silver medals for gallantry.

The lifeboat put to sea in the darkness of early evening into a force 9 south-easterly gale. One of the new 70 foot boats, the *Grace Paterson Ritchie*, had also put out from Kirkwall, 20 miles to the north. It was the last ever seen of the Longhope crew alive while the larger Kirkwall boat's crew were struggling to survive the seas. It was impossible for any lifeboat to lie alongside the stranded merchant ship. The crew were later rescued by coastguards using a breeches buoy while Royal Navy helicopters and a Royal Air Force Shackleton joined the Kirkwall lifeboat as well as the lifeboats from Thurso, Stronsay and Stromness in the search for the Longhope crew which had not sent a signal for many hours. The Thurso crew found the missing boat capsized south-west of the island of Hoy. The overturned boat was taken in tow back to the mainland harbour of Scrabster, west of Thurso, where the bodies of seven of the eight man crew were found inside the hull. That of John James Swanson was missing. Once more a memorial fund was set up and money flooded in from all over the country.

The Longhope tragedy occurred at the same time as a radio fund-raising appeal had been broadcast by the BBC and coincided with Lifeboat Day in London. The result of these various activities and the support of several daily newspapers in London and Scotland led to a massive £56,000 being donated.

The decade ended with the Duke of Kent accepting the Presidency of the RNLI following the death of his mother. Down at Cowes, on the Isle of Wight, a maintenance and repair depot was established for inshore lifeboats to supplement the work done at the main depot at Boreham Wood.

Above: Memorial to the lifeboat crew lost in the Longhope boat in 1969.

Below: The Longhope lifeboat TGB that capsized with the loss of all hands in March 1969, south of the island of Hoy.

Chapter 10

150 YEARS OF SERVICE

The decade in which the 150th anniversary lay started badly for the RNLI. Almost the entire crew of the Fraserburgh lifeboat were lost when the boat was capsized by a massive wave while co-operating with Russian fishing boats in the assistance of a Danish fishing boat.

Reports indicated that the 47 foot Watson type boat, the *Duchess of Kent*, was not rolled over sideways but pitch-poled end over end. The crew of a Russian escort ship managed to right the boat after a time of considerable risk, effort and courage in extremely bad weather only to find four of the six crew dead inside and that a fifth was missing. The sixth man, Jackson Buchan, one of the three Buchans aboard, was thrown out of the boat

The Fraserburgh lifeboat Duchess of Kent *before the disaster in January 1970 when all but one of the crew of six were lost.*

when it rolled. He managed to clamber back aboard the upturned hull and was rescued by the crew of one of the Russian fishing boats.

Plans were in hand in the early 1970s to convert non-self-righting lifeboats to become self-righting by fitting inflatable bags to the top of the superstructure. Tests were successfully carried out at Cowes and conversions put in hand. Trials with the American designed 44 foot lifeboats that resulted from the visit of the Chairman and his deputy to the United States back in 1964 led to the ordering of two boats of this type, called the Thames class, to be built in Britain, 6 feet longer than the American design and powered by twin American General Motors diesels of 390 hp giving a top speed of 17 knots.

The work of rescue at sea went on unabated. During 1973 the cost of the lifeboat service was more than £3.7 million while 1,772 lives were saved and 2,659 calls made on lifeboats, the first figure being the highest ever in peacetime and the second figure the highest ever in one year.

The arrival of 1974, the year of the 150th anniversary, gave the RNLI a chance to evaluate its work over its long history. Since 4 March 1824, when Sir William Hillary held the founding meeting of the Institution in London, 99,825 lives had been saved by lifeboat crews off the coasts of Great Britain and Ireland. The Year of the Lifeboat was 'launched' on 4 March 1974 with a Service of Dedication at St Paul's Cathedral attended by Her Majesty Queen Elizabeth the Queen Mother, the Duke of Kent, President of the RNLI, and the Duchess of Kent. Leaders in religion also attended, the Archbishop of Canterbury preaching the sermon and Rabbi Dr Leslie Edgar reading the lesson.

It was election day and later Harold Wilson called on Her Majesty the Queen to accept her invitation to form a new government. St Paul's was filled by a host of people associated with the RNLI while similar church services of every denomination were held across the land.

Other festivities and fund-raising events followed. Her Majesty the Queen and Prince Philip gave a garden party at Buckingham Palace during the summer attended by 4,000 RNLI supporters. The Queen followed this later in the year at the Palace of Holyrood House in Edinburgh in order that those supporters in Scotland and the north of England could put the royal stamp of approval on their celebrations.

Special postage stamps were issued in Eire, the Channel Islands and the Isle of Man, while exhibitions, displays and celebration balls were held across the country. During the celebrations ashore the business of saving life went on at sea. In 1974 lifeboats were called out 2,909 times and 1,357 lives saved without, happily the loss of any lifeboatmen. It is worth noting that of these rescues 791 people were saved by the inshore lifeboats while 566 were saved by the offshore boats. Launches made were 1,185 by all-weather craft and 1,724 by the inflatables.

Expenditure during the year approached £5 million while fund-raising during the same period led to a surplus on the year of £275,000. However, there were financial storm clouds on the horizon as inflation grew, the stock market was depressed and the building of lifeboats and the price of equipment rose in step with the economic difficulties that the nation was facing. In 1975 expenditure increased to over £5.5 million while income was less than £5.3 million leaving a deficiency of nearly £268,000. This was in spite of the fact that helpers, volunteers, fund-raisers and others collected more money for the RNLI than in the Year of the Lifeboat, 1974. It said a great deal for the affection and generosity of the

British and Irish public towards the Institution in spite of the difficulties that ordinary people were facing on a personal financial level.

A number of economies were introduced, including a slowing down in the building of offshore lifeboats to replace those on service which were beginning to show their age. Approaches were made to large industrial concerns for help to replace funds that might have been expected from the public. One result of this was a donation of £100,000 from British Petroleum, covenanted, towards the cost of a new lifeboat for Aberdeen, reflecting the growth of the oil exploration industry in the North Sea.

Developments of the freehold property, notably the new headquarters under construction at Poole, and the building of new houses for the Spurn Head crew at the Humber estuary continued.

During 1972 the Shoreline membership system had been established alongside the volunteer rescue membership. Shoreline members subscribed a guaranteed minimum sum each year and received the quarterly journal and other information and news from the RNLI. In 1975 membership stood at 28,000. By the 1990s the number was about 200,000 but figures like that, showing regular and substantial support for the RNLI were still a long way ahead. Several new offshore boats were completed during 1975 but although there was a financial surplus, albeit a small one, in 1976, financial Draconian measures were enforced during this year.

In May 1975 the RNLI recorded its 100,000th rescue since its foundation 151 years earlier. It was not a particularly sensational affair. A 13 year-old Liverpool boy Stuart Nixon, was rescued from a rubber dinghy by the crew of the New Brighton (Merseyside) inshore rescue boat.

Special certificates were presented both to Stuart and to the crew of the boat to commemorate the event. By

the end of the year the grand total of lives saved by RNLI crew stood at 100,992.

The summer of 1976 was best remembered for the apparently unending heatwave which settled over much of the country. This meant that many more people than usual made for the coast, consequently putting an extra strain on the lifeboat services, particularly the inshore inflatables working at coastal resorts, although the number of calls made on the service and the number of lives saved were almost exactly the same as in the previous year. Severe storms early and late in the year caused damage ashore to several lifeboat stations, particularly on the North Sea coast.

The administrative headquarters and the maintenance and repair depot were now centralized at Poole, the construction of the depot on the waterfront in West Quay Road being financed by the sale of the old depot site at Boreham Wood. The move to Poole had led to close liaison between the offices of Barclays Bank International, placed conveniently nearby in the town, and the RNLI. The computer analysis of rescue records was transferred to the computer at the nearby bank, the staff of the bank and employees working closely together to help modernize the use of computer systems by the RNLI.

The new Atlantic 21 fast rigid inflatable boats were proving their worth at stations around the coast both in terms of speed, sea-keeping and reliability. Orders were placed for more of these boats as well as six larger offshore boats.

The first fatality of the decade occurred on Christmas Eve off Kilmore, County Wexford, Eire. The 37 foot self-righting Oakley class boat *Lady Murphy* was called out to investigate flares seen to the west of the station in Bannow Bay. A severe gale was blowing from the west-south-west. The call seemed to have been a false alarm and the lifeboat, having completed the search, was recalled. Returning and running ahead of the rough breaking seas the lifeboat was overwhelmed and capsized twice, each time righting successfully while the crew were able to restart the engines which had cut out on both occasions. Crewman Finton Sinnott was killed during the capsize and several others of the crew injured but the boat returned to Kilmore safely.

The celebrations of the Silver Jubilee of Her Majesty the Queen were attended by lifeboats from several stations. Three from the Thames Estuary stations took part in the Thames river pageant while three more attended the Royal Jubilee fleet review at Spithead, off Portsmouth. During the same summer the Queen travelled to Hartlepool to name the new lifeboat at the station, *The Scout*, a Waveney class boat, paid for by the Scout movement.

During the year thirteen medals were awarded for gallantry, Matthew Lethbridge, of St Mary's in the Isles of Scilly, receiving the bar to the silver medal that he already held. When attending the presentation ceremony Coxswain Lethbridge and those of his crew who accompanied him to London were entertained by the Prime Minister Harold Wilson at Number 10, Downing Street. Owning a holiday home in the islands Mr Wilson took a deep interest in the work of the St Mary's lifeboat and was a friend of all the crew.

Severe weather marked the start and end of 1978 but no lifeboat crew lives were lost while 943 people were saved during twelve months that saw a reduction in calls on the service when compared with previous years. The economic crisis in Britain was causing some worries at the RNLI but support continued to come in. The year 1979 started with storms and blizzards in the North Sea where a gold medal, three silver medals and fifteen bronze medals were awarded to east coast crews for assisting merchant ships

during the first seven weeks of the year. Coxswain Brian Bevan, in charge of the Humber lifeboat, had been awarded a silver medal a year earlier. At the start of 1979 he added a gold and bronze award to these and received all three medals at the same ceremony. Because of this achievement he was asked to open the 1980 London International Boat Show at Earls Court, a task which he performed with great modesty and aplomb.

The year 1979 will probably be remembered best for the storm that struck the Fastnet Race fleet of 303 yachts as they sailed between the Isles of Scilly and the Fastnet Rock off the south-west coast of Eire. Winds of hurricane force hit the fleet as the leaders were rounding the Fastnet Rock and the smaller yachts, the majority of the fleet, as they sailed north-west towards the famous rock. Thirteen lifeboat crews were called out from every station from Cadgwith to the south Angle, near Milford Haven to the east and the Irish station at Dunmore East, on the south-east coast of Eire, to the north. The Courtmacsherry boat was also called on from the west of Cork towing one damaged yacht back to its base.

Several books about the storm have been written and about this rescue operation alone. The co-ordination between the RNLI crews, the Royal Navy helicopter crews from RNAS Culdrose, HM Coastguard Rescue Centre at Falmouth, Royal Air Force Coastal Command and other agencies such as the Dutch Navy ship acting as escort to the race, was a credit to all involved. Sixty lives were saved and lifeboats escorted, towed or even 'captured' more than 20 yachts. Those 'captured' had been abandoned but recovered. The storm over and the race leaders battered but triumphant back in Plymouth, the sad business of recovering yachts and the dead continued for almost two days.

The yachting journalists were either on the race or at Plymouth to report it. They were soon joined by representatives of the more sensational media who swooped on the city. Many of those who had spent their lives covering sailing and seafaring matters were amazed at the stories that the ambulance chasing brigade managed to concoct. But for the bravery of the lifeboat and helicopter crews as well as some superb seamanship by many of the yacht crews themselves, the sensation-seeking reporters might have been nearer the truth. The less-informed observers attributed much of the trouble to the fact that 'yachtsmen' are inexperienced seafarers. As it happened many of the fatal Fastnet Race casualties were, in many cases, as experienced as those who went to help them, perhaps a fact contributing to the low loss of life considering how many were at sea, estimated at around 2,900 people.

The troubles during the Fastnet Race, and the aftermath of publicity and enquiries that rumbled on for a considerable time, overshadowed the

Rear Admiral W J Graham.

near-disaster that struck in the Western Isles during the late autumn of the same year. The new 50 foot Thames class boat stationed on the isle of Islay and the 52 foot Barnett class boat from Barra put out in winds of force 11 to 12 to go to the aid of a Danish ship. Her cargo of loose marble chippings had shifted. Both lifeboats were capsized but immediately self-righted without any loss of those aboard while the cargo ship found a safe haven.

During this year Major General Ralph Farrant retired as Chairman of the RNLI, to be succeeded by the Duke of Atholl while Rear Admiral Wilfred Graham took the helm as Director and Secretary of the Institution. Admiral Graham, willingly or otherwise, was a well-known personality in the eyes of the public. He had been Captain of the aircraft carrier *HMS Ark Royal* during the making of the popular television series 'Sailor'. During the series a brave but slightly impertinent Royal Marine produced a ventriloquist's dummy named Wilf which virtually took over the ship's internal television relay system. Whatever the Captain did, Wilf had his views about the situation but, while the dummy reacted to the Commanding Officer in a gently controversial way the Commanding Officer Captain Wilf Graham never reacted to the dummy. The programme opened many eyes to the mysterious workings of the Senior Silent Service and endeared both characters to a vast audience.

Admiral Graham was a sailor's sailor. That came clearly across in the television series about his ship. It also came across at Poole. Many of the employees both in the office premises and at the depot across the road had been in one of the services so understood the thinking of the new executive. The Admiral was in charge, of that there was little doubt, and the office doors showed by signs on them exactly what the occupant of that office was employed to do.

One veteran shipwright, supping a pint in the RNLI 'local' the Brewers Arms at the back of the offices was heard to comment "E'll be 'aving rounds next. That'll be me lot". Rounds are regular inspections by officers of the ship, where they delve into every nook and cranny. They are preceded by a tornado of cleaning, scrubbing and polishing by the ship's crew. The old hand was right. Admiral Graham was often to be found in the depot and elsewhere, not necessarily inspecting but encouraging, asking questions, finding out about problems, the wellbeing of his people and understanding those for whom he was responsible. Never, as far as anyone knows, did he hand down stoppage of leave, rum or pay during these tours. Those at Poole depot described him as the best boss they had ever had, but then he had been a television star too. Today the depot is as clean and organized as the workshop or engineroom of any Royal Navy ship. Those working there are proud of this and put it down to the influence of The Admiral, as they knew him, or,

more simply, Wilf.

Several new boats built to established designs were launched in 1979 while the prototypes of two new classes of boat were also completed. These were the 35 foot semi-rigid inflatable Medina class and the Lochin 33, built by Lochin Marine at Rye in Sussex. The two Medina prototypes were built by W A Souter, at Cowes. Single side band radios were by now fitted to 90 boats with more planned for the following year while VHF whip aerials, which were inclined to break off during capsizes were being replaced by lower profile aerials.

The thirteenth International Lifeboat Conference was held in Holland during August. Twenty-five countries sent delegates. Discussions and papers read covered fire-fighting at sea, search and rescue and medical matters that were related to survival at sea. All delegates supported an application by the Conference management to be considered by the Nobel Peace Prize committee for some recognition. The the next Conference was to be held four years later in Gothenberg, Sweden.

Chapter 11

TOWARDS THE NEXT CENTURY

The year 1980 started well for the RNLI. Superintendent Coxswain Brian Bevan, from the Spurn Head station, opened the London International Boat Show in January, as has already been mentioned. The theme of the Boat Show was safety at sea. The RNLI was able to capitalize on this by displaying on two stands and in the central pool feature where an Atlantic 21 rigid inflatable was used to give a self-righting display three times a day. On one of the two stands the new prototype Medina class lifeboat *Mountbatten of Burma* was displayed, but it was Coxswain Bevan who was the star of the show. Shortly before performing the opening ceremony he was intercepted by Eammon Andrews and invited to make one of the 'This is Your Life' programmes. This was recorded and when broadcast a short time later was seen by an estimated 18.1 million viewers. The effect on fund-raising was not easy to calculate but times were economically hard in the early days of a new Tory government, so any publicity that might encourage fund-raisers and subscribers was welcome.

The Shoreline membership of the RNLI, where the public associated their interest in the Institution with regular annual subscriptions, continued to increase with these subscriptions exceeding £500,000 for the first time. The RNLI was also firmly committed to marketing a number of special items ranging from Christmas cards to souvenir gifts. During 1980 the income from this source exceeded £1 million, another record.

The following year, 1981, was one of records being set both for the number of launchings by lifeboats, 2,290, and 1,072 lives saved but it is sadly best remembered for the loss of the Penlee lifeboat and all her crew at the end of the year, just before Christmas. The year had seen several severe storms. Lifeboats were called out thirty-one times during a storm in September and in mid-December Coxswain Michael Scales of St Peter Port, Guernsey, was awarded the gold medal for the rescue of the crew of twenty-nine from the Ecuadorian motor vessel *Bonita*. His crew all received bronze medals for their efforts.

It was on 18 December, when onshore winds of hurricane force were hitting the south coast of Cornwall that the Penlee boat, crewed by men of the village of Mousehole, were called out to the cargo ship *Union Star*, registered in Dublin. Her engine had failed some eight miles to the south-east of Mousehole. The south-easterly storm was driving the cargo ship along the coast towards the rocks at Tater-du, just four miles along the coast from Penlee Point towards the west.

Coxswain William Trevelyan Richards and his crew of seven launched down the steep ramp at Penlee in their 47 foot Watson type lifeboat *Solomon*

Calm Days. The Penlee lifeboat, Solomon Browne *launching from its slipway near Mousehole. The boat was lost with its entire crew while going to the aid of the cargo vessel* Union Star *in hurricane force winds.*

Brown. There were eight people aboard the cargo ship including a woman and two young girls. A Royal Navy Sea King helicopter was sent from RNAS Culdrose but conditions were so bad that the helicopter crew were unable to lift off any of those aboard the ship.

People ashore at Tater-du saw the lifeboat make several runs towards and alongside the ship which was at this time close to steep cliffs that were being smitten by horrendous seas driving straight towards them. The lifeboat was seen to make another turn away from the ship having taken four of those aboard from it. Then there was silence. Nothing more was seen, or heard on the radio, from the lifeboat. The lifeboat from Sennen Cove, around the corner of Land's End, was called out but her crew were unable to round the corner of Gwennap Head, to the west of the wreck and south of Land's End, because of the sea state and strength of the wind. The search for survivors continued both from ashore and by lifeboats from St Mary's, Isles of Scilly and Cadgwith, on the Lizard peninsula, as well as by helicopters from RNAS Culdrose. Nothing was found that night of either those from the lifeboat or the *Union Star*. It was a total disaster that struck the nation at a time of festivity and goodwill. There can have been few in Britain who did not share a small part of the massive grief that struck the small close-knit community of the village of Mousehole.

The RNLI immediately set about caring for the short-term needs of the dependants of the lost crew, but it was a hard task at Christmas. A 70 foot Clyde type lifeboat, the *Charles H Barrett*, (Civil Service number 35) was stationed at nearby Newlyn to cover for the missing boat, manned by RNLI staff members until a new crew could be formed from a community as small as that of Mousehole. It seemed impossible, but it was eventually achieved.

The missing men were Coxswain William Trevelyan Richards, Second

The wreck of the cargo vessel Union Star, *December 1981. The entire crew of the Penlee lifeboat were lost going to her aid as were the people they were trying to save.*

Coxswain-Mechanic James Madron, Assistant Mechanic Nigel Brockman, Emergency Mechanic John Blewett and crew members Kevin Smith, Barrie Torrie, Charles Greenhaugh and Gary Wallis. All those from the *Union Star* were also lost. The coxswain was awarded the gold medal for gallantry while the rest of the missing crew were awarded bronze medals posthumously. A special gold plaque was given to the lifeboat station.

Messages of sympathy reached Mousehole from royalty, heads of government and from people worldwide. A special disaster fund was set up to help the families of those lost. It was Christmas time. Never was there a better example of the feelings of people during the season of goodwill as money poured into the fund. At the end of 1982, almost exactly a year after the loss of the Penlee boat, the last of five new Arun class boats was accepted from the builders and paid for by David Robinson, the television rentals millionaire and philanthropist who had already provided funds to support a new college at Cambridge University that was named after him. The boat was to be called the *Mabel Alice* and stationed at nearby Newlyn harbour. A new crew had to be trained, mainly men from Mousehole.

Memorial services had been held at the church at Paul, a village close to Mousehole, earlier in January 1982, attended by the Duke and Duchess of Kent. The Duchess gave each widow or bereaved mother an engraved silver cross. During the following month a further memorial service, attended by the nation's leaders, was held at Truro Cathedral but it was not until a year after this service that the *Mabel Alice* was stationed at Newlyn.

David Robinson attended the handing-over and naming ceremony in Cornwall. For a number of years the lifeboat house lay empty but kept immaculately by the crew of the *Mabel Alice*. It was something of a grim reminder of that tragic night for the passing visitor, who could walk around the lifeboat station and notice that the two things still missing were the boat and the oilskin foul weather clothing that would have been hanging on hooks near the boat. The small lifeboat house, on its clifftop eyrie at Penlee Point, became as fitting a memorial as there ever could be anywhere to all lifeboatmen lost at sea. The boathouse is kept available for emergency relief lifeboats.

During 1982, the year before the *Mabel Alice* arrived in Cornwall, fund-raising had gone apace right from the start of the year in which Jimmy Saville, now Sir Jimmy, opened the London International Boat Show accompanied by the crew of the Beaumaris lifeboat. Penlee was on everybody's mind and proceeds from the RNLI stand at the Boat Show broke all previous records for an event of this sort. The money was needed, with the cost of one of the new Tyne class lifeboats put at £430,000 each and with the RNLI having four on order at the time.

Shortly after the Penlee memorial service at Truro a happier event occurred involving people from Cornwall. Mrs Vigdis Finnbogadottir, the President of Iceland, came to Britain and at a ceremony in London presented Coxswain Mechanic Maurice Hutchens and the crew of the Sennen lifeboat her country's silver medal for gallantry for their part in the rescue of the crew of an Icelandic cargo ship during the previous year. The same award was given to Lieutenant Nick Houghton and the helicopter crew from RNAS Culdrose who also took part in the rescue.

If there can be such an event as a successful capsize, then it happened during the spring of 1983. The Salcombe Watson class lifeboat *The Baltic Exchange*, a boat with 20 years of service to her credit, was on call in Start Bay, to the south of Dartmouth, in weather rated as a violent storm. The lifeboat was struck by two massive waves, of an estimated 50 feet in height, while passing the Skerries bank. The first wave swept a crew member from the boat while the second capsized it. The airbag inflated and the boat righted immediately allowing the crew to recover the crew member who had been swept away and then complete their mission before making for the shelter of Torbay. The boat, due for a refit anyway, was taken out of service being temporarily replaced by a lifeboat from the relief fleet. At about the same time as this event the official enquiry into the loss of the Penlee lifeboat was held at Penzance where the lost crew were commended by the court for their courage while others who had taken part in the attempts to

rescue the people of the *Union Star* also received recognition.

Apart from the obvious commendations for the crew of the lifeboat, Lieutenant Commander Russell-Smith, on exchange at RNAS Culdrose from the United States Navy, was recognized for his courageous attempts to rescue those of the *Union Star* while local coastguards were also commended for attempts to reach the stranded ship by descending the cliffs at Tater-du. The crew of the Sennen Cove lifeboat were also praised for their attempts to reach the scene of the disaster. The shadow of Penlee was a long one. While it may have faded a little over the years on a national basis it is, one fears, still evident in that little Cornish community just as the same sad feelings of grief survive in other small fishing ports where lifeboat crews have been lost while attempting to save others.

The mid-1980s were a time of reconstruction and preparation for the years ahead. The various committees of the RNLI were looking far ahead towards the first and second decades of the next century. Some lifeboats were ageing and needed replacing. The 52 foot Arun class was becoming the backbone of the fleet, supported by the new Brede class and later the Mersey class boats all designed with specific sea conditions, operating areas and requirements in the minds of the designers, builders and those that selected the stations where they were to be placed. Prototypes of the new 47 foot Tyne class lifeboat and the new smaller Brede class boat were taken across the North Sea to Gothenburg for the 1983 International Lifeboat Conference creating considerable interest among the delegates attending the event.

The advent of the microchip and other electronic inventions enabled radio and navigational equipment to be reduced in size and improved in efficiency. Though carried on some of the older lifeboats, the earlier types of radio direction finder were rapidly being replaced by modern VHF equipment as well as the latest satellite navigational systems able to pinpoint a vessel's position to within a few yards in any weather. Modern equipment is housed in a case a little larger than an average-sized portable radio making the work of the lifeboat crew easier without costing valuable space aboard. The latter years of the 1980s saw great strides in the area of electronics being made by the RNLI.

Modern materials, be they for boatbuilding or even clothing the crews, also brought about changes. Lighter but more durable foul weather clothing, some developed originally for the pleasure industry, yachtsmen and others, was tested by the RNLI. It is worth noting that the enormous increase in the sport of sailing and power cruising by the public during the 1980s meant that the suppliers of electronics and machinery, as well as clothing, were able to spend money on research, development and improvement that might not have been economically worth the effort if directed simply at the area of commercial shipping. Given the potential market of the million or so people who put to sea for pleasure in their own small craft in British waters each year, the prospects were worth following up. The end effect was the arrival of a mass of equipment at an affordable price and ideal for use by the RNLI.

The increase in the sport of cruising for pleasure led to another change for the RNLI. In the southern half of Britain the majority of rescues made by inshore and deep water lifeboats were of those at sea in privately-owned boats and dinghies as well as bathers, non-commercial fishermen and board sailors. This was particularly the case during the late 1980s, but while the more southerly crews went to the aid of amateurs, in the more northern waters the rescues were still

predominately of professional seafarers, particularly fishermen.

During 1990 almost 2,000 yachts competed in the annual race around the Isle of Wight involving as many as 12,000 sailors, if one picks an average of six people per competing yacht, figures unimaginable in the 1960s. During the race a strong south-westerly wind met a west flowing tide south of the Isle of Wight. Both lifeboats and rescue helicopters were called out. Three yachts in fact sank, fifteen people were lifted ashore and, sadly, one crewman died having been struck on the head by the mainsail boom. It was a busy time for the rescue services.

The yachting fraternity were not slow to appreciate the work of the RNLI in relation to the sport of sailing. By 1988 the various levels of Shoreline membership, ranging from a Life Governor to a junior Storm Force member, totalled 168,174 people with the numbers certain to increase further in the years ahead. The Storm Force section was formed for younger people to enable them to help the RNLI, receive regular news and be able to buy items from the ever-expanding list of gifts and souvenirs offered by the marketing department at the Poole headquarters. During 1988 the income of the RNLI was £38.5 million, the lifeboats were called out 4,224 times saving the lives of 1,366 people in pleasure craft, 157 from fishing vessels and 40 from commercial or Ministry of Defence vessels.

In the pages ahead, where the people who man the lifeboat stations are depicted, it will be seen that rescues and the other work of the RNLI continued apace into the 1990s. In 1989 the Duke of Atholl, who had been Chairman of the management committee of the RNLI for ten years, handed over the position to Michael Vernon, a yachtsman of many years experience and a businessman of considerable standing.

Chapter 12

THE LIFEBOATS OF TODAY

It is fair to say that of all vessels built for non-military purposes anywhere in the world the lifeboats of the RNLI are probably leaders in terms of selection of materials, design, efficiency and safety. They carry the latest equipment, are powered by engines built to the highest specifications and are manned by a band of people selected for their prowess as seamen. Any vessel specifically designed to put to sea in the severest of weather conditions, when many seafarers would be seeking shelter, has to be built to these standards. They simply have to survive when other vessels are foundering, so no corners can be cut.

Ever since 1790, when Henry Greathead's lifeboat *The Original* went on station at Tynemouth, work has been carried out to improve the design and performance of the lifeboat fleet. The earliest boats were steered by an oar, pulled with oars by the crews and occasionally carried sail, if only to steady the boats. The earliest designers, Henry Greathead, William Wouldhave, Lionel Lukin and James Beeching paved the way for the founders of the present day concept, George Watson, Richard Oakley, J R Barnett and James Peake.

During the early days of the RNLI the choice of boat was a question of horses for courses. Then many lifeboats were built locally and often

The Original *1790.*

The Barra Island lifeboat, Arun class Ann Lewis Fraser, exercising at speed.

based on the design of fishing vessels, traditionally 'designed' to cope with local sea conditions. The word 'designed' is used guardedly as many of the fishing boats of the eighteenth and nineteenth century had never been drawn as a plan. Even today the cobles of the north-east coast can be built by eye, craftsmen still using the traditional long saw and adze to shape the timbers.

Initially the choice of a lifeboat for a particular station depended upon a number of factors. Could the lifeboat be launched from a slipway or tractor horse and carriage? Should it be kept afloat in a port or fishing harbour? Would it be operated in shoaling waters?

Although today the slipway launching Tyne is occasionally kept afloat and the carriage launching Mersey can launch from a slipway, lifeboat classes are still designed to cope with differing launching conditions.

Until the new Fast Afloat Boats come into service the largest RNLI lifeboat is the 54 foot **Arun** while the 52 foot Arun is a very popular boat

with crews where these craft are stationed. The first Arun was introduced in 1971, initially built in wood and then in glass reinforced plastic (GRP) except for one, built in steel and now stationed at the most northerly station at Aith in the Shetlands. The design of the Arun won an award from the Design Council some ten years after the first boats of this type were produced. As is the case with all modern lifeboats the Arun is self-righting and is unique with its flying bridge above the wheelhouse which, some feel, make it appear cumbersome, but the boat is anything but cumbersome and is a fine seaboat.

Arun class boats serve on some of the more remote stations and in areas notorious for bad sea conditions. Aith is one example, but there are Aruns at most of the far northern stations including Stromess, Lerwick, Kirkwall, Thurso and Lochinver, the exception being the 47 foot Tyne class boat across the Pentland Firth from Thurso at Longhope. The Aruns, fitted with twin turbo-charged diesel engines of up to 500 hp have a top operating

The Tyne class Longhope lifeboat Lord Saltoun, that went on station in the Orkney Islands in 1987.

speed of 18 knots and a radius of operation of over 110 miles. The Arun carries a crew of up to six men including navigator, mechanic, radio operator and, if necessary, a doctor.

The 47 foot **Tyne** class lifeboat is another design that makes up the pattern of new fast lifeboats that are replacing old slower boats in the RNLI fleet. Whereas the Arun has to be berthed afloat the Tyne is a slipway launching boat but this powerful 18 knots steel boat has also been placed at stations where the boat is berthed afloat. Again, as with the Arun, twin diesels power the boat. It is worth noting again, perhaps, that up on the Pentland Firth and the waters of Orkney two Tyne class boats share the work with the Aruns based there, these being the boats at Longhope and Wick where their crews are as pleased with their vessels as are the crews of their neighbouring Aruns. This reflects the skill of the RNLI naval architects in their ability to select designs and then develop them to provide superb fast seaboats.

As the RNLI changes to an entire fleet of fast lifeboats it seems that the Tynes, Mersey and Arun class lifeboats, later joined perhaps by the new larger fast Afloat Boats, will become the workhorses of the fleet, but it has been the **Waveney** class boats that spearheaded the conversion. The Waveney was a result of a decision made at the 1963 International Lifeboat Conference at Edinburgh where the United States Coast Guard gave details of their latest 44 foot cutter. Later one of these United States boats was sent to Britain for evaluation by the RNLI. During 1990 the original boat was on relief duty at Eyemouth, in Scotland while the Eyemouth 1973 vintage Waveney was being completely refurbished in a local boatyard.

The Waveney is constructed of steel and the design is reflected in later fast boats that have been built for the RNLI fleet since the American boat first appeared in British waters in 1964. It is a credit to American designers that almost thirty years after their first fast boat came to Britain its successors are still fulfilling their roles

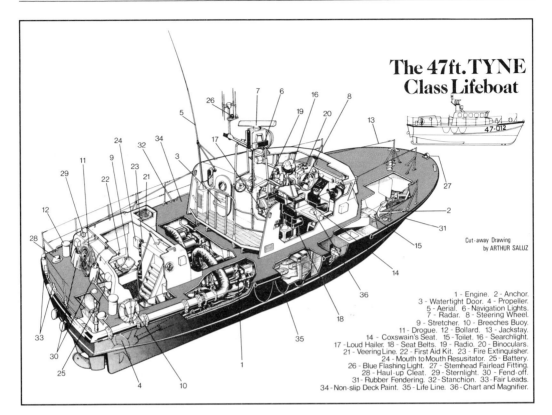

The 47ft. TYNE Class Lifeboat

Cut-away Drawing
by ARTHUR SALUZ

1 - Engine. 2 - Anchor.
3 - Watertight Door. 4 - Propeller.
5 - Aerial. 6 - Navigation Lights.
7 - Radar. 8 - Steering Wheel.
9 - Stretcher. 10 - Breeches Buoy.
11 - Drogue. 12 - Bollard. 13 - Jackstay.
14 - Coxswain's Seat. 15 - Toilet. 16 - Searchlight.
17 - Loud Hailer. 18 - Seat Belts. 19 - Radio. 20 - Binoculars.
21 - Veering Line. 22 - First Aid Kit. 23 - Fire Extinguisher.
24 - Mouth to Mouth Resusitator. 25 - Battery.
26 - Blue Flashing Light. 27 - Stemhead Fairlead Fitting.
28 - Haul-up Cleat. 29 - Sternlight. 30 - Fend-off.
31 - Rubber Fendering. 32 - Stanchion. 33 - Fair Leads.
34 - Non-slip Deck Paint. 35 - Life Line. 36 - Chart and Magnifier.

Below: *Tyne class equipment.*

Above: Tyne class equipment.

Below: Waveney class lifeboat *The William and Jane on station at Blyth, Northumberland.*

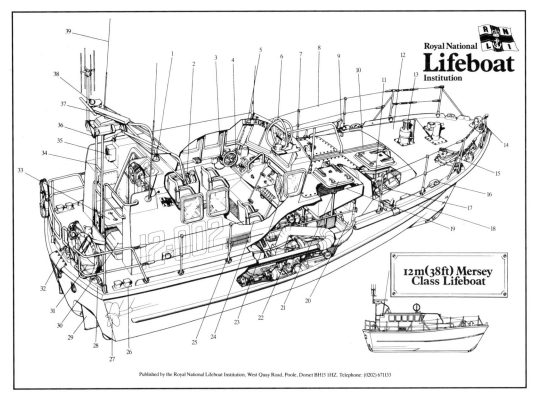

Royal National
Lifeboat
Institution

**12m(38ft) Mersey
Class Lifeboat**

Published by the Royal National Lifeboat Institution, West Quay Road, Poole, Dorset BH15 1HZ. Telephone: (0202) 671133

Below: Hastings' Mersey class lifeboat, RNLB Sealink Endeavour.

around the coast. The Waveney was well ahead of its time in the early 1960s. Today, with its top speed of 15 knots and an operating radius of 95 nautical miles, it has kept well in step with more modern designs. While older lifeboats are being replaced by the new faster classes, the stations operating Waveneys seem set to be among the last to acquire a new lifeboat. All crews seem to like the old American design.

The 38 foot long **Mersey** class lifeboats have been designed for carriage launching from the twenty-two stations that take their boats to sea this way. They are gradually replacing the old Oakley and Rother class boats though with the replacement with a faster boat (the Mersey, with 18 knots is twice as fast as the boats it will replace) some stations, notably Sheringham, may lose their all-weather lifeboat.

The Mersey is built of aluminium or fibre reinforced composite, is self-righting, as are all the new classes, is powered by Caterpillar 285 horsepower turbo-charged diesels and has an operating radius of 90 nautical miles at full power. The boat carries a crew of six who are fully equipped with all the latest navigational aids, rescue, survival and resuscitation equipment.

The 33 foot **Brede** class lifeboat is, as the harbour master at Girvan, Roddy Leitch, commented, a rare breed! There are five on station, at Girvan, Oban, Calshot, Exmouth and Poole. They were designed to fill gaps where the semi-rigid inflatable Atlantic class boats were considered a little too small and exposed for local waters, particularly during winter months. The original Brede was built at Lochin Marine, at Rye in Sussex, from GRP. Indeed the prototype is still working as a general purpose harbour boat at

The Girvan Brede class lifeboat Amateur Swimming Associations, *on a training exercise off the Scottish coast. Subscribed by the Amateur Swimming Associations of Scotland, England and Wales.*

Yarmouth, on the Isle of Wight.

This little 33 foot craft is fast, having a top speed of 20 knots. It also has a respectable operating radius of 70 nautical miles or range of 140 miles at full speed, powered by twin Caterpillar 203 horsepower diesels, a considerable amount of power for a relatively small hull. Carrying a crew of four, the Brede class boat embodies all the safety equipment and most of the electronics of larger boats and is described by the crews as an excellent if somewhat lively seaboat.

The **Thames** class is another rara avis in the RNLI flock, only two being on station, at Islay in Scotland and Dover. They were built in the early 1970s and the design then dropped, the Arun superseding them as the design for a larger class of lifeboat. Both Thames crews are quite happy with their boats although they are expecting something more modern soon.

All the lifeboats mentioned so far are designed with fast semi-planing hulls and full self-righting capability. This will be the form of all lifeboats on RNLI stations by the mid-1990s. Until this goal is achieved there will still be stations operating with the older displacement lifeboats that are being phased out and replaced. These displacement boats are the **Oakley, Rother, Solent** and **Watson** classes. These boats are of a shape that many of the public, who may only see a lifeboat once a year when on their holidays, might consider traditional. Indeed, they are. Often built of wood, often under-powered by today's standards and with a maximum speed of no better than 9 knots, it is not hard to see why they must be replaced as the demands on the RNLI crews change. Further and faster is the name of today's rescue services. Most of these brave old boats are sold, some scrapped. Wandering around the many yacht harbours and marinas along the coast one can often see an old class lifeboat converted to a very seaworthy cruising boat. For example, Newcastle adventurer David Scott-Cowper converted a 42 foot Watson class lifeboat to his special needs and sailed it around the world twice, once on a protracted and delayed voyage that took him through the North-west Passage in the Arctic regions of northern Canada and the United States.

Modern electronic aids aboard lifeboats include radar with a watertight scanner so that it will operate after a capsize, Decca navigator, VHF radio and MF radio, VHF and MF direction finders, and a depth sounder. It is a fact that lifeboats today carry equipment as sophisticated as that found aboard much larger ships, the latest aid to be evaluated being satellite navigation sets that can give the position of the vessel to within two or three feet. A few years ago satellite navigators were the size of a large deep freeze or bigger. Today, thanks to the invention of the microchip, they are no larger than an average radio set and can cost under £500.

The start of 1991 saw the emergence of the prototype FAB 3 lifeboat, 55 feet long and with a speed of 25 knots. It had been fitted-out at the Littlehampton yard of William Osborne Ltd. The boat resembles a scaled-up Arun but many innovations have been incorporated. Twin turbo-charged Caterpillar diesel engines, 1,000 horsepower each drive the hull, built by Halmatic at Portsmouth. This new boat, along with the slightly smaller FAB 4, also nearing completion prior to trials, are the lifeboats that will take the RNLI operations into the next century and beyond.

Chapter 13

THE HEART OF THE LIFEBOAT – THE ENGINES

The heart of any lifeboat is its engineroom and engines. Ever since engines were first installed in lifeboats the RNLI has striven for reliability, a good power to weight ratio and good back-up systems to provide spares when needed. In the days before the slower boats began to be phased out engines were supplied by a number of British manufacturers, such as Thornycroft, Perkins, Parson, Gardner and Ford. The arrival of the boat from the US Coast Guard in 1964, the first Waveney, began a change in the pattern of things.

This first fast boat was powered by American made Caterpillar twin diesel engines of 203 shaft horsepower (shp) each, giving the boat a speed of just over 15 knots. The RNLI began, from that time, to take a long hard look at American engines. While the RNLI naval architects began work on the designs of the several fast boats of the future the engineers were evaluating the Caterpillar power plants. They also examined the power to weight ratio of several engines from another American engine maker, General Motors.

The Caterpillar engines obviously passed all the desired criteria because in 1969 H Leverton Limited, dealers for Caterpillar in Britain based in Windsor, were invited to quote for two 375 shaft horsepower V8 engines fitted with Twin Disc gearboxes to be installed in the first Arun class boat, to be launched in 1971.

Since that time, during the building of 46 Arun class boats, Caterpillar engines were used in every boat of this very successful class though the type of engines changed twice during the years between 1970 and 1989 when the Aruns were being built. The 375 shp engines were superseded for the next 12 Aruns by the more powerful straight 6 cylinder type D 343 TA that provided 470 shp. A further change was then made, installing the V8 cylinder 3408 TA engines that produce just over 500 shp. Caterpillar engines were also installed in the later-designed Brede class boats and the Mersey class. General Motors supplied the power for the slipway launching Tyne class boats, with engines of 425 shp.

The marriage between Caterpillar and the RNLI has obviously been a

H. Leverton's Caterpillar 3412 engine.

happy one because the company, through Levertons, have been asked to provide the engines for the first of the largest Fast Afloat Boats that was being built ready for trials at the start of the 1990s. These are mighty V12 cylinder engines producing over 1,000 shp costing, at 1990 prices, around £55,000 each and that does not include the gearbox which adds another £15,000 to the price of each engine installation.

The success of the relationship between the mighty American engine builder and the RNLI is not simply based upon the proven reliability and specifications of the engines. There is more to it than that. Levertons and a parallel company, Finning Limited, based at Cannock, in Staffordshire, operate a chain of branches and authorized marine dealers who provide excellent back-up to the lifeboat crews when spares are required.

Every working day of the week a 32 ton transporter leaves the Caterpillar stores depot in Belgium for Windsor loaded with machinery parts for the thousands of engines and equipment operating in the United Kingdom. If a spare part is not already in stock at Windsor then, if a lifeboat mechanic sends his order to Levertons by noon on one day, it will be ready for despatch to him from Windsor by mid-morning the following day using the company's own transport. This service is as vital to lifeboat crews as it is the crews of any working vessels such as fishermen, tug operators and other commercial ship operators. The same service is provided for the operators of heavy plant equipment and transport on land powered by Caterpillar. Spares for the earlier engine models fitted to RNLI boats are as quickly and readily available as for the latest types. It is a reflection on the engines themselves that a panic call for spares is very much the exception rather than the rule.

Another feature that has endeared Caterpillar to RNLI crews and

administration is that the whole engine installation is covered by one warranty. Other engine builders are inclined to insist on separate warranty cover for ancillary equipment such as fuel pumps, electronics and filters fitted by them but not made by them. This can cause a confusion of paperwork and delays if something does go wrong.

Reliability is paramount in a lifeboat that must operate in the worst conceivable conditions, often at maximum power, but another factor that enhances the Caterpillar reputation is engine life. The fast boat engines are used, on average, about 150 hours a year, some less, some more. The lifespan of the Caterpillar engines as rated by John Wesson, the Leverton link-man with the RNLI, is 20,000 hours before a major rebuild is considered provident as long as the engine is properly serviced. There is no problem in that direction with the RNLI whose crews keep their boats and lifeboat houses in immaculate condition. These figures give a lifeboat engine easily a 20 year span before major surgery, a point proven by the fact that the first Arun is still on service with her original engines after 20 years, as is the original American built Waveney, now nearly 30 years old.

The suppliers of engines to the RNLI face what might seem to be a marketing man's dream. One can imagine the scope for advertising. "If it's good enough for them, it must be good enough for you" but while pictures of RNLI boats in action are proudly displayed in the offices of engine makers and dealers, the trumpet-blowing is low key in line with the RNLI views who prefer to promote the organization on a much broader span. In spite of this the majority of boat operators, boatbuilders and others connected with marine engineering seem to be very aware of the engines supplied to the RNLI and are suitably impressed.

Chapter 14

THE MUSCLE OF THE LIFEBOAT – THE CREW

Lifeboatmen come from many different walks of life and have varying seafaring skills. The coxswains are usually men who work at sea professionally as fishermen, pilot boat operators, tug masters and pleasure boat skippers but this is by no means the rule. Among coxswains around the coast are a dentist, a Justice of the Peace who runs a fish sales business, a college lecturer and an hotel owner. Crews come from an even wider cross section of the community, in fact from almost every walk of life.

All lifeboat crews carry out training exercises at their stations under the supervision of the coxswains and honorary secretaries but training begins when a crew receives a new lifeboat at the Poole depot. Here the crews of the large offshore boats are put through a week-long course that ranges from classroom instruction covering the operating of equipment

Medallists 1990: Kennett, Thomas, Steenvoorden, Race.

in the boat, and some complicated exercises. Aboard the new lifeboat everything is fully-explained to the crew from emergency procedures in the event of fire, use of equipment that has been explained ashore, use of the navigational aids and tips on achieving the best results from the lifeboat in a variety of sea conditions by using the trim tabs fitted on the stern of the boat.

Chief of Operations, Commodore George Cooper and his staff set a testing series of exercises at sea that include recovering a man overboard, fire in the engineroom, flooding and even capsize, though the capsize itself will have been carried out while the boat is on acceptance trials before delivery to Poole. Following this training course one coxswain said that by the end of the week his brain was crammed with information. He was a little worried that he would not be able to remember all that he had been told, but the course instruction all fell into shape once he and his crew, accompanied by their divisional inspector of lifeboats, had reached their home port on the north-east coast. The whole crew felt completely confident in themselves and their lifeboat.

Inshore lifeboat crews attend their training courses at the RNLI Cowes base. This course is as rigorous as that for the offshore crew, perhaps even more so as they have to practise an actual capsize which involves going upside down in the boat and then leaving the underside of the inverted craft before inflating the airbag on the stern of the Atlantic 21 rigid inflatable in order to right it. Both offshore and inshore crews are trained in helicopter rescue procedures, Search and Rescue helicopters from either the Royal Navy or HM Coastguard providing the aircraft as part of their own training procedures.

The RNLI have several specially-designed mobile caravans which continually tour the coasts of Britain and Ireland giving training courses at a place where it is possible for several crews to attend on alternate days. The several Mobile Training Units are manned by full-time RNLI instructors, each MTU being equipped to teach a specific requirement of the lifeboatmen.

The Mobile Training Units can provide training in radio-telephony and voice procedure up to the standards required by the Department of Trade as well as training in the use of modern navigational aids with which all offshore lifeboats are equipped. Other MTUs are fitted out to provide instruction in first aid which includes the resuscitation of casualties and other obvious requirements in the lifeboatman's work out at sea where people may be injured with broken bones, severe wounds and burns. The first aid course lasts twenty-two hours spread over a period of eight days and ends with an examination and a certificate of proficiency for those who pass.

The RNLI fleet of training units increased during the early spring of 1991 when Lloyds Bank raised the £20,000 needed to fund a new unit for first aid training.

While the crews attend the bases at Poole and Cowes in a regular stream the MTUs are constantly on the move around the country. Courses are also held at Poole for honorary secretaries as well as divisional and deputy divisional inspectors of lifeboats. The drivers of the Talus tractors which push the trailer-launched lifeboats into the sea and recover them attend special training courses at the tractor manufacturer's. Other specialists including district engineers, navigational and radio equipment engineers all attend courses with manufacturers in order to keep up to date with the advance of the technology that forms part of the modern lifeboat fleet.

Occasionally the lifeboat crews are involved with large-scale training

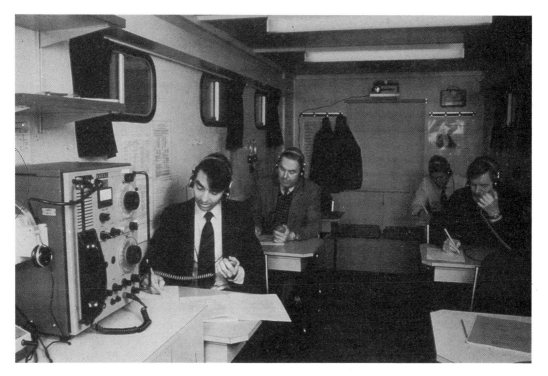

Mobile Training Unit – Radio/Telephony.

exercises involving all the rescue services. During the spring of 1991 such an exercise was held in Mounts Bay, off Penzance, Cornwall. The Isles of Scilly Steamship Company ferry *Scillonian III* was manned by over 280 volunteers who then abandoned the vessel assisted by lifeboats from Penlee (Newlyn), The Lizard and Sennen, helicopters from RNAS Culdrose, the RAF Rescue Co-ordination Centre at Plymouth, British Telecom's radio station at Land's End, the local police, fire services and ambulance services. The local Divisional Inspector of Lifeboats, John Unwin, co-ordinated the operations of the RNLI crews.

Similar exercises are carried out from time to time at other ports, particularly those with busy local passenger ferry traffic. During the regular training exercises performed by all lifeboat crews helicopters from nearby Royal Navy, Royal Air Force and HM Coastguard Search and Rescue stations will often join the training both for the benefit of the lifeboatmen as well as those operating the helicopters. The Search and Rescue helicopter crews generally fly one training sortie during each watch so there is no question of the RNLI incurring extra operating costs when involving helicopters in their own exercises.

Training for the RNLI crews is a continuous process carried out in all weather conditions when every conceivable problem that the crews might meet are rehearsed both by day and night.

Chapter 15

THE BACKBONE: THE HQ AND THE DEPOT

Ever since the RNLI was founded in 1824 it has had an official headquarters somewhere from where all operations were co-ordinated and managed. Until 1975, the administrative offices had been at various locations in the City of London, near the Strand and in Victoria. Following a study by a firm of management consultants it was decided to move from London to the present site at West Quay Road in Poole, Dorset.

Similarly it was also decided that the RNLI depot, where much of the equipment needed by lifeboats is not only stored but manufactured, should also be moved to Poole from the centre at Boreham Wood in Hertfordshire. Apart from the years when the depot was in London's East End neither the headquarters office building nor the depot had been close to water, though the work and traditions of the depot were closely associated with the Royal Navy.

The site at Poole, a mere two hours from London by rail and with water frontage, is ideal and, as the lifeboat fleet is modernized, so the headquarters building has been expanded to almost twice its original

The extension to the RNLI's Poole headquarters was under construction during 1990 and occupied during the spring of 1991.

size containing everything from a small museum section to conference rooms, drawing offices, the centre of the fund-raising operations and the accounting and financial nerve centre. The Operations room and Service Records office are also housed here.

Across West Quay Road at the spaciously laid-out depot new lifeboats are delivered from their building yards for collection by their crews for passage back to their stations following a week of crew familiarization training.

It is not until one visits the Poole headquarters and depot that one realizes the enormity of the work carried out by the RNLI. Apart from designing new boats and many of the fittings and equipment aboard them, these designs have to be tested. All this is handled 'in-house' as is everything from management of the extensive property owned by the RNLI around the country ranging from boathouses, slipways, jetties and crew rooms to roadways and open space around the lifeboat stations.

Permanent crew members and pensioners are all paid directly from Poole as are the payments for crews called out. The Financial Department, not to be confused with the fund-raising section, turns over more than £100,000 per day to keep the entire operation running smoothly and efficiently, boats and equipment properly running and operating. The Fund-raising Department co-ordinates the hundreds of events, donations and other sources of income. Nearby is the Public Relations Department which keeps the nation's media informed about all activities of the RNLI while also producing a quarterly magazine, *Lifeboat*, which is circulated to RNLI Shoreline members and other interested people and concerns. A quarterly lottery is held in conjunction with the circulation of the magazine.

On the top floor of the headquarters building are the offices of the Director, his deputy and staff.

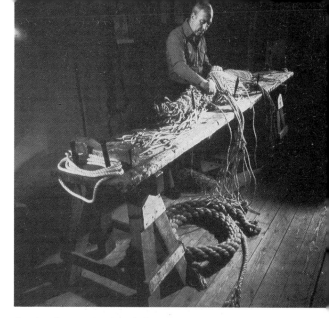

Poole depot rigging loft 1979.

Close by is the Central Operations and Information Room where all lifeboat activities are monitored 24 hours a day, 365 days a year. All information is fed here from Coastguard rescue co-ordination centres and other similar organizations while reports are received here from lifeboat station honorary secretaries. These service reports are generally written by the coxswain of the lifeboat. Details of any service carried out is 'logged' in a computer which is used to analyse local requirements of lifeboats as well as any changes that may have taken place in demands being made on specific stations due to changes in local marine activities.

The communications section handles all electronic navigation and radio equipment used by lifeboats. So complex is some of their equipment that special caravans have been fitted out as communications training centres. These are taken round the coast so that crews can be brought up to date in the use of the latest equipment, be it radio, satellite, navigation or radar.

Although lifeboatmen are often professional seamen, training plays an important part in the pattern of the RNLI. The training centre at Poole gives the crews of new boats a chance to familiarize themselves with their boat. It is an intensive course lasting about a week in which almost every eventuality that may confront a crew is practised.

The depot, where the workshops and stores are accommodated, is as efficiently and skilfully operated as the headquarters offices across the road. A wide range of mechanical work and the manufacture of lifeboat spares takes place in the workshops which include the rigging loft where fenders, ropes and cables are made up to meet the needs of the different classes of lifeboats. While old rigging skills are used, the materials are the latest in natural and man-made fibres and fabrics.

The stores section contains every sort of item that might be needed urgently by a lifeboat crew or simply needed to be supplied for self-maintenance. Strict stock control means that any item from the smallest screws to a complete engine can be despatched from Poole within hours of a request being received to any lifeboat station. Despatch is effected by post, rail or by several vans owned by the RNLI for the purpose. The people in the stores pride themselves that they are very seldom caught short-handed when a request for an item reaches them.

Apart from the stores needed in support of the lifeboats and their stations the depot also includes fund-raising stores where everything from Christmas cards, souvenir pens and car stickers to fund-raising support caravans are sent to RNLI fund-raising branches and guilds nationwide when requested. Fund-raising activities raise more than £30 million a year so the complexity of the fund-raising stores operation is impressive.

All in all, operations in Poole are well-equipped to back up the sterling work performed by all the lifeboat stations around the coast of Great Britain and Ireland.

RNLI medals for bravery. Silver, Gold, Bronze.

St Mary's service to MV Braemar off Isles of Scilly.

Left: Bridlington lifeboat being taken from the lifeboat house by tractor.

Below left: Thurso lifeboat The Queen Mother.

Right: City of Glasgow III *Troon lifeboat –* Arun class.

Below: Port Erin lifeboat launching.

Left: Cartoon by Gareth Davies, son of Coxswain Meurig Davies, of the new Llandudno lifeboat Andy Pearce, Mersey class, named by HRH the Duchess of Kent at Llandudno on 18 June 1991. Disabled by muscular dystrophy Gareth was runner up in the 1990 BBC Radio 4 Today programme Young Person of the Year Award for his work for sufferers of muscular dystrophy. One of Gareth's cartoons was given to HRH the Duchess of Kent at the naming ceremony, specially commissioned by the local RNLI committee.

Below: Pwllheli Mersey class Lilly & Vincent Anthony.

Right: The Barry Dock lifeboat, the first Arun, in London.

Below right: Margate lifeboat.

Above left: Ramsgate Tyne class lifeboat.

Left: The Mersey class lifeboat at Hastings.

Above: Padstow lifeboat Tyne class James Burrough.

Right: Point Law *rescue, Alderney.*

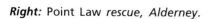

Above: Fund-raisers. The team of Chelsea Pensioners who collected donations for the RNLI every day at the 1991 London International Boat Show, Earls Court.

Left: The latest addition to the RNLI fleet undergoing acceptance trials in the Solent during summer 1991. The Fast Afloat Boat Type 3 is 17 metres long and has a maximum speed of over 25 knots. The lifeboat effected a rescue while undergoing trials, her crew assisting a yacht in difficulty in Lyme Bay off the coast of Dorset.

Chapter 16

THE FUND RAISERS

Fund-raising by hundreds of volunteers nationwide provides the lifeblood of the RNLI . . . money. The country is divided into RNLI branches and guilds for the purpose of fund-raising and organizing sponsored events. There are hundreds of them ranging from the small branches in country villages to the larger branches of the cities. The fund-raisers come from every walk in life from the Chelsea Pensioners who gallantly pass the collecting boxes round the London International Boat Show to young children performing a sponsored maypole dance at a village fete in the West Country.

The Central London committee headed by seven ladies, who in turn lead a panel of around forty members, manages to raise large sums of money each year for the RNLI. In 1990 they sent £215,000 to Poole headquarters as a result of their activities.

Typical of a Central London member is Mrs Pat Telfer, wife of retired stockbroker Charles Telfer. She has served twice as one of the vice-chairmen on the branch committee for a total period of five years. At the time of the Gulf War she was very busy making arrangements for the Lifeboat Day collections in Central London on 12 March 1991 but thought this just as well as she had two sons serving at the sharp end of the operations as young army officers. RNLI work gave her some escape from the worry. (In fact she probably had more to worry about than she realized

as the elder of the two, Richard, serving as a Lieutenant with the Royal Scots Dragoon Guards, was later awarded the Military Cross as a result of his service in the Gulf.)

On London's Flag Day all the membership is out at strategic points with their distinctive yellow RNLI oilskins. The greatest rivalry is between those who collect at the two railway stations on the Central London territory, Charing Cross and Victoria.

The two stations are considered the high points of the various pitches manned, each station providing the RNLI with over £4,000. In all the ladies of the Central London Branch expect to collect over £20,000 on this one day.

None of the ladies involved are paid anything, not even expenses for travel or postage when organizing functions, or the many telephone calls that keep the branch rolling along. When asked whether she had ever tried to calculate what the personal cost of operating the branch was, Mrs Telfer said that it was probably better not to think about it.

The 1991 President of the branch was Lady Oswald, wife of the First Sea Lord, while the Chairman, and they insist on that title, was Mrs Valerie Aisher, wife of the illustrious yachtsman Robin Aisher. In fact the 1991 membership list of the Central London committee has a distinctly salty tang to it, reading a little like an extract from the Lloyd's Register of

Anne Butler, Chairman 1989-1990 and Pat Telfer, Vice-chairman, Ladies Central London Committee.

Yachts and their owners. Organizing the fund-raising activities is no self-gratifying excuse for holding a few select social functions. It is sheer hard work. Between a lecture on antiques with lunch at the Royal Air Force Club in Piccadilly in January and the Christmas Carol Service in the Old Church, Chelsea, in December, 1991 saw the ladies of the Central London Branch organize a beer festival, a clay pigeon shoot, a tennis tournament, an opera performance at the Fishmonger's Hall, a bridge drive and a Christmas fair.

The highlight of the year is the Lifeboat and Mermaid Ball, held at the London Hilton Hotel, on Park Lane, in December. Advertising has to be sought to support the lavish programme sold at the event. Prizes have to be found to be presented in the various tombola and raffle events held during the occasion. Selling the tickets, over 800 of them at £65 each, is less of a problem. These are sold out on a first-come-first-served basis almost as soon as available. It is a popular event. The prizes are lavish, the top prizes in a Short Odds raffle can be worth as much as £12,000

each, all donated to the cause.

After all the hard work organizing the success of the evening, there are the brighter moments for those who have made all the effort. In recent years Pat Telfer put a party together to form a table at the Lifeboat Ball. Arriving late at the table, one of the guests, David Darby, wanted to buy a ticket in the main lottery of the evening, with tickets at £100, the first prizes including a fast dayboat, outboard motor and trailer and a visit for two to New York, all donated for the occasion. Unfortunately David Darby had not the funds at hand to buy a ticket so Charles Telfer bought two, gave him one and kept the other for himself. The ticket he gave to his friend won the boat, outboard motor and trailer worth a total of about £12,000. David Darby sent Charles Telfer a cheque for the £100 and then set about learning the ropes about boating!

At the end of the year, when the efforts of about fifty people have raised enough money to pay for virtually half the cost of a new fast Mersey class lifeboat it all seems very worthwhile.

Local branches are always seeking new members and people to help and take part in fund-raising events. The RNLI will often provide back-up material to help promote the cause and the sales of the many gifts that are sold are part of the nationwide fund-raising effort. This help includes the provision of RNLI flags, sales kiosks and, occasionally, an inshore lifeboat on its trailer to form the centre of a lifeboat display at a village fete or fair, though this depends upon the availability of such a boat from the local regional office or depot.

The London and other big city branches and guilds are the exception rather than the rule. Harbours with lifeboats and those nearby avidly support local boats. Towns inland may adopt a specific lifeboat station and associate with it. Villages inland, where some of the population have probably never seen a lifeboat, hold events to raise funds for the lifeboat service. There is something of a jumble in the minds of many people when they try to distinguish between the many charities be they medically supportive, connected with the church or the preservationists. No-one seems to have much doubt about the RNLI with its distinctive lifeboat lapel badges, collecting boxes in bars and restaurants and the lifeboats in their familiar colours in the small fishing ports and larger havens around the coast.

The Younger Fund-raisers: Storm Force

Storm Force is the name of the organization of young people who support the RNLI. Any lifeboat coxswain who has had a visit from Storm Force members to his lifeboat and station will tell one that it is an appropriate title. Small hands, sometimes sticky from sweets and ice creams, manage to get everywhere on the dazzling paintwork and polished metalwork of the lifeboat.

At the start of 1991 there were over 15,000 young members of Storm Force spread throughout Britain and Ireland. Each person either pays a £3 per year subscription out of their own pocket money or is sponsored for that amount, or more, by a relative or friend who may already be a member of the adult membership club Shoreline. The two organizations run parallel in their activities. Fund-raising events almost always overlap in the form of sponsored walks and swims, garden fetes and the many other activities that RNLI supporters of all ages organize and take part in. Shoreline parents may well sponsor Storm Force children in events.

Just as there are parties, dances and dinners organized on a national and local basis for the adults, so there are rallies held for the children. Just as Shoreline members have their ties, badges, jerseys and other items bearing the RNLI flag logo so Storm Force members can buy T-shirts, hats and badges with their own logo.

It was late in April 1991 when one of the biggest events in the history of Storm Force took place. British Rail's InterCity Sector decided to name one of their HST 125 locomotives, No. 43160, *Storm Force*. It was also decided to hold a national contest among Storm Force members, through their own newsletter, to find a child to name the engine.

Contestants had to write to the RNLI telling them why they would like to name the locomotive. It was won by seven year-old Laura Scaife, from Barnsley, Yorkshire, who wrote saying that she thought the day out would cheer up her grandfather following the death of her grandmother. Laura, her grandfather, and the rest of the family were invited to Poole. Displaying confidence that belied her young age and watched by a large crowd, Laura named the train before setting off aboard it for the National

Storm Force train.

Exhibition Centre at Birmingham via a number of stops en route to collect Storm Force members. Eighty-five children, each with an adult, left Poole. On arrival at Birmingham they were met by local RNLI members having been divided into groups to tour a series of displays of lifeboat activities including one of a 'D' class inshore boat presented by the crew of the Port Talbot lifeboat and later a display afloat on a nearby lake.

The event was attended by representatives from the RNLI headquarters, including the Deputy Director, Ray Kipling, executives from British Rail InterCity and the City of Birmingham. The event was organized by the RNLI's public relations department staff and Tracey Brooks of InterCity, who must have felt like latter-day Pied Pipers as they gathered children from across southern England and bore them northwards to the Midlands. The rally at Birmingham over, the train then returned tired but happy children back to their home stations.

The Storm Force concept seems to have emerged through the activities of children who watch the BBC Blue Peter programme and who, over the years, have raised funds to provide five inshore lifeboats.

Chapter 17

THE LIFEBOAT STATIONS –
Northern Britain, Isle of Man and Wales

Spurn Head and northwards

Most lifeboat stations have one or even two features special to them. Spurn Head, that tail of land that hangs down from the north at the entrance of the Humber river estuary, has several. Geographically it is unique. The lifeboat station and the crew's homes lie at the tip of the remote point, four miles down a narrow road which in severe winter storms has, on several occasions, been cut by the sea. Because of the remote geographical location of the station the crew of the **Humber** lifeboat, as the Spurn Head boat is known, are the only entire lifeboat crew fully-employed by the RNLI. At every station where one of the offshore lifeboats is based there is either a mechanic or coxswain mechanic on the RNLI payroll, but at Spurn all seven men in the crew are employees of the RNLI.

Superintendent Coxswain Brian Bevan, in charge at the Humber station, is the most highly decorated coxswain or lifeboatman in service, having earned a gold, a silver and two bronze awards. While the framed certificates commemorating these awards hang modestly in the sitting room of his home his proudest possession, placed centre stage on his sitting room mantelpiece is an invitation to attend one of the private lunches that the Queen holds for a

selected group of guests. For him, in spite of having opened the London International Boat Show, saved many lives in fearsome conditions, been subject to the television programme 'This is your Life' and attended the

Coxswain Brian Bevan, the most highly decorated lifeboatman in the RNLI, holding a gold medal, silver medal and two bronze awards.

RNLI awards presentation ceremonies, this was the high point in his life.

He remembers the day vividly. He sat next to Sir John Junor, former editor of the Sunday Express.

"Sir John was a great help to me," he recalls. "He helped me to relax, guided a rough lifeboatman through the business of knowing which glass, knife and fork to use with each course and then helped me back to the train at Kings Cross Station afterwards by lending me his company car. In fact it was a very relaxed occasion. The Queen was very easy to talk to and she had certainly done her homework about Spurn Head and me!"

The 1987 Arun class 52 foot lifeboat at Spurn Head is the second Arun that has been stationed there. The lifeboat, the *Kenneth Thelwall* was part of the largest-ever bequest to the RNLI from the estate of Kenneth Thelwall, who lived at Walkington, near Beverley, Humberside. In 1987 £3 million was left to the RNLI. This paid for the new Humber lifeboat at Spurn Head, another boat at Ramsgate and the extension to the Poole RNLI headquarters.

The houses at Spurn Head, built in 1975, are bright and comfortable, well-insulated against the vicious winter weather. They need to be. The crew take one day off per week, always therefore leaving six men to man the boat. Annual holidays are arranged on a similar basis. Until recently the lifeboat crew shared the Head with the lighthousemen of Trinity House living at the mighty Spurn Head light, and the coastguards at their lookout station. Now the lighthouse is no longer operational and the coastguard post has been taken over by the Humber pilots.

Spurn Head is a busy station, averaging a call-out per week, sometimes more, which is double the average of most other stations. Calls range from pleasure craft in difficulty offshore from the treacherous estuary waters to landing sick people from passing vessels. Fishing boats from all the nations that fish the North Sea are all part of what Brian Bevan calls 'The Business'. Fourteen service boards, recording the activities of the lifeboats based at Spurn Head over the years, cover thirteen yards of the wall of the crew room.

When the winter winds are howling across the North Sea from the east, driving snow and sea spray across the narrow isthmus that leads to Spurn Head and rattle houses miles inland, spare a thought for the families at Spurn where the children of the crew have to travel eight miles to school by bus each day and it is a four mile journey each way to the mainland and back for even the basic essentials of life. However Spurn Head is a coveted, respected and proud station. It is obvious that the crew would not wish to be anywhere else.

Brian Bevan will be fifty-five years old, the retiring age for coxswains, during the 1990s and is among many of the lifeboatmen who are protagonists of raising the retirement age. Like others he feels that with the quality of life as it is today and people's general good health, the age limit should be extended where justified. He does not necessarily feel this in his own special case, but, like coxswains all along the coasts of Britain and Ireland he worries that there may not be enough young experienced people coming up behind them to take their place.

Forty miles north of Spurn Head lies **Bridlington**. Whereas the Humber lifeboat at Spurn Head is operated in something approaching isolation, Bridlington, where the Mersey class lifeboat *Peggy and Alex Caird* is launched across the seafront and beach by tractor, is very much part of a northward stretching chain of lifeboats. The Mersey class lifeboat, with a speed of 17 knots, covers the southern end of the coastline stretching from Bridlington to Whitby which includes the stations at

The new Bridlington Mersey class lifeboat Peggy and Alex Caird.

Flamborough, Filey and Scarborough.

Like Filey, ten miles north of Bridlington, and Scarborough, sixteen miles north, Bridlington is the RNLI public relations department's dream station. These three lifeboats are all launched from carriages hauled to the water from the boathouses by tractor. This not only allows the public to see the launching of the boats from close quarters but it also means that the lifeboat houses, in seafront promenades busy with holiday-makers, are an attraction in themselves. Each has a sales kiosk in the lifeboat house, or Filey will have one once their lifeboat house is rebuilt, where brisk trade is carried on with the sale of lifeboat souvenirs. A master of these sales is Douglas Gray at Bridlington, whose efforts have achieved over £40,000 in one year.

Bridlington has a small 'D' class inshore inflatable lifeboat to support the main lifeboat which proves its worth in the rescue of swimmers, board sailors and small inshore fishing craft. This is only operational in the summer months, the tourist season, but plans are afoot to improve the inshore lifeboat shed and attain all-the-year-round status for the boat.

Launching time for the lifeboats moved by tractor to the sea is not as long as some might think. From the time the crew members are summoned from their work places or homes by electronic pager the average time to have the lifeboat in the sea and ready for service is about thirteen minutes, though better times than this have been achieved.

The anomaly on this stretch of Humberside and North Yorkshire coast lies at **Flamborough**, just around the mighty Flamborough Head to the north of Bridlington. Here the station operates an old Oakley class boat from

The steep Flamborough slipway.

a slipway that might alarm climbers of the Matterhorn, it is so steep. It launches the boat into a narrow cove that reminds one of the Cheddar Gorge as cliffs tower on either side and the entrance to the cove faces north-east, straight towards the worst of North Sea weather. The boat, built in 1963, has a best speed of eight knots, slow when compared with the boats at the stations either side at Bridlington and Filey with their best speeds of seventeen knots. (The new Mersey class lifeboat goes on station at Filey in 1991 replacing the Oakley stationed there since 1962.)

The RNLI policy of replacing as many slower boats as possible with Fast Boats by 1991-2 might mean that Filey and Bridlington can easily cover the waters guarded by the Flamborough lifeboat. In 1990 thoughts were being passed around that the Flamborough station might be given an Atlantic 21 rigid inflatable. The total removal of any type of boat from Flamborough

would be a great sadness to the community where the lifeboat is as much a part of community life as the church and the village inn.

The **Filey** station, where a life-saving boat was first stationed in 1804, two years before Bridlington, is an historic place. The 1990s plans of the RNLI will not only lead to the replacement of the ageing boat but also the rebuilding of the lifeboat house and crew room. Coxswain Graham Taylor and his crew eagerly await the arrival of their new Mersey class boat. They have achieved a launching time of eight minutes with their tractor and carriage-borne Oakley class boat across the promenade and beach.

Six miles north of Filey another seafront tractor launching station guards seafarers off **Scarborough**. The Scarborough station first operated a lifeboat in 1801 and has several claims to historical fame both of a heroic and disastrous nature. In 1912 the retiring Scarborough coxswain, John Owston, was profiled in the Lifeboat magazine after forty-one years of service. Born in 1844 he was sixty-eight years old when, after being swept from the lifeboat and safely recovered during the rescue of several fishing boat crews he realized that age was against him. So much for the present day retirement age of fifty-five.

Coxswain Owston was responsible for the rescue of 230 people during his time as lifeboatman, 28 of these in a storm in 1880 when he and his crew saved fishermen as a result of five separate missions. This rescue earned him a silver medal.

Scarborough has had its tragedies too. In December 1954, when returning from a mission to assist fishermen, the Liverpool class lifeboat *E.C.J.R.* was returning to the harbour entrance when the boat capsized drowning Coxswain John Sheader, Second Coxswain John Cammish and Signalman Francis Bayes. Local people drove their cars to the beach to illuminate the sea but to no avail as far as the lost crewmen were concerned. Coxswain Sheader was a man of sixty-three years of age with forty-two years of service with the lifeboats.

In November 1969 Coxswain William Sheader, a distant relative of Coxswain John Sheader, took the Oakley class lifeboat *J G Graves of Sheffield* to sea in answer to a call to assist a converted ship's lifeboat in trouble among rocks in South Bay, to the south of the town. One survivor was found close inshore among rocks where, had the lifeboat been capsized in the dangerous seas, she could never have self-righted due to the depth of the water. Having landed the man, who was in poor shape, Coxswain Sheader put out to sea again and recovered a further man who died later in hospital. Again the lifeboat put to sea in now horrendous conditions to search for a third survivor but he could not be found. On entering the harbour after this

final rescue attempt the lifeboat escorted two cobles into port, one near sinking. This operation earned Coxswain Sheader a silver medal.

Like the other stations on the north-east coast of England with slow lifeboats at the start of the 1990s, Scarborough awaits the arrival of a fast Mersey class boat in 1991 or 1992.

Whitby, one of the most historic ports associated with the RNLI and a busy fishing port and tourist centre, lies seventeen miles north-west along the coast from Scarborough, the harbour entrance facing almost due north. The port is associated with Captain James Cook, although he was born in the village of Marton, some thirty miles from Whitby and, in fact, closer to Scarborough. The Tyne class lifeboat *City of Sheffield*, new in 1988, lies on the east side of the Lower Harbour near the swing bridge.

The first lifeboat station was established at Whitby in 1802 and, as already mentioned, was not affiliated to the RNLI until a disastrous accident in the harbour mouth in 1861 when only crewman Henry Freeman survived a capsize to become the first RNLI coxswain of the Whitby boat.

The close association between the Whitby lifeboat and the boat further north at Runswick is best remembered from the days of the *Rohilla* incident during the First World War. A large deep water lifeboat that used to be stationed at Runswick has now been replaced by a fast Atlantic 21 rigid inflatable boat, perhaps giving a clue to the future of the Flamborough station further south. The present day Staithes and Runswick station lies about half way between Whitby and the next station housing an offshore boat at Teesmouth, thirty miles up the coast. Whitby is fully-equipped for the next decade with a modern fast boat, as is Teesmouth. While the Whitby boat lies afloat in the harbour the Teesmouth boat is launched from a slipway.

The Teesmouth station lies on a spit

Above left: *The Whitby relief Tyne class lifeboat* Owen and Ann Aisher *going to the aid of the fishing vessel* Sophie Louise, *which had rudder problems. The fishing vessel was towed down the coast to safety off Scarborough. The lifeboat was on call for over nine hours.*

Left: *The* Zetland *lifeboat now at Redcar.*

Above: *The Teesmouth station.*

of land at the entrance to the River Tees some four miles north-west of Redcar where the only surviving lifeboat designed in 1789, the *Zetland*, survives in a museum housed in the old lifeboat shed. The *Zetland* was built in 1800 and brought to Redcar by local fishermen who paid £200 for her. On station at Redcar for seventy-eight years, from 1802 until 1880, the *Zetland* was used in the saving of over 500 lives.

In 1854 a storm hit the north-east coast driving the merchant ship *Jane Erskine* aground. Local fisherman put to sea in their cobles to attempt a rescue but were soon themselves in trouble. The *Zetland* was launched not only to rescue the entire crew of the cargo ship but also twenty fishermen, a total, including the lifeboat crew, of

fifty-two people coming ashore aboard the lifeboat. Today Redcar has an Atlantic class rigid inflatable on station to support the Teesmouth boat *Phil Mead*.

The approach by land to the **Teesmouth** station is forbidding. During southerly or south-westerly winds the acrid fumes from the nearby British Steel works and an oil refinery waft across the bleak sulphur-seared grass where wild dogs roam, living on the rabbits that frequent the promontory. Lifeboatmen cannot be choosers of the position of their stations. The demands of the job dictate that aspect of their work. When the wind turns to the north and east at Teesmouth the smoke from industry is replaced by salt spray and sea mists.

Hartlepool's Waveney class lifeboat.

Notwithstanding, Coxswain Peter Race earned a bronze medal for gallantry from this station during the summer of 1989 while the helmsman, Rodney Thompson and crewman, Peter Hodge, aboard the Redcar Atlantic 21 rigid inflatable were awarded thanks of the institution on vellum for their part in the same operation. The fishing boat *Gang Warily* had fouled its propeller in a force 7 north-easterly wind and was drifting among rocks and 12 foot waves towards cliffs. Coxswain Race took the lifeboat under the cliffs while Acting Mechanic Christopher Jones took the small inflatable from the lifeboat to attempt a rescue of the two crew of the fishing boat. For this he received a thanks on vellum. The lifeboat took one of the crew from the Atlantic 21 who was injured. Eventually Crewman Hodge swam ashore among the rocks to the aid of the two survivors from the fishing boat.

Massive redevelopment is taking place at **Hartlepool**, four miles north of Teesmouth by sea. The old fishing port lies north of the more modern industrial docks which have been virtually destroyed to make way for the building of a marina leisure complex. The Hartlepool lifeboat house is due for renewal as part of the RNLI plans for the 1990s and the Waveney class boat is also due to be replaced. The Maiden family have held the position of coxswain at Hartlepool for about fifty years, Robert Maiden having been coxswain for thirty-two years until 1972 when his son, also Robert, took over until retirement in the early 1990s. There are two of his sons in the lifeboat, Robert and Ian so the tradition seems to continue.

The Hartlepool lifeboat work ranges from the saving of pleasure craft, fishing boats and board sailors. Recently the crew saved those aboard the merchant vessel *Arne* which broke its anchor cable and drifted onto the Seaton Bank off Hartlepool in severe weather. Robbie Maiden's best memory is of the day when the

Hartlepool's Atlantic 21 inflatable used for inshore rescue work.

restored warship *HMS Warrior*, now at the Royal Navy dockyard museum at Portsmouth, began her voyage south under tow from a tug having been refitted in Hartlepool. A modern Royal Navy warship, loaded with the families of local dignitaries and the men who had worked on *HMS Warrior*, formed the escort. A swell had built up and it was not possible to transfer the guests to an awaiting tug as the tug would have damaged the warship's boarding ladder. The lifeboat was called alongside, taking off fifty-eight people. There were already sixteen people aboard the lifeboat including press photographers and crew. A total of seventy-four people were landed from the 44 foot lifeboat, Robbie Maiden claiming an unofficial record.

Hartlepool is a cheerful station, as most are, but special pride is taken in the occasion when four of the crew with others from local RNLI stations, flew to New York to compete in and win the International Lifeboat Rowing Races in 1980. Ron Latcham, a Hartlepool boat crewman of small stature, coxed the winning boat while the mighty Robbie Maiden rowed. The winners' commemorative plaque has pride of place in the boathouse.

The Hartlepool station has an Atlantic 21 rigid inflatable as well as the larger boat, the Atlantic 21 being used for inshore rescue work, the crew of the Atlantic 21 and the larger boat being interchangeable.

The **Sunderland** station, established in 1800 and three years older than Hartlepool, prides itself as being the oldest lifeboat station. In 1990 a Waveney class boat, *Wavy Line*, was put on station at Sunderland, replacing the slower older 1963 Watson class boat *Willam Myers and Sarah Jane Myers*. A special ceremony was held on the Sunderland waterfront on the north shore of the River Wear estuary. The newer faster boat will enable crew to operate more closely with the crews at Hartlepool to the south and Tynemouth to the north where an Arun class boat is on

Sunderland: Waveney class boat Wavy Line.

station. To emphasize the link between Sunderland and Tynemouth, the Tynemouth crew came south to Sunderland to attend the ceremony aboard their boat.

At about the same time as the dedication of the lifeboat at Sunderland, **Tynemouth** celebrated the 200th anniversary of the building of the first purpose-built lifeboat to the design of Henry Greathead at Tynemouth in 1790.

On Sunday 8 July 1990, a special annual Sea Sunday church service was held at St Hilda's Church, South Shields, attended by the local lifeboat crew who crossed the River Tyne in their Arun lifeboat to be there. The Director of the RNLI, Commander Brian Miles, was there having attended the previous day's ceremony at Sunderland. It was while there, at Sunderland, that he spoke of the recent death of Sunderland man Selwyn Ewart, Fleet Maintenance Superintendent to the RNLI. The RNLI flags were flown at half mast along

the north-east coast where many knew him well.

The address at the South Shields church service was to be given by the sometimes-controversial Bishop of Durham, the Right Reverend David Jenkins. All present wondered whether even in a service dedicated to the RNLI he could manage to put a controversial slant on the occasion. He did. Discussing the cost of the new design of the larger fast lifeboats, still in an embryo stage of development, he asked why a charity dependent upon voluntary contributions should be required to provide the £1 million needed to build each of these boats made to save life while Her Majesty's Government sanctioned the spending of millions on the manufacture of weapons designed to destroy life. The Lord Bishop had obviously been better briefed on the matter of nuclear weapons than on the whole thinking and spirit that is and always will be the RNLI.

After the service a retired coxswain

Director Brian Miles with the Sunderland crew.

summed it up: ''If the Government paid for the RNLI and the Department of Trade and Industry managed to get its hands on the boats we would have to fill in half a dozen forms before being allowed to put to sea.''

The Tynemouth crew took the matter in their stride just as they have overcome countless problems while saving life during the past two hundred years. Coxswain Martin Kenny of the Tynemouth lifeboat seemed neither concerned nor surprised. Others felt it sad that the work of the RNLI had become entangled in a political comment made at a religious ceremony by a leader of the church. Very sad, and a far cry from RNLI ideals.

Up the coast at **Blyth**, where the Waveney class boat the *William and Jane* lies to the harbourside berth by the old boathouse, a busy small commercial port keeps the lifeboat crew on the alert.

Blyth has a steady rate of calls and lies on the direct flight path into the western approach to Newcastle airport as well as the southern extremity of a low flying training area used by the Royal Air Force. There have been occasions when they, with the Tynemouth lifeboat, have been called out to await the safe arrival of aircraft from over the North Sea low on fuel trying to make it to Newcastle, or to search for ditched military aircraft. They have recovered the bodies of several Royal Air Force personnel, not a task they enjoy there being no satisfaction in it. Like the feelings of the Search and Rescue helicopter crews, the recovery of dead people affects all involved.

There had been another lifeboat station a few miles north of Blyth at Cambois but this was closed after the First World War, the responsibility for the coast north of Blyth to Amble falling upon the Blyth crew. Both the Amble station lifeboat sixteen miles north of Blyth and the North Sunderland lifeboat, a further twenty miles north at Seahouses, are occasionally restricted from putting out by low tides. On these occasions Blyth takes the strain.

Amble, a small fishing port at the entrance to the River Coquet, has seen considerable change during recent years. A yacht marina has been built just upstream from what was Harrisons Shipyard where, until recently, traditional cobles were built for fishermen. The yard has been taken over by new owners, Marshall Branson, where lifeboats are still refurbished. Like most of the north-east coast stations rescue operations now involve more leisure craft and less commercial vessels. Historically one of the most notable operations occurred at Amble in September 1969.

Coastguards at Amble harbour entrance were watching a yacht struggling towards the harbour in rough seas but while the yacht crew made the port safely an RAF motor pinnace, manned by a crew from nearby RAF Boulmer, capsized to the north of the port. Both the inshore lifeboat and the Watson class boat were launched, the former reaching the capsized craft within minutes of putting out. Two survivors were found clinging to a life buoy and were taken aboard the inshore boat. They were rushed ashore as they were in poor shape. A rescue helicopter was called from RAF Boulmer while Coxswain William Henderson, aboard the Watson *Millie Walton*, rescued one more man found clinging to the upturned hull.

Coxswain Henderson, fearing that men were trapped under the hull, tried to tow it to the harbour. The tow broke at the first attempt. The upper works of the pinnace then struck the bar at the harbour mouth and the tow broke again. The wreck then drifted past the south pier while local skin divers attempted to swim under the hull. They were taken from the water by the lifeboat crew in an exhausted state.

Four hours after the pinnace had capsized Royal Navy divers with cutting

gear were at the wreck having flown from the Royal Navy base at Rosyth on the north shore of the River Forth near the Forth road bridge. They carried their equipment across the rocks to the wreck and in just over an hour managed to cut a hole in the bottom of the vessel's hull rescuing one man who had been trapped beneath but had managed to survive for over five hours in an air pocket. There was no sign of the remainder of the crew, three men, whose bodies were later found among rocks further offshore.

This operation earned Coxswain Henderson and James Stewart, a crewman, a bronze medal while Robert Stewart and Andrew Scott, the crew of the inshore boat, also received bronze awards. It was a fine example of co-ordination between lifeboats, the RAF Search and Rescue crews and the Royal Navy where local fishing boats had also assisted both in attempts to tow the stricken vessel as well as help with radio communications. A life buoy from the pinnace can still be seen in the Amble lifeboat house. In 1990 Amble operated a Waveney class lifeboat, the *Margaret Graham*, but a newer boat was being awaited by Coxswain John Connell and his crew.

Further up the Northumberland coast from Amble Coxswain Robert 'Dougie' Douglas had been coxswain for many years at **Seahouses** but was facing retirement on reaching the age of fifty-five during 1992. His tractor launched Oakley, built in 1963, was expected to be replaced, like him, in the few years ahead. A new Mersey class boat, *Grace Darling*, had been funded for the station by the Grace Darling Anniversary appeal and other legacies and gifts.

Coxswain Douglas was adamant that the retirement age should be extended. As a fisherman working for twelve hours and more per day in an open coble in most weather conditions off the coast made famous by Grace Darling, he feels that he could handle the lifeboat for at least a further five years. He is also concerned that with the drift away from fishing by the younger people in his community there could be a dearth of up-and-coming potential lifeboatmen with experience of local conditions and waters. He sees no reason why, even if his sight may not be as good in the years ahead as it was at the age of fifty-three, he could not go to sea in the lifeboat even if only to assist and advise the younger crew. The North Sunderland lifeboat, as the one at Seahouses is officially known, is the nearest to Bamburgh where Nathaniel Crewe, Bishop of Durham, left his money in trust to set up the first lifeboat station and where the Darling family are buried.

The Grace Darling museum at Bamburgh certainly emphasizes the drama of the occasion when Grace and her father William Darling put out from the Longstone lighthouse to attempt to save passengers and crew

from the cargo passenger ship *Forfarshire* in 1838. Her ornate Victorian tomb stands in Bamburgh churchyard perhaps sadly some yards from the family grave where her parents and other relatives lie, but from her grave one can see the Longstone lighthouse whereas from the family tomb one cannot.

Coxswain Robert Douglas, back at his home in Seahouses, while in no way wishing to be disparaging or to detract from the courage of Grace Darling, pointed out in the down-to-earth manner typical of Northumbrian fishermen, that she had probably rowed from the lighthouse to Bamburgh and even Seahouses in a coble many times.

Grace was probably as experienced a seafarer in small boats as her brother, a fisherman, who was at sea fishing at the time of the disaster. The fact that she tended the boat in the sea while her father clambered on the wreck and rocks to seek survivors certainly

Grace Darling's tomb in Bamburgh churchyard.

Entering Eyemouth on a stormy day.

proves this. Had her brother not been away at sea it is probable that he would have been with his father and not young Grace whose memorial to some is not in the churchyard at Bamburgh but is the Longstone lighthouse and the Big Harcar rock where the *Forfarshire* was wrecked.

The **Berwick-upon-Tweed** station, the next station of the chain along the north-east coast of England and the south-east coast of Scotland, actually lies on the south bank of the Tweed estuary at Tweedmouth, the village across the River Tweed from Berwick. Here a larger class of lifeboat has been replaced by an Atlantic class rigid inflatable while eight miles further up the coast in Scotland the **Eyemouth** station has a recently completely refurbished Waveney class boat, the *Eric Seal*, paid for in 1972 by the Civil Service, the thirty-sixth boat funded from this source and named after the head of the Post Office and Civil Service Lifeboat Fund at that time.

The entrance to the narrow harbour

of Eyemouth is a horrific place in strong winds from the north and north-east. A witness to this was a rescue performed by the first Eyemouth lifeboat in April 1877, a year after the boat, the 30 foot pulling boat *James and Rachel Grindlay*, was put on station having been built at nearby Burnmouth for £1,000 and taken to Eyemouth overland on its carriage drawn by six horses and soldiers watched by a crowd of 5,000 people.

Coxswain James Maltman put out to sea early in the following spring when twenty-one fishing boats working off Eyemouth were caught in a severe north-easterly gale. Few were Eyemouth boats and their crews were ignorant of the pilotage into Eyemouth harbour. The lifeboat crew put one of their men onto each boat, one at a time, and piloted them into the safety of the harbour, returning to sea at once to fetch another boat home. All twenty-one fishing boats were saved together with a total of

120 men.

Disaster overtook success at Eyemouth four years later when another storm struck the coast on 14 October 1881. Again the fishing fleet was out and caught offshore in a northerly gale. Most of the Eyemouth fleet was at sea including almost the entire lifeboat crew who were mainly local fishermen. The fishing fleet was wrecked and a total of 189 men lost including 129 men from Eyemouth. It reduced Eyemouth's status as one of Scotland's premier fishing ports and it was years before the community began to recover from the disaster. A memorial service is still held each year. Among those lost was William Nisbet, the second coxswain to have been appointed at Eyemouth.

The entrance to Eyemouth harbour is still as fearsome as ever in northerly gales but a Waveney class boat manages the Roadstead well where a massive ground swell can build up producing a long stretch of white water and rollers of large proportions. Apart from calls to help fishing vessels and passing merchant shipping once more, as elsewhere, it is the leisure sailors whose demands on the crew are increasing as more and more people put to sea for recreation.

The last lifeboat station on the long chain northward from Spurn Head to Scotland is that at **Dunbar**. The first lifeboat was established there in 1808, but before that Dunbar had been the Murrayfield or Twickenham of English and Scottish armies. The Scots even routed the place themselves when eleven hundred years ago King Kenneth of Scotland sacked it. In 1296 King Edward I of England stormed and took it while in 1338 Black Agnes, Countess of March and Dunbar, held off the Duke of Salisbury and his troops during a prolonged six week siege. Her husband was away at the time but the situation was saved when reinforcements arrived by sea. During 1650 the Covenanters defended the town and castle against Cromwell's Roundheads but by an error of tactics, the Scots outnumbering the visitors by two to one, they allowed the away side to win. Cromwell, so pleased with his victory, granted the town £200 to build the harbour which is today a small fishing port and lifeboat base with space for a few yachts and smaller fishing vessels. A hole blown through the old castle now serves as a new harbour entrance, the entrance to

Dunbar Harbour, home of the Solent class lifeboat Hugh William Viscount Gough *(and the ghost of Black Agnes!)*

the north-east having been filled in with rock and ballast. Rumour has it among local people that the ghost of Black Agnes runs a commercial guest house at the back of the town.

Dunbar, proud of its history and its links with life-saving, has one unique claim to fame all of its own. The crew were on passage from Dunbar to Dumbarton, on the Clyde, via the Caledonian and Crinan canals, delivering a relief boat, when they received a call while on the west coast of Scotland to go to the assistance of a vessel in Loch Striven to the north of Rothsay. They claim to be the only lifeboat crew to have provided a service on both coasts of Scotland.

The station also claims to hold the record for the longest continuous time spent on one call when the liquid gas carrier *Inga Tholstrup* ran aground in the Firth of Forth. The lifeboat was called out early on Monday 10 November 1988 and stood by the stranded ship until the following Friday. During this operation Second Coxswain Orlando Sammels was badly injured in a fall in bad weather and had to be evacuated ashore by helicopter.

During the early 1990s Dunbar operated a Solent class 48 foot boat, the *Hugh William Viscount Gough*, but like other stations running older boats the crew are hoping to receive one of the new Fast Afloat Boats as they come on stream. A crew member at the station reflected the comments of other lifeboatmen down the whole of the 200 mile stretch of coast from Dunbar to Spurn Head. The business of saving life and helping seafarers is changing from commercial vessels and fishing boats to yachts, dinghies and board sailors.

A total of sixteen large-boat stations covered this long stretch of the North Sea coastline at the start of the 1990s interspersed with smaller stations operating inflatable inshore boats. There are ten inflatables in all not on larger boat stations as a second line of

defence, but most independent small boat stations are only manned during the summer months.

North-east Scotland

The offshore lifeboat stations at **Anstruther, Broughty Ferry** (Dundee), **Arbroath** and **Montrose**, stretch along the Scottish coast from the entrance of the Firth of Forth.

Anstruther operated an ageing Oakley class lifeboat until 1991 when it was planned to put a new Mersey fast all-weather lifeboat on the station. The slower Oakley meant that with a fast Arun based only 24 miles northwards round Fife Ness on the Tay, life became relatively quiet in recent times. The diminution of the fishing fleets has meant that much traditional rescue work has gone but is being replaced with the growth of pleasure boating activities in the Firth of Forth.

Certainly the description of Anstruther station as quiet in the excellent history written by Michael Welch is apt. During the service of the Oakley class lifeboat *The Doctors*, between 1965 and 1984, only 54 calls were handled but perhaps the arrival of the new lifeboat with twice the speed, should provide the men of Anstruther and their supporters with a more lively life with the RNLI.

The stations at **Arbroath** and **Broughty Ferry** have both had their tragic moments over the passage of time. In 1953, while on a call to investigate distress flares sighted offshore, the Arbroath lifeboat was capsized with the loss of six of the seven man crew. At Broughty Ferry the lifeboat was lost when on a call in December 1959 when on the way to the North Carr light vessel that was reported adrift in severe weather. The lifeboat capsized in the entrance to the Tay Estuary and all eight of the crew drowned.

Montrose and **Arbroath** were originally established in 1800 and 1803 respectively with lifeboats designed and built by Henry Greathead while the two stations further south were founded later. The RNLI took over management of the Montrose station in 1869, establishing a second station.

Aberdeen is the operations and communications centre for much of the oil industry operating out in the North Sea. Fleets of helicopters and oil rig supply and support ships ply the coast. Many of the incidents that lead to the need for rescue services occur out of range of the Arun class lifeboat *BP Forties* or, if close to the coast, can be dealt with by passing oil rig traffic, be this helicopters or support vessels which can reach the scene before the lifeboat. Because of this the Aberdeen station is not as busy today as it was in past years. The last award-winning service occurred in March 1976 for which Acting Coxswain Charles Begg received a bronze medal.

On the evening of 12 March 1976 the coastguards informed the Aberdeen lifeboat that the fishing vessel *Karemma* had broken down outside Aberdeen harbour, and the lifeboat slipped her moorings and headed out of the harbour. The wind was force 7 and as the lifeboat left the harbour she met very rough seas and had to adjust her speed frequently. The fishing vessel was drifting towards the beach and a tug had made an unsuccessful salvage attempt. Because of the nearness of the surf the crew of the *Karemma* agreed to abandon their vessel and with skilful manoeuvering the lifeboat came alongside and took off two men.

A large rolling sea then swept the *Karemma* on to the lifeboat, filled the lifeboat wheelhouse, rushed into the cabin and separated the two vessels. The seas were becoming steeper as the vessels neared the shore and another skilful manoeuvre brought the lifeboat alongside the casualty. A rope was made fast between the two vessels

and two more survivors were taken off before another sea forced the *Karemma* down on the lifeboat, broke the rope, and separated them again.

For the third time careful control of the engines and rudder brought the lifeboat alongside and the fifth survivor was taken off before the lifeboat left the casualty. The lifeboat had to manoeuvre carefully to gain sea room before she could return to harbour, streaming a drogue due to the very confused seas.

The whole service was carried out quickly and efficiently and Second Coxswain Charles Begg who was in command of the lifeboat, showed great courage, determination and seamanship in overcoming the hazardous conditions to effect a successful rescue. He was awarded the bronze medal of the RNLI. Throughout the service, Mechanic Ian Jack was at the engine controls, assisting Charles Begg in the manoeuvres and for his part in the service he was awarded the thanks of the RNLI inscribed on vellum.

The crew worked together as a perfect team and medal service certificates were awarded to Assistant Mechanic George Walker and crew members William Cowper, Andrew Walker and Frank Cruikshank.

Two silver medals were awarded two years before this rescue for the saving of another trawler, the *Netta Croan*, afire off the port. The official RNLI report of the incident says it all.

'At 20.50 on 13 April 1974, a report was received that the trawler *Netta Croan* was on fire and out of control and the lifeboat proceeded to her assistance. The crew of the trawler were unable to steer her or stop the engines, and a helicopter and tender standing by were unable to effect a rescue because of the flames and the erratic course. The lifeboat chased the casualty without being able to catch her, but as she circled to starboard the lifeboat cut across and approached the vessel. Coxswain Bird handed over the wheel to Mechanic Jack, a man experienced in closing moving vessels after several years on a pilot boat. The coxswain then stationed himself at the port wheelhouse door to see both the casualty and the helmsman. The lifeboat was taken alongside the main deck of the casualty at full speed and all survivors were taken off, and the lifeboat cleared all within one minute.

The whole manoeuvre, carried out at speed, was under very real danger from the flames, the possibility of exploding fuel tanks and the possibility of the trawler sheering and putting the lifeboat under her bows. A search was carried out for a further crew member who had attempted to jump into a liferaft earlier, but this was called off at 2 am on 14 April.

The winch operator in the BEA rescue helicopter, which illuminated the casualty throughout the rescue, described the operation as a "fantastic job". With great courage, determination and seamanship, Coxswain Bird and his crew achieved what others, in faster, larger and more manoeuvrable craft were unable to do, while giving no regard to the dangers they were putting themselves into.

In addition to the award of the silver medal to Coxswain Bird and Mechanic Jack, the thanks of the Institution, inscribed on vellum, were awarded to:- Assistant Mechanic G Walker and crew members F Cruikshank and A Walker.'

The ever-increasing sophistication of helicopters, less and less restricted in operating in darkness and extreme weather and the fact that there are so many based at Dyce Airport, Aberdeen, has meant that calls on the Aberdeen lifeboatmen have decreased during recent years though it would certainly be improvident to consider reducing the status of the station or even closing it in such a busy port.

The **Peterhead** lifeboat station, north of Aberdeen has had its moments of tragedy and heroism. Established as an RNLI station in 1865 a second station was set up during 1911. It was the lifeboat from the new station that was totally wrecked while going to the aid of a Royal Navy ship. Three of the crew of twelve were drowned. A fourth died some years later as the result of an illness caused by the incident.

During the Second World War the Peterhead lifeboat crew carried out the rescue of 106 people from three ships in trouble in hurricane force winds. This rescue, in January 1942, earned Coxswain John McLean the station's first gold medal, a silver medal to Mechanic David Wiseman and bronze medals to the six other members of the crew. The most recent award-earning service was carried out by the Peterhead crew aboard the Solent class lifeboat *RNLB The Royal British Legion Jubilee*, then on station, in August 1987. The lifeboat went to the aid of a fishing vessel and stood by while an RAF Sea King helicopter from RAF Lossiemouth winched the eight crew of the vessel to safety in pitch darkness, a full northerly gale and 30 foot seas.

The official RNLI account of the rescue follows but it is worth noting that after the event the fishing vessel crew told how they experienced 'abject loneliness' when the lifeboat crew failed to see them sheltering in the battered wheelhouse and set out to look for survivors in life rafts.

'At 29 minutes past midnight on Thursday 27 August 1987 Moray Coastguard overheard the fishing vessel *Constant Star* inform Peterhead Harbour Control that she had run aground on the Skerry Rock and required immediate assistance. Peterhead lifeboat station honorary secretary, Captain Alexander Auld authorized the pageing signal to call out the lifeboat crew.

Twelve minutes later Peterhead's temporary station lifeboat, *RNLB The Royal British Legion Jubilee*, a 48 ft 6 in (14.8m) Solent class lifeboat built in 1971, slipped her moorings and proceeded at full speed.

The wind appeared to be blowing strongly from the north-north-west as the lifeboat set out. As she turned into the Outer Harbour the coxswain was able to see and head for the lights of the fishing vessel *Challenger* at the scene of the stranding. Once clear of the harbour the lifeboat experienced the full strength of the north-easterly gale force 8. The sea was rough with crests reaching 30 feet high around the casualty.

Constant Star was found lying fast on a north-westerly heading, without lights and listing 15 degrees to port. Large wave crests passed over her with only her white masts visible. Two fishing vessels were lying clear in shallow water. The lifeboat crew used the searchlight and illuminating flares to search the vessel for any survivors as the lifeboat steamed slowly northward. The casualty was caught by a series of high waves and was swung to starboard, ending up on an easterly heading with an increased list to port.

The coxswain made three runs alongside the casualty but no survivors were seen. He reported to the Coastguard that the life rafts were missing. A search began and *Challenger* reported seeing a light one mile south of Buchan Ness Light. The lifeboat steamed to the south and found a light/smoke float and two lifebelts but no survivors. The *Challenger* found a life raft but the raft was not fully deployed from its canister. At 1.22 am a Sea King helicopter arrived from RAF Lossiemouth and was instructed by the Coastguard to conduct a search out to eight miles south. Numerous fishing vessels in the area were also searching for the second life raft. Coxswain McLean decided to return to the casualty and posted two lookouts on the foredeck. The casualty's wheelhouse was almost demolished and the vessel was nearly submerged. The coxswain took the lifeboat to

within 100 feet, as close as conditions would allow and the lookouts James Clubb and Sid Chisholm saw a movement near the wheelhouse. It was just then that a particularly large sea broke over the lifeboat causing, it was found later, injuries to three lifeboatmen. The news of the sighting was transmitted to all concerned at 1.59 am. The lifeboat took up station close to the south-west of the casualty's stern in case of a mishap during the winching operation. The helicopter arrived and the winchman was lowered down. He was almost washed overboard as he placed the survivors into the strops but in four double lifts the eight survivors were lifted off the vessel and landed ashore into the care of ambulancemen.

Peterhead lifeboat arrived back at station at 2.25 am. She was refuelled and ready for service at 2.41 am.'

Coxswain McLean is no relation to the previous coxswain of the same name but when he retired in the summer of 1991 his nephew, James Clubb took over the position from him. Peterhead honorary secretary, Captain Alexander Auld is happy to remember that the station was the first where, while he himself was in the RNLI crew, the present Director, Brian Miles, was working at his first RNLI posting as Deputy Inspector for Scotland making his first ever station visit in 1964.

The **Fraserburgh** and Peterhead lifeboat stations lie equi-distant either side of Rattary Head, the headland on the north-east corner of Grampian. The two stations have long records of deeds of extreme gallantry. Both stations now operate slipway launched Tyne class lifeboats, the *City of Edinburgh* at Fraserburgh and the *Babs and Agnes Robertson* at Peterhead. The Fraserburgh station has an historically sad uniqueness about it. Since the end of the First World War the lifeboats from Fraserburgh have been capsized three times while working from the fishing port, first in

1919, again in 1953 and most recently in 1970. A total of thirteen lives were lost in these three disastrous incidents. During the 1970 capsize, when the lifeboat *Duchess of Kent* was at sea to assist the Danish trawler *Opal*, five of the six crew were lost including Coxswain John Stephen and bronze medal holder Mechanic Frederick Kirkness. Following this disaster the Fraserburgh station closed from 1970 until 1978 when a new crew were trained and the lifeboat *RNLB The Royal British Legion Jubilee* was based there prior to the arrival in 1985 of the current Tyne class boat.

Although a fishing port Fraserburgh is in the front line of the oil business with many oil rigs off the north-east Scottish coast, but intense helicopter operations, together with the many oil rig support and supply vessels, the lifeboats are not as involved with oil rig rescues as might be imagined. Fishing boats are the main factor in lifeboat business in the area.

The loss of Coxswain Andrew Noble and Acting Second Coxswain Farquhar in 1919 occurred when the lifeboat from Fraserburgh was going to the aid of HM Drifter *Eminent*. The 1953 capsize occurred during an operation to help a trawler. A recent rescue operation took place when the Fraserburgh crew saved eight from the fishing vessel *Mystic* and then put back to sea to save the boat itself once the crew had been safely landed. The RNLI official report, published in March 1989, two months after the rescue, tells of the rescue that typifies the work carried out over the years by the Fraserburgh crews. The report is reproduced with full permission of the RNLI. The rescue earned the current coxswain at Fraserburgh, Albert Sutherland, a special thanks on vellum from the RNLI.

'Fraserburgh's 47ft Tyne class lifeboat *City of Edinburgh* was launched at 4.45 pm on Friday 13 January 1989 after Moray Coastguard had reported a fishing vessel, *Mystic*,

taking in water and in need of help three miles north of Fraserburgh harbour.

Near the harbour the wind, force 7 from the south, created only a slight sea and low swell, as some protection was afforded by the land. Visibility was good but the sky was overcast and the night was very dark.

The casualty could not be seen, but Coxswain Albert Sutherland soon picked her up on his radar and direction finder and steered towards her. The skipper reported that his vessel was listing badly and his crew were taking to the life raft. At 4.55 pm the lifeboat approached the fishing vessel. The wind now clear of the land, south force 8, gusting 9, and against a 2 knot tide, was creating a rough sea with an 8 foot swell.

The 74 foot trawler lay stopped across wind and tide with head to the westward. She was down by the head, with a severe list to port, rolling heavily. A life raft was secured to the starboard quarter, with seven men in it. The skipper was trying to release the painter. The coxswain manoeuvred around the casualty's stern, carefully avoiding the life raft and the gallows, and came alongside the after end of the shelter. The skipper was helped over the lifeboat's port side and the coxswain immediately came clear of the casualty.

The life raft had now come clear of the fishing vessel. The coxswain placed the lifeboat on the lee side of the life raft and each time the swell raised the raft a survivor was helped aboard. When all survivors were safe the lifeboat crew manhandled the life raft onto the after deckhouse, and the coxswain headed for harbour.

At 5.06 pm the lifeboat secured in Fraserburgh harbour and passed the survivors and the life raft into the care of the Fisherman's Association.

Soon after the men were landed the skipper of the fishing vessel, in discussion with Coxswain Sutherland, realized that his boat was now quite likely not to sink and at 5.16 pm the lifeboat cast off and headed back to the casualty. Three attempts were needed for the coxswain to place two men aboard the casualty in the same place as before. These men were the skipper of *Mystic* and Second Coxswain James Sutherland (brother of the coxswain). The lifeboat was then placed head to wind on the port bow of the casualty, while a line was passed and secured on *Mystic*'s port bow. Progress with the tow was slow, never more than three knots, as the heavily laden vessel dived into the swell, but some lee was found as the harbour was approached. The towrope parted as the lifeboat and tow approached the harbour entrance, but was reconnected. The casualty then sheered away as she was being lined-up for the harbour, but the pilot boat assisted in bringing her in.'

It is not common for a lifeboat to put back to sea to salvage a broken down vessel. The prime job of RNLI crews is to save life, but *Mystic* was a local boat, owned, prior to this rescue, by the honorary secretary of the Fraserburgh station.

Along the north coast of Grampian lies the fishing harbour of **Buckie** where one of the lifeboats donated by philanthropist David Robinson lies. The funds donated by David Robinson for the Buckie lifeboat, the Arun class *Charles Brown*, also paid for the lifeboats at The Lizard and Penlee (Newlyn) in Cornwall. In what is still a relatively busy fishing port the Buckie crew have a history of saving fishermen and their boats, although in

The Buckie lifeboat, Arun class Charles Brown, *donated by Mr David Robinson, towing a* casualty of the 1985 Round Britain Powerboat Race back to port. The powerboat began to sink as the lifeboat slowed to enter Buckie. It was safely berthed in the harbour.

John F Kennedy on relief duty at Invergordon lifeboat station.

1987 Coxswain John Murray received a bravery award for the rescue of two yachts along the coast off the harbour at Macduff.

It is the station at **Invergordon** in the Cromarty Firth, that completes the north-east Scottish chain which runs north from the Firth of Forth. The Invergordon station has what might be best described as an 'open-and-shut' history, opening in 1911, closing in 1968 and re-opening in 1976. It is one of the quieter stations mainly due to the fact that the RAF station at Lossiemouth is only 35 miles away across the Moray Firth to the east. RAF Lossiemouth operates a Search and Rescue helicopter squadron covering both marine and mountain rescue work. The area is also involved in supplying the oil rigs in the North Sea so there is a constant flow of marine traffic off the coast of the area, much of this fully capable of handling any situation where a rescue operation might be required. In 1991 the relief fleet Waveney class lifeboat,

The White Rose of Yorkshire was on temporary station duty.

Northern Scotland and the Northern Isles

The most northern lifeboat station in the British Isles is at **Aith**, fifteen miles north-west of Lerwick, capital of the Shetland Islands. The first boat was based at Aith in 1933 but the station now proudly operates an Arun 52 foot boat, the *Snolda*, the only Arun in the RNLI fleet to be built of steel. The boat was placed on station in 1985 and officially named the following year by HRH the Princess of Wales while HRH the Prince of Wales opened the new pier and lifeboat crew house which had earlier been severely damaged in a storm.

The *Snolda* was paid for by donations from oil companies operating rigs in the area and a charitable trust. Aith is a small community at the south end of Aith Veg, a north running sea inlet. Until the summer of 1990 there were five members of the Henry family among the crew. Kenny Henry was coxswain, his son Hylton second coxswain, another son, Kevin, full-time mechanic and another son, Barry, on stand-by as a crewman. There is also a cousin aboard. Kenny Henry has now retired as coxswain, Hylton taking his place.

A memorial to a Faroes seafarer, Ove Joensen, has been placed on the lifeboat crew house. Ove made three attempts to row from the Faroes to Copenhagen, Denmark, but on the first two occasions he had to be rescued by the Aith lifeboat where he made many friends. He eventually achieved his ambition in 1986 but, sadly, was drowned off the Faroe Isles a year later.

The Aith lifeboat, with twenty crew on call from the village where fishing and farming are the main activities, covers the waters to the north and west of Shetland, some of the wildest waters in the British Isles.

Three years before a boat was put on station at Aith the first Shetland station was opened at **Lerwick**, in 1930. In 1990 it celebrated its 60th anniversary with a dinner dance attended by local dignitaries, including the Lord Lieutenant of Shetland, Magnus Shearer, who was then honorary secretary of the Lerwick boat, and the RNLI Director, Lieutenant Commander Brian Miles, well known in the islands for his service aboard a 'roving' 70 foot lifeboat that served in the area some twenty years earlier. A service of thanksgiving was held in Lerwick on the next day.

One of the highlights of the celebrations was the presentation of an inscription of appreciation on vellum to Coxswain Mechanic Hewitt Clark, a charming but taciturn man who had served on the boat at Lerwick since 1967 and been coxswain since 1979, earning two bronze awards

Above: The memorial to Ove Joensen.

Below: Lerwick – Coxswain Hewitt Clark.

during this time. The vellum appreciation was given for his rescue of thirty-three Nigerians off a fish freezer ship, aground off the islands at night in severe weather. Hewitt Clark had to make thirty-three runs alongside the ship, the *Azu*, taking one man off at a time.

The Lerwick lifeboat, the *Soldian*, an Arun named after a rock off Shetland, was mainly financed in 1978 by thirty or more oil companies operating in the Brent and Ninian oil fields to the east of Shetlands. Close liaison is maintained with both the local Coastguard, which operates helicopters, and the Norwegian rescue services across the North Sea. Lerwick is considered to be a busy station by present standards, work varying from assisting fishing vessels and the oil industry vessels to ferrying casualties from the off-lying islands to the mainland of Shetland.

Although only fifteen miles from Aith as the crow flies, the Lerwick and Aith lifeboats are very independent of one another, their respective operating areas being divided by the fifty mile length of the Mainland island of Shetland that stretches from the Point of Fethaland in the north to Sumburgh Head to the south.

About fifty miles south-west of the Shetland Islands lie the seventy or so islands of the Orkney group. Here there are three lifeboat stations very much more inter-connected than the two on the Shetland Islands. Before the loss of the Longhope lifeboat on the night of 17 March 1969, there were stations at Longhope, Stromness and Stronsay, an island in the north-east Orkneys. When the **Longhope** boat was capsized with the loss of all her crew there were insufficient people in the community at the south of the island of Hoy to man a new boat without training.

The 70 foot lifeboat *Grace Paterson Ritchie* was based at **Kirkwall** in a roving commission around the Orkneys, Shetlands and the Scottish north coast, but after the loss of the Longhope boat a lifeboat was placed on permanent station at Kirkwall where crew were readily available. When crew were trained from the Longhope community to replace those lost, a boat was put there while the Kirkwall boat remained and the Stronsay boat withdrawn much to the dismay of the islanders, but logistically it made more sense to have a boat in the centre of the islands than, literally, out on a limb.

Today the Kirkwall lifeboat, the Arun class *Mickie Salvesen*, donated by the Salvesen family, new on station in 1988, covers the northern and western approaches to the Orkney islands while the **Stromness** boat, another Arun, *The Joseph Rothwell Sykes and Hilda M*, covers Scapa Flow, the western side of the islands and the notorious Pentland Firth where the Longhope lifeboat was capsized. Stromness is an attractive fishing town with a winding flagstoned high street typical of the island towns and villages. The lifeboat is very much a focal point of the local inhabitants. The old slipway launched lifeboat was replaced by a boat moored out in the harbour so the old lifeboat shed is being converted into a meeting hall.

During the First World War the Stromness lifeboat station was involved in a naval fiasco that in itself led to political repercussions which rumbled on for years. The warship *HMS Hampshire* left Scapa Flow on the evening of 5 June 1916. A severe storm was blowing from the north-east. Lord Kitchener of Khartoum had embarked the ship for passage to Northern Russia in an effort to boost the morale of the Russian Government which had been flagging, particularly in their attitude towards Britain and her allies.

Because of the direction of the winds, blowing at severe gale force, it was decided that the ship, with two escorts, would sail west of the Orkney Islands, passing the village of Birsay, the north-east point of the Orkney isle called Mainland, before passing Westray and then heading north for the Shetlands. The seas were so bad that the escorting destroyers had to turn back but *HMS Hampshire* continued alone, the storm force winds by then having backed to the north-west. Just before 8 pm the ship struck a mine thought to have been laid recently by a German U-boat, possibly the *U75*. She sank within fifteen minutes, Lord Kitchener being among those lost. Altogether only twelve people survived of the crew of 655 men. It is thought that as many as two hundred men escaped from the ship aboard rafts but almost all were drowned or fatally injured as the rafts were swept ashore in wild seas onto the rugged coast.

Local people thought they may have been able to save many of these men by snatching them from the waves as they came ashore, but they were prevented from doing so by armed troops who threatened them with rifles as they approached the shore.

Meanwhile news of the disaster had reached Stromness where the honorary secretary, George Linklater Thompson, JP, prepared to launch the lifeboat. However on hearing this Captain F M Walker, commanding officer of the Western Patrol, based at Stromness told Mr Thompson,

"You have no right to interfere in naval matters. It's none of your bloody business, and what's more, if you attempt to launch the lifeboat it's mutiny. Mutiny, do you hear? Any more nonsense or argument and I'll have the whole lot of you locked up."

During the conversation 643 men, including Lord Kitchener, were already dead or drowning a mere thirteen miles up the coast north of Stromness with no-one to give them help.

The islanders of Orkney erected a memorial to Lord Kitchener and the crew of *HMS Hampshire* on Marwick Head overlooking the place where the ship sank. The money raised for this monument, a tower, came from local public subscription, but none of it from naval or other government funds.

The most recent Longhope lifeboat, tucked away on the south side of the island of Hoy, is a Tyne class vessel, new in 1987, the *Lord Saltoun*, another legacy of the Salvesen family.

Across the Pentland Firth from Stromness and Hoy lies the small fishing and ferry port of Scrabster where the **Thurso** lifeboat lies in the harbour on moorings. Again, as at Stromness, the Thurso boat was once launched from a shed down a slipway but in 1956 a new Watson class boat housed in the shed was, with the shed, destroyed by fire. The shed was rebuilt and the lost boat replaced. Today the Thurso boat is a 1988 built Arun named *The Queen Mother*. The lifeboat was named personally by HM the Queen Mother at a special ceremony in the summer of 1988 and Her Majesty keeps a lively interest in 'her' lifeboat.

Not only does the Queen Mother like to hear of any activities involving the Thurso lifeboat but every summer she opens the gardens of her nearby holiday home, the Castle of Mey, a few miles east of Thurso along the north Scottish coast. All 'takings' at the entrance are given to the RNLI. Her interest in the Thurso lifeboat is much appreciated by the local people. On the occasion of her 90th birthday, in August 1990, the crew of the lifeboat sent her a birthday card signed by them all and were represented at the special birthday parade held in London in July 1990.

Links between the mainland and the boats of Orkney are strong. The coxswain of the Thurso lifeboat, Billy Farquhar, was aboard the Thurso boat on his first-ever operation in March 1969 as a crewman with the RNLI during the sad business of towing the capsized Longhope boat back to Scrabster and the recovery of the bodies from the wreck. Though over

twenty years ago it was a baptism of
fire that Coxswain Farquhar is certain
he will never forget.

Eastwards from Thurso Bay, past the
northern-most point on the British
mainland, Dunnet Head, and round
Duncansby Head southwards down the
Caithness coast lies the **Wick** station
with its slipway launched Tyne class
boat *Norman Salvesen*, another
Salvesen legacy. The Wick boat
completes the lifeboat network that
covers the Shetland Islands, the Orkney
Isles and Scotland's northern shores.
The lifeboat, Coxswain Walter McPhee
in charge, is launched from a slipway
which faces east towards waters often
beset with breaking waves and a
heavy ground swell if the wind is
blowing from an easterly direction,
but this does not deter the men of
Wick where the first boat was placed
on the station in 1848.

The final lifeboat station on the
mainland coastline of Caithness and
Sutherland is on the west coast at
Lochinver. Lochinver is one of the
most attractive harbours in far
northern Scotland, set at the head of
a sea loch across the Minch channel
from the Hebridean station at
Stornoway, a station with which the
Lochinver crew liaise closely in times of
trouble out in the Hebridean waters.
Lochinver is a busy fishing port from
which more than 40 fishing boats
operate including several of over 90
feet in length. Harbour Master Captain
Alistair Campbell is honorary secretary
for the lifeboat, the *Murray Lornie*, a
1989 Arun class vessel that lies moored
in the harbour close to the fish dock
where Coxswain Neil Gudgeon works.

Coxswain Gudgeon confirmed the
comments of other lifeboat crews in
the far north that the latter years of
the 1980s had been quiet when
compared with earlier years. All
attributed this to several factors even
though there had been many severe
storms in the area. Those putting to
sea these days have more sophisticated
equipment both for navigation and

weather predictions. There has been a
reduction in fishing fleets which used
to provide most of the lifeboat's work
in these waters. Coastguard and
military helicopters from the Royal
Navy and Royal Air Force Search and
Rescue squadrons are larger, have
greater range and fewer operating
limitations than in their earlier days. In
spite of this all lifeboat crews train
regularly, keep their boats and
boathouses in pristine condition and
remain quietly proud to be part of the
RNLI.

Hebrides and Scotland's west coast

Stornoway is the most north-westerly
of the Scottish lifeboat stations and
one of the more remote in terms of
having other stations in the area,
although the mainland station at
Lochinver is just over thirty miles away
to the east of the Isle of Lewis. During
the night of 24-25 April 1990 a
Bulgarian fish factory ship, the
Condor, with a crew of twenty-eight,
ran onto rocks about thirty miles south
of Stornoway. The Arun class lifeboat,
Sir Max Aitken II, was called out at
just before 2 am on 25 April and
headed south into a freshening south-
westerly wind towards the casualty.

The lifeboat reached the *Condor*
after a two and a half hour passage.
It was evident to both the lifeboat
crew and those aboard the factory
ship that the ship was sinking by the
bow. The master of the *Condor* gave
the order to abandon ship so the
lifeboat lay alongside taking the crew
off by a pilot ladder in increasingly
rough seas and rising wind. All
twenty-eight were safely aboard the
lifeboat as the ship began to sink. The
extra weight of twenty-eight people
and their personal belongings aboard
the lifeboat meant that the passage
back to Stornoway, due north with
the wind now blowing at gale force

from astern, could not be made comfortably at full speed but lifeboat and survivors reached Stornoway safely after almost three hours of leaving the sinking ship.

Much of the work of the Stornoway lifeboat involves fishing vessels but early in 1991 some of the weight of work was eased for the Stornoway lifeboatmen when a new station opened on **Skye**, forty-five miles south-east.

The new station at Portree, on the Isle of Skye, opened for evaluation in mid-February 1991, when crew members from Portree completed a training course at the RNLI headquarters at Poole and then took their relief fleet Waveney class lifeboat *Connel Elizabeth Cargill* back to Skye. Evaluation of a station generally lasts a year after which the RNLI decides whether or not to put a lifeboat on permanent station or abandon the idea. Portree will certainly be well placed to not only liaise with Stornoway and Lochinver to the north in the waters of The Minch that lie between Skye, the Isle of Lewis and Cape Wrath, but will also work with the stations in Barra and Mallaig to the south-west and south respectively.

The station at **Mallaig** is busy and among the more recently established in Scotland having opened in January 1948. It was three years after this that Coxswain Bruce Watt and his crew performed a remarkable rescue of sixty-two people from the steamer *Tapti*, aground on the island of Tiree in terrible weather. The present coxswain at Mallaig, Tom Ralston, is amazed that no medal was awarded for this rescue but puts it down to the modest self-effacing character of Coxswain Watt, a characteristic one finds everywhere among RNLI crews.

Tom Ralston is a local wholesale fish merchant and Justice of the Peace. He took over the work of coxswain mechanic in 1985 at Mallaig, where the Arun class lifeboat, *The Davina and Charles Matthews Hunter*, has

been stationed since 1982.

During the notorious hurricane force winds of October 1988, which hit Scotland almost exactly a year after a similar storm hit southern England, Coxswain Ralston earned a bronze medal for gallantry and seamanship while saving the crew of two of the fishing boat *Galilean* which was being swept onto a lee shore in nearby Loch Nevis in winds gusting at 90 knots. Not only did the Mallaig crew save the two fishermen but they saved the vessel, earning the entire crew a MacMillan Silk Cut Award for Seamanship.

It was while second coxswain in August 1982, that Tom Ralston took the Mallaig lifeboat to sea to rescue the yacht *St Just*. It was the station's longest recorded service, the lifeboat staying at sea for almost twenty-eight hours. A rescue operation typical of stations on coastlines strewn with off-lying islands took place off Mallaig during the holiday period between Christmas Day and New Year's Eve in 1990. A woman on the island of Rhum, fifteen miles west of Mallaig harbour, had fallen, putting her arm through a plate of glass. She suffered severe lacerations to her wrist. The emergency services were alerted and two helicopters, one from RAF Lossiemouth and a civilian one from Stornoway were sent out but driving snow and gale force winds reduced visibility in the darkness to zero. Both helicopter crews had, reluctantly, to abort their missions and return to their bases. The Mallaig lifeboat crew were alerted and put to sea into the storm at 2 am.

Coxswain Ralston drove the lifeboat at full power into steep seas which first put the Decca navigation equipment and then the radar out of order but the crew pressed on using old fashioned methods of navigation, a chart, a compass and a good lookout. After an hour at sea they reached the island jetty where the casualty was waiting in a survival bag in the back of a Land Rover. She was aboard within minutes and with two of the crew looking after her in the cabin below deck the lifeboat was off back to Mallaig, now with the wind astern, taking forty-five minutes for the passage.

A doctor and ambulance were awaiting the lifeboat at Mallaig where the woman was attended to before being taken in the ambulance the fifty miles to hospital in Fort William, the journey taking three hours in blizzard conditions, the ambulance being preceded by a snow plough. At 5 am the lifeboat was refuelled and was back on her mooring when Coxswain Tom Ralston returned home to begin celebrating his fifty-fifth birthday, the present retirement age for RNLI coxswains. At the start of 1991 the Mallaig lifeboat station had recorded over 400 calls and saved 188 lives.

Sixty-five miles due west of Mallaig, at Castlebay on the island of Barra, lies the **Barra Island** station which has had the Arun class lifeboat *Ann Lewis Fraser* stationed there since 1988. Fishing vessels and cruising yachts constitute most of Barra's rescue business but every four years the Round Britain two handed yacht race calls at the small port which, on one occasion, kept the lifeboat crew busy when a severe gale blew up causing considerable danger in the anchorage.

It was in November 1979 that an extraordinary incident happened off the waters of Barra. The Barra Barnett class lifeboat, today replaced by an Arun class lifeboat, was called out to assist the Danish coaster *Lone Dania* in difficulty between Barra and the island of Islay, near the island of Tiree. The seas were enormous, estimated by the coxswain of the Islay lifeboat, also answering the distress call, to have been averaging 30 feet in height with occasional peaks and troughs of 60 feet. The wind was hurricane force 10 to 12. The night was very dark.

As the Barra lifeboat headed south-east towards Tiree, forty miles away,

the Islay boat, with a greater speed, headed north-west. The Barra station at Castlebay and the Islay station at Port Askaig are about the same distance from the sourthern tip of Tiree. During the operation, which the coaster survived unaided, both lifeboats capsized in the storm while still many miles apart but both self-righted without loss of life, each using its own method. The older Barnett from Barra used the airbags built into the top of the superstructure while the more modern Thames class lifeboat *Helmut Schroder of Dunlossit*, still at the station in 1991, recovered from the capsize simply because of its in-built watertight superstructure which is designed in such a way that the boat cannot stay inverted. It was the first capsize experienced by either class of lifeboat. Later the RNLI investigators into the incident were delighted to report that the capsizes were simply due to the sea and wind conditions and not to a design fault. The lifeboats had performed exactly as expected once capsized, but it illustrates the perils that lifeboatmen face.

Today there is a station at **Tobermory**, at the north of the island of Mull, lying half way between Barra and Islay. This station was first opened in January 1937 but closed in 1947 because of a problem finding enough people to man the lifeboat. It was reopened in 1990, a Waveney, *Ralph and Joy Swann*, being taken there from Ramsgate on temporary station duty. The 54 foot Arun class lifeboat *City of Bradford IV* was placed on station at Tobermory on 7 February 1991. Even with a fast offshore lifeboat at Islay and now an 18 knot Arun at Barra it seems that the RNLI decided that the 100 miles between Barra and Islay was too much for the two lifeboats to cover between them, particularly as there is no land westwards from either Barra or Islay until one hits the northern coast of Labrador, Canada.

Barra Island lifeboat after capsizing November 1979.

Islay, as the station at Port Askaig is registered on RNLI files, lists some rare events in its relatively brief history which began when it was founded in 1934. Typical of island stations the run-of-the mill jobs are those of ambulance work but Islay has another. The ballot boxes after General Elections have to be collected from nearby Colonsay and taken to the mainland. Barra has the luxury of an airfield, be it all a tidal beach where flight schedules depend on the state of the tide.

In 1950 Coxswain Duncan McNeil received a special award for the bravest act by a lifeboatman during any year. Coxswain McNeil attached a line to a drifting mine and then towed it ashore where it was deactivated. Seven years later the Islay lifeboat crew received a case of rum, always a popular drink with the RNLI

crews, for the longest service of the year which totalled 26 hours.

The nearest mainland lifeboat station to those out at Tobermory and Islay is at the picturesque port of **Oban**, a busy terminal for the ferries that operate around the Inner and Outer Hebrides. A Brede class lifeboat, the intermediary size between the larger Tynes, Merseys and Aruns and the semi-rigid inflatable Atlantic class, is based at Oban. In fact Oban is using its third Brede class boat, the most recent boat, *Nottinghamshire*, going on station in 1989.

The Oban coxswain and crew made an award-winning rescue at the end of January 1985 when the fishing vessel *Shemara* ran aground on a reef of rocks, Lady's Rock, at the south-west end of Lismore Island where the Sound of Mull, Loch Linnie and the Firth of Lorne meet. Early on 31

January a westerly gale was blowing across the island of Mull as the 33 foot long Brede class lifeboat *Ann Ritchie* put to sea, heading north-west to the casualty in mounting seas. Coxswain Patrick MacLean found the *Shemara* had run aground and was listing severely to port. The fishing boat skipper advised Coxswain MacLean to make his approach on the starboard side but the coxswain decided otherwise and made 15 or 16 runs along the port side in deeper water, eventually taking off all eight of the crew including one suffering from angina. The lifeboat was met by an ambulance once back at Oban at 4.30 am.

By virtue of its position in the shelter of the attractive waters east of Mull, Oban lifeboat crew have found an increase in calls to yachts and other leisure vessels as charter increases in the area and the west coast of Scotland enjoys a massive increase in visitors in their own yachts and power cruisers.

At the southern end of the 55 mile long Kintyre peninsula lies the **Campbeltown** lifeboat station on the east side of Kintyre in Campbeltown Loch. The station has a long and interesting history interspersed with deeds of great courage as well as some curious events. In 1916 a bullock caught its head in the RNLI flagstaff halyard and was strangled. The owner of the beast was paid £10 compensation for his loss. In 1937 two people aboard a yacht's dinghy were hunting sharks. They harpooned one which then set off with the dinghy in tow until the lifeboat caught up with the procession and saved the dinghy and occupants. The moral? Always carry a sharp knife aboard one's dinghy when hunting sharks off the Scottish coast.

More recently Coxswain Mechanic Alexander Gilchrist was awarded the silver medal for gallantry for the rescue of the crew of the trawler *Erlo Hills* adrift with engine failure in storm force northerly winds.

In order to complete the description of the Scottish west coast and Hebridean stations it is perhaps best to use the official RNLI description of the rescue of the crew of the fishing vessel *Erlo Hills* and a later rescue, in 1988, of the fishing vessel *John Hannah VC* which typify the work of these stations on the islands and remote promontories of the Western Isles and west Scottish coast. The following description was released by the RNLI in February 1982, after the rescue operation in October of the previous year.

'SILVER MEDAL SERVICE BY CAMPBELTOWN LIFEBOAT

At 7.06 on the morning of 2 October 1981, the Campbeltown Arun class lifeboat *Walter and Margaret Couper* set out from Campbeltown Loch with Coxswain Alexander Gilchrist in command after the station's honorary secretary was informed that the trawler *Erlo Hills* with fourteen men aboard was ashore north-west of the Mull of Kintyre. At that time there was a force 5 wind with moderate sea conditions.

The reported position of the trawler turned out to be incorrect and eventually a British coaster the *Caol Mor* reported she had sighted the trawler ashore off Rathlin Island (off the north coast of Ireland). The coaster was asked by the coastguard to stand by until the lifeboat arrived.

Once clear of the shelter of the Mull of Kintyre the lifeboat encountered worse conditions with wind force 7 and poor visibility in the heavy rain squalls. Just at this time the lifeboat's radar failed so that all navigation had to be done by Decca navigator. At 9.25 the lifeboat arrived on the scene and found the trawler with her bows aground but her stern still afloat. Wind had increased to gale force 9 when Captain Nixon of the coaster *Caol Mor* asked Coxswain Gilchrist to pass a towline to the *Caol Mor* and the lifeboat to keep the coaster's

THE LIFEBOAT STATIONS 135

bows pointing into the wind. Finally
Captain Nixon had to slacken the
towline and bring his coaster round in
a circle over it in order to get back to
the windward side of the casualty. He
showed great skill during this
manoeuvre, passing within feet of the
reef upon which the trawler lay. At
11.00 the *Erlo Hills* was pulled clear
and out to sea. Her skipper then
confirmed he had power so the
coaster released the towline and
continued on her passage. The lifeboat
would remain with the trawler, it was
decided, and escort her into
Campbeltown. Short, steep breaking
waves were constantly being thrown
up by the strong tidal eddies and
force 9 winds.

Shortly after the *Caol Mor* had
departed it became clear to Coxswain
Gilchrist that all was not well aboard
the trawler. She began going round in
circles and then her engine failed.
Immediately she began to drift back to
the shore; the trawler's skipper
refused to let the lifeboat take the
crew off, so Alexander Gilchrist moved
in and on the second attempt, when
only 200 yards from the shore, he
secured a tow. Both lifeboat and
trawler were constantly being struck
by 15 foot waves and because of the
Erlo Hills' damaged steering gear the
lifeboat was only just making headway
as she pulled the trawler clear. As the
casualty's crew would not abandon
ship Coxswain Gilchrist realized that
the only way to save them would be
to radio to the *Caol Mor* to return
and tow them to safety. Before she
had arrived back on scene, however,
the coxswain had to let go of the tow
because the risk of the lifeboat
capsizing due to the effect of the tow
was too great to continue. By now the
casualty was out of immediate danger
as the state of the wind and tide was
keeping her from drifting back to the
shore.

The trawler had an English skipper
and Spanish crew and during this time
the skipper had been making radio

link calls to Spain and the south of
England. When the coaster returned to
the scene and asked the lifeboat to go
in and pick up a towline from the
casualty, the trawler's crew resolutely
refused to pass it to them. For two
hours the trawler's skipper refused a
tow, radioing all the time to his
owners. During this time the coaster's
captain decided he had to leave for
Campbeltown because he was running
very low on fuel. The Portrush
(Northern Ireland) lifeboat was now on
her way but Coxswain Gilchrist
remained standing by the drifting
casualty.

At last at 3.10 the trawler's skipper
radioed that he would obey all
instructions from the lifeboat.
Coxswain Gilchrist again recalled the
Caol Mor who by now would only be
able to tow the trawler into the
shelter of Church Bay on the south
side of Rathlin Island because she was
so low on fuel. Wind had increased to
storm force 10 with 25 foot waves. On
four occasions the lifeboat passed a
towline between the two vessels with
Coxswain Gilchrist bringing the lifeboat
only feet from the coaster's stern
which at times was high above the
lifeboat, her propeller thrashing out of
the water. Waves broke across the
after deck of the lifeboat, engulfing
the crew as they passed the line. Each
time, however, the towline parted
under the strain and by 5.10 the *Caol
Mor* had to leave as she was
dangerously low on fuel.

Now the trawler's skipper was
prepared to abandon ship; with
fenders along the starboard side of
the lifeboat and the crew in position
to grab the survivors, Coxswain
Gilchrist approached the casualty
through the 30 foot waves. Six
approaches were made and each time
the lifeboat with exceptional timing
had physically to drag the reluctant
Spanish crewmembers onto the
lifeboat. At 5.30 all fourteen survivors
had been taken off and the lifeboat
set a course for Campbeltown. The

passage had to be made at reduced speed because of the conditions, and frequently the lifeboat was heeled right over by the heavy breaking waves. She arrived at station at 8.30 over 13 hours after setting out and the survivors were landed and given accommodation for the night.'

The second award-winning rescue occurred seven years later. While the RNLI report is more succinct it is no less dramatic than that of the rescue of the crew of the fishing trawler *Erlo Hills*.

A full account of the service follows:

'At 8.32 pm, on 30 September 1988, Clyde Coastguard informed Mr J McWhirter, honorary secretary of the Campbeltown lifeboat station, that the fishing vessel *John Hannah VC* was disabled and at anchor off Davaar Island and had requested assistance.

Maroons were fired at 8.35 pm and at 8.40 pm, Campbeltown's relief lifeboat, the 52ft Arun class *Sir Max Aitken* was launched on service.

The weather was overcast with occasional showers though visibility was generally good, with a gentle south-westerly breeze and a slight sea running in the loch.

After clearing the harbour, Coxswain Mechanic Alexander Gilchrist headed east down the loch and proceeded at full speed for Davaar Island. Arriving at the reported location at 8.50 pm, no trace could be found of the casualty. After consulting the Coastguard, Coxswain Gilchrist headed south to search the shore. At 9.15 pm the Coastguard reported that the fishing vessel had been found at anchor close to Keill Point and the lifeboat made all speed, arriving at 9.37 pm.

Weather conditions had worsened, with a strong onshore southerly breeze, force 6, and a southerly swell. The casualty was anchored about 35 yards from the shore, rolling heavily in surf and rough seas, with her stern overhanging a reef. The tide was running strongly east at 2-3 knots and

Coxswain Gilchrist considered the situation too dangerous either to attempt a tow or to launch the inflatable 'Y' boat from the lifeboat or to use a breeches buoy.

From radio conversations with the casualty's skipper, it was apparent that his crew were very inexperienced.

In view of all these factors, Coxswain Gilchrist decided to make a series of runs to the casualty down wind, while keeping his stern up wind in deeper water. Assistant Mechanic Brodie was instructed to monitor the echo sounder while the second coxswain and crew manned the foredeck.

On the first run, none of the survivors would jump and Coxswain Gilchrist had to reverse smartly to avoid being swept into shallow water. On the second run two survivors were grabbed and pulled aboard the lifeboat by the crew, before the lifeboat reversed clear.

On the final run the last survivor misjudged his jump, missed his footing but clung to the bow of the lifeboat as she reversed. He was hauled aboard and all the survivors were given hot drinks and kept warm.

The lifeboat headed east and arrived at Campbeltown Harbour by 11.00 pm. The survivors were landed, the lifeboat refuelled and made ready for service again at 11.30 pm.'

Despite the imposition of fishing quotas on European fishing fleets and the threat of restrictions on time allowed to fishermen to spend time at sea carrying out their work, the calls on the lifeboats of the Hebrides and the west coast of Scotland still involve fishing vessels. This is likely to remain the case in the years ahead.

The Scottish golf course coast

The Scottish south-west coast from the Firth of Clyde to the Mull of Galloway is perhaps best known to the British public at large from television golf programmes which show the rock Ailsa Craig, over 1,000 feet high, looming in the distance while commentator Peter Allis waxes lyrical! Three lifeboat stations cover this coast, the most northern being at **Troon** where the Arun class boat *City of Glasgow III* is based in the tidal basin to seaward of the Troon Marina. The boat is the centrepiece of two inshore lifeboats, one based at Helensburgh and the other at Lamlash on the island of Arran.

One of the most memorable rescues by the Troon lifeboat, commemorated in a fine painting by marine artist David Cobb, was that of the crew of the Dutch dredger *Holland I* in severe onshore westerly winds. Coxswain Ian Johnson and his crew were called out in the afternoon of 12 September 1980, when the dredger began to drift towards breaking water and the shore. The lifeboat at Troon at that time was a Waveney class 44 foot boat. Coxswain Johnson took the lifeboat in on a number of runs, taking off the

dredger crew one at a time, one of his crew grabbing the survivors and pulling them on to the lifeboat over the bow rails each time the lifeboat closed with the dredger. This rescue earned Coxswain Johnson a silver medal for gallantry while the prints of the subsequent painting of the event raised much appreciated funds for the RNLI.

One of the most common calls today made on the Troon lifeboat is from the International Airport at nearby Prestwick in times of aircraft emergencies. When rescue services are assembling ashore the Troon lifeboat takes up station at sea to the west of the main east to west runway.

Apart from international and other passenger traffic that uses Prestwick, the airfield is a major flying training centre for future airline pilots although the opening of Glasgow Airport to international flights has meant that a number of flights, notably of larger passenger aircraft, have moved there. However, Prestwick is still considered a busy airfield.

The Troon lifeboat Sir David Richmond of Glasgow, *a petrol engined Watson class vessel, undergoing trials off Cowes prior to delivery to the Ayrshire station in 1929. The mast will carry a jib and mainsail while oars are also aboard.*

South from Troon lies the small fishing port of **Girvan** some ten miles due east of the Ailsa Craig rock which dominates the seaward view from the town. Here the harbour master, Roddy Leitch, is RNLI assistant coxswain and full-time RNLI mechanic to the 33 foot Brede class lifeboat *Amateur Swimming Associations*, a rare Brede, as Roddy Leitch puts it as there are not very many Brede class boats on Scottish stations, the only other one being round the Mull of Kintyre up on the Firth of Lorne at Oban, Argyllshire.

Having a smaller boat than the Arun at Troon or the 47 foot Tyne class boat down the coast at Portpatrick the Girvan crew admit feeling 'squeezed', although they have taken their boat out on calls west of the Mull of Kintyre and were put on stand-by when Richard Branson made his dramatic descent from his transatlantic balloon journey, skimming the fields of Rathlin Island off Ulster fifty miles west of Girvan before ditching in the sea. Girvan was awash with avid journalists and photographers that day but otherwise it is a comparatively quiet station averaging about twelve calls per year.

Scotland's most southern lifeboat station lies at **Portpatrick** on the west coast of the Galloway peninsula and a few miles south-west of the busy ferry terminals at Stranraer and Cairnryan on Loch Ryan. The station is best remembered for the tragic loss of the ferry *Princess Victoria* in 1953 when 133 people lost their lives and only 43 survived. The ferry routes across the shortest passage between the Scottish, Welsh or English mainland to Ulster are still very much on the minds of Coxswain Robert Erskine and his crew of the 47 foot Tyne class lifeboat *Mary Irene Millar*.

One and three quarter million passengers pass through the Stranraer and Cairnryan ferry terminals each year to Larne, on the north coast of Ulster. It is only 18 miles from Portpatrick to the Ulster coast and the Portpatrick crew liaise closely with the lifeboat at Donaghadee across the water. Indeed Coxswain Robert Erskine comes from the Irish port but was captured by a girl from Dumfriesshire, so settled in Portpatrick. Because of the nature of the waters between the Scottish and Ulster coasts, and the amount of traffic through the channel, Portpatrick can be a busy station averaging two or three calls a month, but it is that call from a ferry, which they hope never comes, that is never far from the minds of the Portpatrick crew when wild westerly weather strikes the south-west coast of Scotland.

The Manx Wheel. The Hub

At the centre of the northern part of the Irish Sea, between the north-west coast of England and the shores of Northern Ireland, lies the Isle of Man. Apart from fairies, steam railways, cats without tails and its own parliament the Tynwald, the island has another attribute that surprises some people. It operates five RNLI lifeboat stations, four of them working with all-weather boats.

Thirty miles long from north to south and ten miles wide, the island acts as the hub of a wheel of lifeboat stations, the spokes radiating out to the sixteen mainland stations on the coasts of Ireland, Scotland, England and Wales that lie on the Irish Sea shores. For this very reason the Isle of Man has been a centre of maritime activity since the earliest inhabitants of the area ventured afloat. Relatively late-comers to these activities were the Vikings, who colonized the island and gave it the basis of its present parliamentary system. During the recent millenium celebrations the Norwegians recognized the fact by presenting the islanders with an exact replica of a Norse longship which was successfully rowed and sailed from Norway to the island. To put the royal stamp of approval on the festivities King Olaf of Norway visited the island.

The first Manx lifeboat station was at **Douglas** where Sir William Hillary lived while he founded the RNLI as we know it. He is buried nearby and the site of his house, Fort Anne, overlooks the station, the harbour and the Tower of Refuge, which he had built on the rocks lying off the harbour entrance. Appropriately the Douglas lifeboat, a 1988 slipway launched Tyne class vessel, is named *Sir William Hillary*.

The Douglas boat deals with every type of rescue and, as with the other Manx stations, is ready to face everything from problems with ferries to ditching aircraft. The Isle of Man is a 'way point' for both international transatlantic flights as well as more local transit traffic flying between England and Ireland and other routes north and south across the Irish Sea. The Cregneish navigational beacon stands on a hill behind Port St Mary to the south-west of Douglas while Ronaldsway Airport, lying between the two harbours, is a busy commercial airfield. Apart from the busy ferry and aircraft activity the area supports many fishing ports and is increasingly becoming a yachtsman and power cruiser owners' playground as moorings and berths in southern British waters become harder and harder to find. It all seems to happen around the Isle of Man and liaison with the mainland stations is not uncommon.

Port St Mary and Port Erin lie on the south-western corner of the Isle of Man. **Port St Mary**, on the east side of the last promontory of the island before rounding the dangerous waters off the Calf of Man and heading up the western coast of the island, is a small fishing port harbouring one of the 54 foot Arun class lifeboats. There have only been four Aruns built to

this length, the rest being 52 foot long. The boat is moored between two pilings, an uncommon way of berthing a lifeboat, but it works. The most recent of RNLI stations on the Isle of Man, Port St Mary is preparing to celebrate its centenary in 1996. When asked what he thought might be an appropriate way of marking the occasion a member of the crew said that he thought that they might grant an extension of opening hours at the lifeboatmen's local inn, The Albert! There were more ambitious thoughts elsewhere in the community.

Port St Mary and **Port Erin** are a team. They lie three miles apart by road but nearly ten miles if one sails there round the Calf of Man, the small Manx National Trust island lying off the south of the main island. The two stations often work together as was amply illustrated during the autumn of 1990. In the early hours of an October morning, with a strong south-west wind blowing, rough seas building and visibility poor, one of the Irish Sea ferries running between Belfast and Liverpool reported that a young lady passenger was missing and was suspected of having fallen overboard. The position given was south of the Calf of Man. The Port St Mary and the Port Erin boat, a slipway launched Rother with a speed of only 8 knots, were both launched. The crews carried out a combined search in darkness over a prescribed pattern. Dawn broke over a cold rough sea.

After several hours of co-ordinated but fruitless endeavour a recall signal was received aboard the lifeboats. The missing passenger was, as later reported on the radio in the north-west region, found to have been in 'someone else's cabin'. Cold and frustrated but, surprisingly without obvious recrimination, the lifeboat crews returned to their home ports. What happened to the 'missing' person was not reported.

Port St Mary, being close to the Isle of Man airport at Ronaldsway, is a

A motor ketch with a crew of three ran into the harbour at Castletown Bay, Isle of Man, after engine failure. The Port St Mary lifeboat tried to give assistance with the help of their inflatable carried aboard.

station with aircraft very much on the minds of the crew. Once in a while the whole island rescue service system carries out an all-island aircraft alert exercise, such is the recognition of the position of the island in relation to the aircraft routeing already mentioned. The site of the 'crash' can be anywhere in the mountainous area or the sea or the flatter country to the north and west of the island. A sea situation involves all the island lifeboats and if not all boats, then certainly many of their crews. Police, a rescue helicopter, the fire service, and RNLI are all involved while local hospitals are put on full alert to receive casualties. One can only be grateful that the situation has never arisen in reality but there is no point in pretending that it never could. One only has to remember the awful Lockerbie air disaster to appreciate this.

The aged Port Erin lifeboat lies in a lifeboat house on the south shore of the attractive Port Erin bay with its dangerous reef formed by the remains of a collapsed stone breakwater close by. During the time of the happily thwarted rescue of the 'missing' ferry passenger the future of the Port Erin station and that of **Peel**, 10 miles northwards up the Manx western coast, was in a state of flux. The fishing port of Peel operated an Atlantic 21 inflatable while as mentioned, Port Erin had the Rother. Both local opinion and thoughts further afield at the Poole headquarters quietly indicated that the situation at the two stations might become interchanged, Peel being sent a fast offshore Mersey class boat while still maintaining an inflatable while Port Erin could be equipped with an inflatable, probably an Atlantic. Certainly, taking an outsider's viewpoint and appreciating the changes being made all around the coasts of Britain and Ireland as the new fast classes of lifeboats take station, this makes sense, considerable

sense.

The rationalization of the 1990s places the fast boats about 20 miles apart, sometimes more, sometimes less, depending upon geographical characteristics. This fits at Port Erin and Peel, bringing in Port St Mary, 20 miles from Peel to the south, and Ramsey, 30 miles away northwards round the northern-most headland of the island, the Point of Ayre. No doubt by the mid-1990s all will be resolved.

There is no such uncertainty at **Ramsey** up on the island's north-east coast where the honorary secretary, Harbour Master Brew watched with satisfaction as the new lifeboat house rose steadily, an attractive edifice costing £250,000. Much of this was paid for out of local fund-raising efforts. The new Mersey lifeboat went on station in July 1991 while a new submersible Talus tractor preceded it to be used in trials at both Ramsey and Peel with a Mersey 'on loan' from the mainland. The whole new package, preparing Ramsey for the years ahead, brought the total expenditure, from one RNLI source and another, to almost £1 million. The pride and happiness among the local lifeboatmen and supporters was almost tangible at the beginning of the 1990s. Although Ramsey is not as busy as some stations, when calls do come to Ramsey they can be hazardous due to the reputation of the Irish Sea and its weather.

The Manx Wheel. The Rim.

The Isle of Man wheel rim begins at Portpatrick. Three inflatable lifeboats at Kirkcudbright, Kippford and Silloth then cover the shoaling waters of the Solway Firth before one finds the next all-weather lifeboat at **Workington**. Workington, primarily a commercial harbour operated a tractor launched

Watson until 1990 when a Solent class boat was put on temporary station duty, awaiting the arrival of the 47 foot Tyne class *Sir John Fisher* due in 1991.

It has been decided that the Workington Tyne should be launched from davits on the harbourside with strong slings placed under the boat. No other lifeboat is yet launched in this way, but extensive tests with the system were carried out by the RNLI using cranes and strops with success so work was put in hand at Workington to erect the unique davits in readiness for the new boat.

When compared with other stations Workington is not as busy as some but is still a vital station geographically as there is very little shelter for larger vessels during westerly gales along the Cumbrian coast once past Barrow in the south and sailing northwards towards Whitehaven and Maryport. A 'C' class inflatable is based 11 miles down the coast from Workington at St Bees but this can have launching problems in severe south-westerly and westerly winds.

The next station down the Cumbrian coast is at **Barrow**, not amid the busy shipyards but perched far out on Roa Island, a small community that time seems to have passed by. The Tyne class boat *James Bibby* is housed in the lifeboat house which is one of the few prominent features of the vast flat expanse of Morecambe Bay. An inflatable, essential for working in the shallow waters of the bay notorious for its quicksands, supports the all-weather boat. The Barrow crew are as likely to be recipients of awards for their work from the RSPCA as the RNLI. Over the years a number of animals ranging from horses and cattle to dogs have strayed out on to the sands and been trapped by the fast incoming tide. People also stroll out across the sands unaware of the dangers while inshore fishermen, amateur and professional, provide their share of customers of the Barrow

lifeboats. The rescue business at that station is varied, increasing in the tourist season when small boat and board sailors put to sea.

At Morecambe a 'D' class inflatable takes care of the problems of the holiday-makers getting into trouble in the bay but at **Fleetwood** a new Tyne class boat has replaced the Waveney that was there from 1976. Coxswain Bill Fairclough, while delighted with the new boat, thought the Waveney, with its higher control position, better for one of the tasks which the Fleetwood boat often has to carry out. Holiday-makers are sometimes swept from the Blackpool promenade in severe weather. Searching from the lower profiled Tyne is not often as easy as it was from the higher Waveney.

Fleetwood, with its own fishing fleet, ferry terminal, holiday complexes, caravan camps and resorts all around it, is a busy station. The lifeboat, the *William Street*, was funded by a trust set up by a Lancashire businessman of the same name. The capital in the trust fund was about £6.25 million and the lifeboat was paid for by just one year's interest from the fund. The new Tyne installed, Fleetwood faces a bright future as a lifeboat station, as does the station at **Lytham St Anne's** where another new Tyne lies on a mooring near the entrance to the narrow small estuary. Between Lytham and Fleetwood, in the centre of the Fylde peninsula coast at Blackpool there are two 'D' class inflatables on station, their primary duty to be ready to deal with the holiday-makers who get into trouble off Blackpool beach, and there are many of them.

The Lytham lifeboat was new at the beginning of 1990 and is supported by a 'D' class inflatable. The next station down the coast is at **Hoylake**, on the Wirral peninsula. This area of north-west England has received a real shot in the arm from the RNLI, new boats arriving from Poole, taken home by

Naming ceremony of the Fleetwood Tyne class lifeboat William Street *on 12 May 1990.*

their own crews, in a steady stream from the beginning of the 1990s.

While Hoylake lies just north of the seaward end of the Dee Estuary there are inflatables at West Kirby and Flint to deal with trouble in the shoal waters in the estuary. In 1990 there was no fast all-weather lifeboat on the north coast of Wales until one reached Llandudno. **Rhyl**, halfway between Llandudno and the River Dee was operating a venerable Oakley class boat over 20 years old and launched from a carriage and tractor across the beach. A fast all-weather boat was expected, but no-one was prepared to put a date to its arrival.

Llandudno, where, in 1990, Coxswain Meurig Davies unwillingly faced compulsory retirement on reaching the age of fifty-five, the lifeboat launching procedure is certainly entirely different compared with most other stations around Britain and Ireland. The

Llandudno lifeboat is housed with its Talus tractor in the town centre almost a mile from the promenade of the holiday resort and even further from the beaches on the western shore of the Orme peninsula which is dominated by Great Orme's Head. The reason is practical and simple. If it is too rough to launch to the east then the lifeboat, a Mersey new on the station late in 1990, can be rumbled down the town's roadways and launched on the western shore.

The massive tides of the Liverpool Bay area mean that at times the lifeboat can be taken across over half a mile of sands before reaching the sea but at high water, launching from Llandudno promenade, the boat can be at sea within 10 minutes of leaving the lifeboat house. Asked whether there was ever a problem with traffic Coxswain Davies responded with a wry smile and the comment that few

motorists will argue with a package of lifeboat and tractor weighing over 25 tons coming down the main street.

The town centre launching operation at Llandudno is an RNLI public relations man's dream on a level with other resort stations such as Bridlington and Scarborough, on the east coast, where a comparable situation exists, the boats launching from the main promenade. Llandudno's new Mersey class boat was named *RNLB Andy Pearce* by HRH The Duchess of Kent in a special ceremony at Llandudno on 18 June 1991.

It is as one approaches Anglesey that reminiscences begin among lifeboatmen about the rescue of the Greek freighter *Nafsiporos* in December 1966. Already described in earlier pages, the episode emphasized the connecting spokes between the stations on the Isle of Man and those around the edge of the Manx Wheel. When the alarm was raised it was the lifeboat from Douglas that put to sea

to start the search, later to return to port having not sighted the stricken vessel in poor visibility. The search was taken up by the lifeboat crews from Moelfre and Holyhead who, after a stupendous effort in terrible conditions, successfully saved the crew. On that occasion the Beaumaris and Llandudno crews were also put on stand-by but not called out.

Beaumaris, the southern-most station on Anglesey operated an ageing Watson, built in 1960, at the start of the 1990s as well as an Atlantic inflatable that is ideal for the difficult waters of the treacherous Menai Strait. However, in June 1991, the RNLI announced plans to withdraw the Watson from service following the arrival of fast lifeboats at Moelfre and Llandudno.

The future of the lifeboat at the remote village of **Moelfre**, on the east coast of Anglesey, is well set. The coxswain, Will Roberts, is a small fiery character with a marked sense of independence which must surely come

from living in a place that is as quiet as a churchyard in winter but attracts visitors in the summer months. During a recent rescue of a vessel in difficulties between Llandudno and Moelfre the coastguards had called out the Llandudno boat, but the direction given that the Llandudno crew should have sailed by to reach the casualty was inaccurate. Will Roberts opened the lifeboat house at Moelfre, let the Tyne class boat *Robert and Violet* down the slipway to the water's edge and started his own direction finder. Getting a good bearing he launched the boat and set off to find the casualty and tow it to safety before the Llandudno boat arrived. It is the Llandudno coxswain, Meurig Davies, who tells the tale with a smile.

Holyhead, the busy ferry and fishing port on Holy Island at the north-west corner of Anglesey, is a busy lifeboat station now, operating a new Tyne class boat, the *St Cybi II*, a donation from the Civil Service, Post Office and British Telecom Lifeboat Fund, the fortieth boat provided by this fund-raising organization. Before the Tyne the station had an Arun class boat. The crew prefer the Tyne when comparing the two. A magnificent painting of the rescue of the crew of the Greek ship *Nafsiporos* adorns the crew room at the station.

The ferries operating out of Holyhead to Ireland have occasionally needed help from the lifeboat crew, the most recent occasion being in January 1990 when fire broke out in the engineroom of the Sealink ferry *St Columba*. The lifeboat, at sea for twelve hours standing by the vessel, worked in co-operation with a helicopter from nearby RAF Valley, one of the busy Royal Air Force Search and Rescue centres and also a training station for Search and Rescue aircrew.

Apart from the lifeboat station, which provides the trainees at RAF Valley with help when they practise wet winching, Holyhead is the local Coastguard centre for the area while lifeboats from around the Manx Wheel

Porthdinllaen lifeboat station.

and further afield are serviced and refitted there.

The final, most southerly station on the Irish Sea coast of Wales and England that faces the Isle of Man is at **Porthdinllaen** out on the north shore of the Lleyn peninsula. The fact that it is not even on many road maps is not surprising. It is not even on a road. The station is approached through Morfa Nefyn and then along a private gated road over a golf course to a low cliff top. From there on it is a rough track down to the lifeboat house that contains a Tyne class boat, the *Hetty Rampton*. When compared with some the station is not busy, though in the summer months, with the rapid increase in coastal sailing and the expansion of Pwllheli as a sailing centre around the other side of the peninsula, calls can come thick and fast if a north-westerly

summer gale springs up. There is little or no shelter from westerly winds on the whole north coast of the peninsula from Bardsey Island on the western-most tip to Caernarfon at the south-west end of the Menai Strait, a distance of about forty miles. Anything, from a ferry with a power failure to a small yacht with a broken engine, would be in dire trouble if off that coast in strong westerly winds. Thus, though not run off their feet at Porthdinllaen, their being there is vital.

Cardigan Bay and the South Wales stations

The most northern station in Cardigan Bay, that coastal crescent on the west coast of Wales, is at **Pwllheli**. Until the end of 1990 an elderly Oakley class boat, *The Royal Thames*, was on the station but during 1990 extensive alterations were made to the boathouse in the local yacht yard in preparation for the arrival of a new carriage launched Mersey class boat at the start of 1991. Pwllheli is a relatively quiet station but has become more active with the increase in yachting and motor boating in the area.

Pwllheli was hoping to become the centre for the Olympic regatta had Britain been chosen as the venue for the 1994 Olympic Games. It was an optimistic hope and one can only wonder whether the small town could have coped with the invasion of competitors, worldwide media and all the camp followers of the five-ringed circus. The massive holiday camp a short distance eastwards along the coast might have been requisitioned to take the strain of the accommodation problem while improvements to the harbour might have managed to provide the necessary facilities for the yachts and dinghies involved, not forgetting the many committee boats, support vessels, press and television craft and other essentials of a successful regatta. Coxswain Brian Green, who took over from Coxswain Billy McGill with the arrival of the new boat, was confident that the local RNLI branch could provide adequate rescue facilities even if it meant putting a second, even third relief boat temporarily on the station.

West of Pwllheli lies the holiday village of **Abersoch** where the Atlantic class rigid inflatable is based, dealing for the main part with the rescue of holiday-makers in various guises, be they divers, swimmers, sailors or cliff climbers. It is not for these rescues that the station made national news recently but for quite another reason. Crew member Dilwyn Owen had suffered from kidney failure and was awaiting the chance of a kidney transplant operation. The telephone call came through to Abersoch to inform Dilwyn that a kidney was available but he was nowhere to be found. One of his colleagues decided that the best way of finding him was to fire the lifeboat maroon rocket to summon the boat's crew. All, including the elusive Dilwyn, appeared. He was soon on his way to hospital in Liverpool where the operation was successfully carried out. The station honorary secretary, Captain Pat Grimason was delighted, commenting that it was probably the only time that a potential loss of life had been prevented by a lifeboat station without the boat even putting to sea.

A 'C' class inflatable lifeboat is based at Criccieth, near the massive holiday camp complex but the next all-weather station southwards is at **Barmouth** where the Rother class boat *The Princess of Wales* is stationed. The honorary secretary, Lieutenant Colonel Colin Walker, admits that being off the shipping lanes means the station is quiet when compared with those at Tenby, Angle or St Davids in South Wales, but the north-east corner of Cardigan Bay can be a treacherous place for a vessel in difficulty in a south-westerly or westerly gale.

Although the Rother class boat on the station is one of the last to be built, and therefore a relatively modern boat, the Barmouth crew are due to receive a new Mersey class boat in 1992. They feel that the wider operating range and the greater speed of the Mersey would increase the amount of work handled by the station.

Recently a whole fleet of small fishing vessels was caught outside the estuary entrance in a storm and was escorted to safety by the lifeboat although one, who tried to make it without help did, as one of the lifeboat crew put it, almost end up on the wrong side of the wire.

South from Barmouth the middle of Cardigan Bay is covered by an Atlantic 21 at Aberdovey, a 'D' class inflatable at Borth and a 'C' class inshore inflatable at Aberystywth. It is not until one reaches **New Quay** that the next all-weather lifeboat station is found. Here, up until 1990, a 30 year-old Oakley, was on station with a 'D' class inflatable. The Oakley, the *Calouste Gulbenkian*, was launched by carriage and slipway but it was due to be replaced by a new Mersey class fast carriage launching boat during 1991. The inshore inflatable is used mainly for tourists during the holiday season who find themselves in trouble swimming and sailing but the all-weather boat has served well in recent years. During a recent winter storm the Ministry of Defence barge *Longbow*, loaded with very expensive experimental missile tracking equipment broke adrift off Aberporth nine miles down the coast. The New Quay crew went out and stood by the barge until tugs arrived from Milford Haven to secure a tow and take the barge to shelter. A faster boat at New Quay, capable of 17 knots, is an improvement to be much appreciated by the crew.

The Arun class boat *Marie Winstone*, based at **Fishguard**, covers the wild

The Arun class Marie Winstone *based at Fishguard.*

Welsh coastline between the St David's station to the south-west and Cardigan to the north-east. The Fishguard crew often work in conjunction with the St David's crew, although on Christmas Eve 1989 they were called to a coaster in difficulty in a storm almost on the doorstep of the St David's station, standing by until more substantial help could arrive from Milford Haven. Mechanic Chris Williams recalls the incident with a wry smile, common of lifeboatmen who have worked on another station's territory.

Fishguard is a busy ferry port with all the implications this means to the lifeboat crews, although rescue work covers a wide range of vessels from pleasure craft to fishing boats. On one rare occasion the crew were called out in thick fog to take a pilot out to the world's oldest sailing ship still working under sail, the *Inca*, which was having difficulty in finding her way into Fishguard Harbour. The mighty

buttress of Strumble Head lies to the north-west of the station, no place to be drifting around lost even on a calm sea.

To the west of Fishguard, past Strumble Head and out on the end of the peninsula that forms St David's Head lies the **St Davids** station two miles from the small cathedral town whose name the station bears. The lifeboat house is set in a narrow inlet at St Justinian's, sheltered to the west by Ramsey Island. It is one of the more dramatic settings for a lifeboat station that houses a slipway launching Tyne class boat, *Garside*, that was new at the station in 1988 and named by HRH the Duke of Kent. The slipway launching of the old boat that was replaced by the Tyne has featured in several posters depicting the RNLI.

The new boat was not long on station before making a rescue that earned Coxswain David Chant a bronze medal for gallantry. In February 1989, winds of storm force were blowing from the south-west when the fishing vessel *Stephanie Jane* suffered a mechanical failure while near the South Bishop lighthouse to the west of Ramsey Island. The trawler crew dropped an anchor but it failed to hold in the severe weather.

Not only did Coxswain Chant and his crew manage to take the four crew off the fishing boat in very difficult conditions but they also managed to put a line aboard the casualty and tow it to shelter. In 1985 Coxswain Chant's predecessor, Coxswain Fred John carried out a similar rescue of a fishing boat and its crew of two who were aboard, while the lifeboat's inflatable boarding boat was used to rescue a further person who had been swept ashore. This rescue was performed using the Watson class boat *Joseph Soar* which was replaced by the new Tyne class boat, the *Joseph Soar* then going on station at Shoreham, Sussex. The boat is now being sold.

Across St Bride's Bay and at the southern side of the entrance to

Milford Haven lies the lifeboat station of **Angle**, close by the small remote village of the same somewhat curious name. The lifeboat house is tucked under the shelter of a small cliff approached along a dirt road. Plans are well in hand to rebuild the slipway and lifeboat house. The old slipway had become dangerous as the concrete supports began to show signs of deterioration. The new Tyne class lifeboat, *The Lady Rank*, will be rehoused some yards south-east of the present position.

Milford Haven and Pembroke Dock at the eastern end of the Haven are busy areas in shipping terms. Pembroke Dock has a ferry terminal and ship repair yard while there is heavy oil tanker traffic into the Haven which has several oil refineries and oil storage farms around its shores. The Angle lifeboat, with Gerald 'Farmer' Edwards as coxswain, has gone to the aid of everything from a passenger missing from a ferry to fishing boats, ditched military aircraft and pleasure craft. The fact that the area is so busy

Launching the Angle lifeboat in Milford Haven prior to her naming ceremony.

Alan Thomas, Tenby.

with commercial traffic of every size means that there are usually harbour tugs, pilot vessels and other support vessels continually on the move, or at any rate manned and standing by for work. This fact may sometimes mean that these boats rather than the lifeboat may attend incidents but the Angle station still keeps busy.

The only silver medal for gallantry awarded by the RNLI in 1989 was earned by Coxswain Alan Thomas of **Tenby** for the assistance and crew rescues involving three fishing boats during a violent storm from the north-west in September of that year. Initially the Coastguard requested the lifeboat crew to go to the help of the fishing boat *Seeker* in trouble off Worms Head, sixteen miles south-east of Tenby Harbour. The Tyne class lifeboat, *The RFA Sir Galahad*, put out and located the casualty while the fishing boat *New Venture* was

attempting a tow. A third fishing boat, the *Silver Stream* was standing by.

When the lifeboat reached the scene the original casualty was already ashore but the *New Venture* was herself now in trouble close to the beach at Rhossili, as was the fishing boat *Silver Stream,* her skipper trapped in the wheelhouse by trawl gear that had fallen against the back of the wheelhouse door. He was dragged from the wheelhouse window by the lifeboat crew. The boat, abandoned, then joined the *Seeker* on the beach while the Tenby lifeboat began to escort the *New Venture* on the long battle against the wind to Tenby Roads, two of the lifeboat crew being put aboard the fishing boat to help the exhausted crew who were later landed at Tenby once their boat had been secured in a safe anchorage. Both the fishing vessels driven ashore were later refloated when the storm abated.

Apart from receiving his silver medal at the 1990 RNLI annual general meeting at the Royal Festival Hall, Coxswain Alan Thomas also received the Miss Maud Smith Award for Courage, a small financial gift instituted in 1943 by Maud Smith in memory of John, 7th Earl of Hardwicke, a descendant of Admiral Earl of Hardwicke, Chairman of the RNLI in 1861. Coxswain Thomas also received the Silk Cut Award for Rescue at Sea.

Amid its successes Tenby has had its sad moments in recent years. The lifeboat house bears a photograph of Second Coxswain John John who died while on service in the lifeboat in the summer of 1988. Flares were reported off Worms Head. The lifeboat put to sea immediately to make the fifteen mile passage across Carmarthen Bay. During the operation Second Coxswain John suffered a brain haemorrhage and died. The call on the lifeboat crew had been a hoax.

The lifeboat station at Tenby opened

in 1854 as part of the Shipwrecked Fishermen's and Mariner's Benevolent Society and joined the fold of the RNLI two years later. Since that time, nine silver and five bronze medals have been earned by crew members for gallantry, the Tenby lifeboat called upon over 1,400 times and over 630 lives saved.

Across Carmarthen Bay from Tenby lies the inflatable based at Burry Port near Llanelli, facing the popular recreational area of the Gower Peninsula. This boat is used for seasonal work, as is the next inshore boat along the coast at Port Eynon on the southern shore of The Gower while on the east of The Gower, facing into Swansea Bay from the west, lies the all-weather lifeboat station in the attractive holiday village of **The Mumbles**.

The 1985 built Tyne class lifeboat, *Ethel Anne Measures*, is supported by an inflatable. In 1947, it will be remembered, the entire crew of The Mumbles lifeboat were lost along with forty-one crew of the coaster that they were trying to save. A memorial still remains in the lifeboat house by the pier to those crewmen lost but The Mumbles holds other memories. During the summer of 1981 the holiday passenger ferry, the *Prince Ivanhoe*, taking tourists on a cruise along the shore of The Gower, hit rocks close to the shore. The master had the sense to run the ferry ashore, the engineroom already flooding rapidly. The Mumbles lifeboat was called but lifeboats, life rafts and a dinghy were lowered from the ferry and all 575 people aboard safely reached the beach. One lady passenger had the presence of mind to take photographs of the event as she bobbed about in a life raft. She later framed the pictures and sent them to The Mumbles lifeboat crew as a souvenir for their lifeboat house. Apart from being coxswain of the lifeboat Alan Jones is also responsible for the nearby lighthouse as an employee of Trinity House, the authority that keeps navigation equipment operating in British waters.

East of The Mumbles lie a string of three inshore lifeboat stations at Aberavon Beach (Port Talbot), Porthcawl, and Atlantic College, St Donat's Castle. While Aberavon and Porthcawl both have 'D' class boats the station at St Donat has, appropriately, an Atlantic 21 for it was at Atlantic College that the prototype of this boat was designed. The boat on the station is manned by students from the college.

The last all-weather lifeboat station at the eastern end of the coast of South Wales is at **Barry Dock**, just west of Cardiff where the original Arun class boat lies, named *Arun* and proudly bearing the number 52-01. This was the boat that was taken to the Isles of Scilly for evaluation by Coxswain Matt Lethbridge and is unique in that the deck is flush from bow to stern unlike the rest of the Arun fleet which have a deck that drops down nearer the waterline from a point beneath the front of the superstructure making the business of pulling people from the sea easier for crews. Several converted RNLI boats lie nearby the lifeboat station the boats now retired from the fleet and sold by the Institution. These include one of the original sailing lifeboats that was converted to her present form in 1900.

Among recent rescues carried out by the station were two made during the winter of 1989-90. In December 1989 the crew of the yacht *Pelinore* reported to Swansea Marine Rescue Co-ordination Centre that the yacht was sinking six miles off Nash Point, twelve miles west of Barry. The wind was blowing at storm force from the south-west. A Search and Rescue helicopter was called from RAF Chivenor, North Devon.

The motor vessel *Belle Ranger* reached the scene and her crew managed to take the yacht's crew of two off the *Pelinore* while the helicopter crew lowered a pump aboard the sinking vessel thus controlling the incoming water. The Barry Dock lifeboat, the relief boat *Duchess of Kent*, an Arun, with recently-appointed Coxswain Ray Finn at the helm, had been trapped by tidal restrictions for a short while at Barry but arrived at the casualty to take the two yacht crew from the *Belle Ranger* and put a towline aboard the yacht. The tow parted in the extremely rough conditions so it was decided to wait for the weather to moderate, as forecast, before attempting to reconnect the line and put lifeboatmen aboard the yacht. Sadly the weather stayed atrocious and the yacht sank, the Barry Dock lifeboat returning to harbour with the casualties. The lifeboat crew were congratulated in writing by Chief of RNLI Operations, Commodore George Cooper, for their efforts.

A month later, in January 1990, the pipe-laying barge *Jimmie Mac* lost three of her four anchors while lying out in the Bristol Channel off Cardiff in winds gusting at up to 100 knots. The Barry Dock lifeboat put out in terrible conditions and headed for the barge, standing by until two tugs from Barry Dock were able to pass through the locks between the non-tidal and tidal basins at the dock and reach the barge putting towlines aboard. The lifeboat crew were asked to stay with the tugs and the barge during the long business of towing the barge to the safety and shelter of Barry Harbour. Certainly Coxswain Ray Finn started his new appointment with a baptism of fire.

The Barry Dock crew are proud of their Arun boat but wonder whether they are in line for something more modern as even the earliest of the new fast offshore boats the *Arun* that they operate is now twenty years old. Theirs is the last fast all-weather boat station on the coast of the Bristol Channel before the channel ends at the Severn Bridge thirty miles to the north-east. There is a seasonally busy inflatable lifeboat at Penarth, between Barry Dock and Cardiff. After that lies the entire mouth of the River Severn including the holiday beaches of Gwent and north Somerset as well as the busy port of Avonmouth covered by the inshore boats at Penarth and Weston-super-Mare 10 miles across the mouth of the long estuary. Perhaps Barry Dock could well need a boat both bigger and faster than their faithful Arun to cover that responsibility during the storms in the winter months. Certainly a regular visitor to the lifeboat house, Assistant Mechanic David Brooks, thinks so. He should know. He joined the Barry Dock lifeboat at the end of World War II and retired from the crew in 1962. Happily sailing through his 80s he still makes one of the best cups of tea in any of the RNLI lifeboat crew rooms and is there when the crew come back from a call, day or night.

Chapter 18

THE LIFEBOAT STATIONS –
South and West Britain and Ireland

South from Spurn Head

Skegness is the only lifeboat station with a fast all-weather boat between Spurn Head and the next station southwards, 25 miles across the mouth of The Wash at Wells-next-the-Sea. There are two stations north of Skegness, at Mablethorpe and Cleethorpes, each working with 'D' class inflatables.

Skegness has no harbour and is not mentioned in the leading pilotage handbook for yachtsmen and small craft users, but it has an active lifeboat station on the seafront where, in July 1990 the crew took delivery at Poole, after a week of training, of the Mersey class boat *The Lincolnshire Poacher*. The money came from local fund-raising efforts and a gift of £360,000 from Van Geest Charities, managed by the banana importing company.

Calls at Skegness, which vary greatly in number from year to year, are equally divided between pleasure craft and commercial vessels, mainly fishing boats, but the most memorable event was in 1978 when the pier at Skegness was washed away and the lifeboat put out on a very long call to stand by the merchant ship *Glorioso* whose ballast had shifted in a force 11 severe storm. The Skegness boat is launched from the beach with a carriage and tractor, a slight embarrassment being caused in recent years when the tractor sank into the sands on the

beach while the crew of the lifeboat, the old Oakley class *Charles Fred Grantham*, had to stay at sea aboard their boat for 24 hours.

1990 was also the year of the new boat for the station across The Wash at **Wells**. In July, HRH the Duchess of Kent named the new Mersey class boat *Doris M Mann of Ampthill* at a special ceremony, a particularly proud moment for Coxswain Graham Walker and his crew but, perhaps, a prouder moment for 84 year-old Frank Taylor.

Frank Taylor served for 45 years in the Wells lifeboat, starting his time in the last pulling boat. His son Ronnie and grandson Mark 'Hooker' Taylor are also lifeboatmen where the last horse launched lifeboat came off station in 1936.

The Duchess performed the naming ceremony wearing an attractive green summer dress, raising the eyebrows of some of the older seafarers present. Perhaps someone should have told the Duchess, wife of the RNLI President, that green is considered an unlucky colour aboard a boat!

The Wells boat is now stationed at the end of a long sea wall stretching to the mouth of the narrow tidal harbour. Outside the entrance lie miles of shelving sandbanks where the 'D' class inflatable is busy in summer months rescuing holiday-makers cut off on the sandbanks by the tide. Wells is an historic station although, founded in 1869, not one of the oldest. During a 22 hour service in the severe winter

The Wells lifeboat Doris M Mann of Ampthill.

of 1914 the crew were all suffering from frostbite on their return to port while the boat was at risk of being capsized by a one inch covering of ice.

In 1950 the Wells lifeboat featured in a special RNLI issue of historical stamps produced to portray the activities of the RNLI through the years. The Wells stamp showed the coxswain rescuing a survivor from a ditched Lancaster bomber. During the Second World War the crew were on stand-by most nights and dawns once the bombers from Britain began raiding Germany, passing over the Norfolk coast on their way out and back on their missions, although the RAF had their own rescue vessels along the eastern coasts of England and Scotland.

Wells is the first station, reading from northwards, on the Norfolk coast, the next being **Sheringham**. A good example of lifeboat co-operation occurred during 1956 when the coaster *SS Wimbledon* was in trouble 13 miles off Cromer. Several ships stood by the

coaster but her master was swept overboard, recovered from the sea but later died, after the Sheringham Coxswain Henry 'Downtide' West had asked the Sheringham boat to bring out more fuel and return ashore with the injured master of the *SS Wimbledon* and a doctor who had attended him. The Sheringham boat also transferred eight of the crew from the stricken ship to one of those standing by before saving ten more and returning ashore. Henry West received a silver medal for gallantry for this rescue.

While in 1990 Wells-next-the-Sea received one of the latest lifeboats, Sheringham station had the oldest Oakley *Lloyds II* which was transferred from the Ilfracombe station. The people of Sheringham fear that this may be a sign that they may lose their station altogether as their ageing boat was not replaced by a faster modern boat but by another old one. They eye the fast new Mersey class boat at Wells, and the fast Tyne class boat along the coast to the east at Cromer, with some concern for the long life-saving tradition of their community.

Henry 'Downtide' West, remembered for the SS *Wimbledon* incident, was succeeded by the equally delightfully named Henry 'Joyful' West as coxswain in 1963. He, in turn was succeeded by his brother Jack, in 1985. Brian Pegg took over a year later to retire in 1989 after thirty-nine years RNLI service. His place as coxswain was taken by Clive Rayment.

The most recent exploit performed by the Sheringham boat was in 1989 when a Swedish roll-on/roll-off car transporter, *Torgothia*, drove straight on to the Haisborough Sands. The ferry was attended by the Sheringham boat. This time the ferry was eventually refloated without loss, but the lifeboats from Cromer and Sheringham stood by for two long days.

At Sheringham, their lifeboat shop at the RNLI station takes over £20,000 per year from the sale of gifts, donations and souvenirs, while they recently discovered the old sailing and pulling lifeboat *J C Madge*, on their station from 1904 to 1936, lying neglected as a converted houseboat in the Norfolk Broads. She has been brought home and is being restored to her former glory for the enjoyment and admiration of passing holiday-makers and local people. It will be sad if Sheringham has to forgo an all-weather lifeboat even for sensible economic reasons, but they would, it seems, accept a fast Atlantic 21 rigid inflatable just to stay alive and keep the RNLI flag proudly flying.

Along the Norfolk coast, four miles to the east of Sheringham, is the famous town of **Cromer** where the name Henry Blogg is legendary. As lifeboat coxswain and holder of the George Cross, the British Empire Medal, the RNLI gold medal and four silver medals, his name is still very much revered. One must wonder what he would have made of the modern Tyne class lifeboat *Ruby and Arthur*

The Sheringham lifeboat J C Madge *on service to* The Ulla *24 February 1916.*

Reed II which, during its first year on the station in 1985 attended an oil tanker on fire 75 miles from the coast in a force 12 storm. He would probably have been impressed having spent his time as coxswain of the early sailing and pulling boats.

Blogg, who joined the Cromer crew in 1894 and became coxswain in 1909, was part of the Davies family who still man the Cromer boat. Today Richard Davies is coxswain, his cousin Billy is second coxswain and his son John is a crewman. Tradition prevails. Life is quieter now at Cromer than in the frantic wartime years. The people of Cromer will be as sad as those of Sheringham if the Sheringham station loses her big boat. They have shared many rescues over the years though the Cromer station was established in 1804, thirty-four years before Sheringham. It is worth noting that the 'D' class inflatable based with the Tyne class boat at Cromer was provided by the Sheringham and Cromer Round Table.

The Cromer boat launches down a slipway from the end of Cromer pier while southwards along the beach lies the lifeboat museum and shop were a turnover of over £50,000 per annum has been achieved. One cannot visit the museum without leaving with the feeling that the spirit of Henry Blogg survives, so synonymous is he with the town and its valiant history of life-saving.

Off Cromer lies the famous, or infamous, Haisborough Sands where for centuries, ever since man began putting out to sea, the unwary have come to grief, such as in the 1941 merchant ship convoy disaster. In spite of this there is no all-weather RNLI lifeboat for another thirty miles down the Norfolk coast until one reaches **Great Yarmouth and Gorleston**. There is a 'D' class inflatable, funded by the Leicester branch of the RNLI, at Happisburgh operating there in the summer months only. There is an all-weather lifeboat at Caister, just up the coast from Great Yarmouth, but this is not an RNLI boat.

The Caister station is something of an anachronism. In 1969 the RNLI decided that the Great Yarmouth and Gorleston station could handle operations without another boat only four miles up the coast. The reaction of the Caister people was typical of a small community losing their lifeboat. They fought back, kept a boat on station and some 10 years after the closure began raising funds to buy a new boat and support it without RNLI funds. The leading light in this effort was 'Skipper' Woodhouse. He made television appearances, won the support of stars performing at the Great Yarmouth summer season music halls as well as local mayors of larger towns and cities. Late in the summer of 1990 they accepted their new vessel, a Lochin class boat. Almost £500,000 had been raised or promised and Caister, was back ready for service with a modern boat.

The Great Yarmouth and Gorleston boat lies at Gorleston, a village south of Great Yarmouth at the entrance of the River Yare. Commercial docks line both shores of the estuary while pleasure craft put to sea from yacht harbours further up river. The Waveney class lifeboat *Barham* was named to commemorate those lost during World War II aboard the warship *HMS Barham*.

Be it pleasure craft, commercial vessels or holiday-makers in trouble off Great Yarmouth beach the all-weather lifeboat has an Atlantic 21 on the station to provide support. It was, perhaps, the provision of an inshore and all-weather lifeboat at the Gorleston base that led to the demise of the station at Caister in the eyes of the RNLI.

Lowestoft lies ten miles south of the Great Yarmouth and Gorleston station. A Tyne class lifeboat, *Spirit of Lowestoft*, lies afloat at the inner south pier near the Royal Norfolk and Suffolk Yacht Club with which the crew have a good relationship. The Lowestoft station is a busy one which the crew attribute to the greater range of the Tyne over the older slower boats of earlier times. Historically the station has two claims. Established in 1801 it operated the first pulling boat rigged with sails, the *Frances Anne*, built locally by Batchelor Barcham under the supervision of Lionel Lukin after the earlier Greathead design had proved unsuitable for beach launching from the shore at Lowestoft. The boat cost £200, was 40 feet long with a 10 foot beam and served for 40 years from her launching in 1807.

Lowestoft also operated the first motor-powered lifeboat. It was this boat, together with a sailing and pulling boat from Gorleston, that was involved in the rescue, or attempted rescue, of the crew of the coaster *Hopelyn*, aground on the Scroby Sands north of Gorleston.

On 19 October 1922, the coaster ran aground on the Sands. Coxswain William Fleming and his Gorleston crew battled for two nights and a day to try and save the twenty-three people aboard but without success. The Lowestoft boat was called up from the south under the command of Coxswain John Swan who, with his motor-driven boat, was able to hold alongside the wreck and take everyone off in spite of ferocious weather conditions. Both coxswains were awarded gold medals for their efforts. It was a fine example of how the two boats have co-operated over the years, both facing shoals near their stations.

More recently, on 19 October 1988, the current coxswain of the Lowestoft boat, John Catchpole, was awarded the bronze medal for rescuing five people from the coaster *Medina D* which ran aground on local sands and rolled over minutes after Coxswain Catchpole and his crew had managed to get alongside and save the people aboard. One of the characters at Lowestoft is Billy Keith, for twenty-four years one of the crew and now caretaker of the lifeboat house and unofficial but avid archivist of the station.

The next station south from Lowestoft is at **Aldeburgh**, best known for its music festivals, Pimms Number 1 and weekend hideaways of the upwardly mobile people, young and old. In 1990 fisherman James Churchyard was coxswain, soon to retire after serving twenty-seven years with the lifeboat where the most memorable rescue was that of seventy-four people from the ship *Magdapur* which hit a mine off the coast at the start of the Second World War.

Aldeburgh has a 1982 Rother class boat, *James Cable*, mainly funded by local people, which is launched by tractor from the beach. This is supported by a 'D' class inflatable which is used to assist holiday-makers in difficulty off the popular beach. The tranquillity of the place in summer belies the storms that can beset the Suffolk coast in winter when the Aldeburgh crew are called to stand by and assist a variety of vessels passing the Aldeburgh Napes, dangerous shoals lying some four miles offshore and littered with wrecks from every age.

Harwich, the next station south, is busy in every sense of the word. Seven ferry routes run from the port or from nearby Parkstone Quay and Felixstowe across the Orwell estuary. Apart from this there is a considerable amount of other commercial traffic in the area as well as a number of large yacht marinas in the reaches of the River Orwell. Tugs, harbour launches and pilot boats add to the traffic working closely with the lifeboat crew if trouble arises. The Waveney class boat *John Fison* is due to be replaced shortly by one of the largest Fast Afloat Boats, an extended version of the very successful Arun class. This reflects the importance which the RNLI and local harbour authorities attach to Harwich. It is no coincidence that the honorary secretary at Harwich is Captain Rod Shaw, the harbour master for the port.

The Harwich lifeboat station has a curious history. There was a purpose-built lifeboat at Harwich, the *Braybrooke*, in 1821 but the service was withdrawn in 1825. The station reopened in 1875 and a second station opened in 1890 which operated the first steam-powered lifeboat, the *Duke of Northumberland*. The first station was then closed just prior to the First World War while the second station continued to operate until 1917 with the lifeboats *City of Glasgow I* and *II*. It was not until 1965 that the RNLI placed an inshore inflatable boat at Harwich for the summer season only, but the volume of traffic at the port was increasing steadily.

The small inflatable did sterling work which led to the decision by the RNLI to put an all-weather boat at Harwich in 1967. There has been an inshore and all-weather boat there ever since. It was on the night of 19 December 1982 that an event occurred off Harwich that perfectly illustrates the special problems that the Harwich

crew has to be prepared to handle. Two car ferries, *European Gateway* and *Speedlink Vanguard*, collided in the approaches to Harwich harbour, the *Vanguard* ramming the *Gateway* amidships. *European Gateway* began to list and soon capsized in shallow water in a way similar to the later disaster at Zeebrugge in 1987.

Every alarm bell in the area rang. Pilot boats near the scene of the disaster were soon on hand, joined by the Harwich lifeboat, harbour tugs and other vessels including another ferry. *Speedlink Vanguard* managed to launch a ship's lifeboat to assist, much to the credit of her crew.

The unhappy task of the lifeboat crew was to recover bodies. Thanks to the proximity of other vessels to the collision all survivors had been taken off the *European Gateway* by the time the lifeboat arrived. After the event, the whole community of Harwich rallied to offer every sort of help to survivors, from free taxi services to off duty nurses returning to work. The coxswains of the two pilot launches received bronze medals from the RNLI. Coxswain Ken Lee, of one pilot boat,

The aftermath of the collision. The ferry European Gateway.

managed to get alongside the ferry as she rolled over in cold rough seas to take thirty-six people aboard his boat, transferring them to the ferry *Dana Futura* where they were treated for shock and cold.

Only six people died in the disaster which is a credit to those who took part in the rescue, but, as one lifeboatman put it, six is six too many. The lifeboat crew, having recovered two of the five bodies accounted for, received a letter of appreciation from the RNLI signed by the Chairman, the Duke of Atholl.

Life is not all gloom and doom at lifeboat stations. During the summer of 1983 an event occurred that deserves mention in any work covering the activities of the RNLI and its stations, if only to point out that amid the dedication and courage of the crews and the effort of those who keep them afloat, there are moments of total farce and amusement that would do credit to the Whitehall Theatre in London.

The local lifeboat committee decided to charter a pleasure launch for an evening cruise up the River Stour. Ninety-nine people embarked the passenger ferry *Brightlingsea*, including seven Master Mariners holding Foreign Going tickets, two local harbour pilots and the Commodore Captain of a ferry company operating from nearby Parkstone Quay. The channel to Mistley, their destination, takes a 60 degree turn just before reaching the quay. There was, in his capacity as a guest, a river pilot on the bridge when the turn was reached but no turn was made. The ferry went aground on mud. An impromptu committee meeting of RNLI worthies and Master Mariners was convened. Passengers were invited to move forward to admire the charm of Mistley, the Master Mariners thereby deeming it unnecessary to shift cases of wine to keep the ferry on an even keel.

Full astern power was applied with

no success. The sunset over the Stour is a memory that stays with many aboard as the mud was churned up by the propellers. A further committee meeting was held where it was decided that the inshore lifeboat might be discreetly called out to take off the women and children aboard in true nautical tradition. Coxswain Peter Burwood was contacted via a little-used radio channel. He agreed to launch the inshore lifeboat. It had been deemed unnecessary to give a Mayday call as this might have alarmed the harbour authorities. Anyway, many of them were aboard the ferry.

The inshore lifeboat arrived close to the stranded ferry with blue light flashing and with a flourish of spray. The three-man crew were greeted with applause and the raising of wine glasses.

Further discussions had been held to decide how to transfer an elderly lady, who had recently had a hip replacement operation, to the lifeboat. Meanwhile the lifeboat crew had acquired a wooden dinghy from nearby to use as a platform across the mud from the ferry to the lifeboat. That in position the elderly lady with the hip replacement remarked, as she shinned down the ladder, that it had been a wonderful experience. One lady insisted on taking her packed supper with her while the Master Mariners asked for a docking bottle each. The first request was granted, the last refused while a card school in full swing in the lower cabin were told that they could not stay overnight.

During the stranding one of the guests had asked that a telephone call be made ashore asking for coaches to be sent to Mistley to transfer the survivors back to Harwich. The coaches duly appeared. It transpired that the guest owned the coach company so all returned to the starting point in comfort, one lady still clutching her doggy bag, the lady with the replacement hip feeling no pain and several people convinced that the whole event had been planned that way.

A brief inquiry was later held ashore where the absence of the two local pilots was noted. The ferry successfully floated off the mud bank on the next flood tide and made its way surreptitiously back to its berth under cover of darkness without mishap or the presence of seven Master Mariners, one Captain Commodore or two pilots aboard.

Enough of the more hilarious aspects of RNLI activity, but it is good to know that amid the hard work and effort by supporters there are such moments. The incident was officially logged in the service record of the inshore lifeboat as follows:

5 July 1983. Ferry Brightlingsea. Landed 99.

While the Harwich all-weather lifeboat handles the longer range calls, the Atlantic class lifeboat receives more calls for inshore operations, many of these to assist the crews of yachts, dinghies and board sailors. In 1988 one elderly board sailor was

rescued with his board a total of nine times. On one occasion it was not possible to take his board ashore and it was lost. He promptly purchased a new one and set out again only to be rescued once more. He has been given some sound advice by Captain Rod Shaw, the honorary secretary at Harwich.

Some rescues from Harwich have had their humorous side. During the winter of 1979 the pirate radio ship Radio Caroline aboard the converted coaster *Mi Amigo*, anchored in the Thames Estuary, began to take on water in a storm while the ship's pumps had failed. The Harwich lifeboat took off three disc jockeys, two crewmen and a canary called Wilson.

More recently, in 1984, the Harwich offshore lifeboat made one of its longest services when the British coaster *Gladonia* broke down 30 miles off the Dutch coast. After a voyage of about 60 miles the lifeboat crew reached the scene and stood by in a north-westerly gale until a Dutch tug was able to take the coaster in tow. The crew then escorted the tug and coaster towards Great Yarmouth,

The end of the RNLI charity fund-raising night out.

returning to Harwich after almost 17 hours at sea.

Between 1965, when the station was reopened, and the summer of 1990 the Harwich station answered 517 calls with the inshore lifeboat and 322 with the all-weather boat, saving a total of 345 lives surely confirming that the RNLI decision to reopen the station was the right one.

The final all-weather lifeboat station on the Lincolnshire, Norfolk, Suffolk and Essex east coast chain lies at **Walton-on-the-Naze** while three Atlantic inshore boats are based at Clacton, West Mersea and Southend-on-Sea. A further boat, a 'D' class inflatable is based at Burnham-on-Crouch, and two more at Southend. All the inshore boats are on all-the-year-round service.

The Walton and Frinton lifeboat, as it is known, is the only lifeboat that lies at anchors in the open sea in the shadow of Walton pier, protected to some extent from easterly winds but not from westerlies. The busiest time for the Walton crew comes at weekends when the amateur sailors of the east coast estuaries and marinas set out along the shoal-strewn shores of Essex and the Thames Estuary.

The Walton station is also the link with lifeboat operations across the Thames Estuary at Sheerness and Margate, on the north coast of Kent, while there is a Thames Coastguard station at Walton. As with other stations with older lifeboats Walton hopes that their 1970 built Solent class boat, *City of Birmingham*, is to be replaced by something faster and more modern. As recently as 1990 the lifeboat was unable to attend a German yacht stranded on sands offshore simply because they had not got the speed to reach the yacht within reasonable time and the rescue work was handled by a helicopter from RAF Manston in Kent.

In 1988 there was another ferry 'scare' on the east coast when fire broke out in the engineroom of the *Nordic Ferry* when the ship was five miles off Harwich. The weather was bad, a south-westerly gale forecast. Lifeboats were called out from Harwich, Aldeburgh and Walton together with three tugs and several other vessels while three helicopters were put on readiness. Fortunately firemen, landed from a fire tug, were able to put out the fire without it becoming necessary to evacuate either passengers or crew from the ship. Moving the 348 people aboard the ship might well have presented a major problem to those involved in the rescue had it proved essential, but the whole operation showed how the lifeboats and other rescue services are now fully co-ordinated. This sort of modern-day call perhaps emphasizes the need for a faster lifeboat than the Solent class, maximum speed less than 10 knots, on the north shore of the Thames Estuary.

The long stretch of coastline from Skegness in the north to the Thames Estuary in the south is steeped with lifeboat history involving some of the oldest purpose-built lifeboats and the most heroic of lifeboat crews. Now, as is the case throughout RNLI operations, new faster boats are replacing the older types, in some cases the coverage of the coast has been necessarily trimmed due to the introduction of these new craft while ashore the lifeboat houses and crew rooms are being rebuilt or modernized. All this is part of the overall long-term plan to ensure that the lifeboat service is as effective as it can be before the start of the twenty-first century.

The Kent Stations

Sheerness, on the north coast of Kent at the entrance to the River Medway, is one of the latest additions to the RNLI stations around the coasts of Great Britain and Ireland. In 1969 a lifeboat was sent to Sheerness harbour for evaluation trials to be made. In 1971 a lifeboat station was opened at the port with both an all-weather and inshore inflatable lifeboat. Initially the temporary lifeboat *Ernest William and Elizabeth Ellen Hyde*, a boat based on a Keith Nelson hull, served for the trials until replaced with another boat, *Gertrude*, a legacy of Lady Stuthers. Between the start of trials in 1970 until 1974 the boats were called out 154 times saving 81 lives.

In 1974 Sheerness received a Waveney class lifeboat, the *Helen Turnbull* with which, in August 1975, Coxswain Mechanic Charles Bowry won the station's first medal, a bronze award, for the rescue of a yacht's crew off the West Barrow Bank in a south-westerly gale. In the winter of 1978 he was awarded a second bronze medal for the rescue of two people from a cabin cruiser during an easterly gale riven with driving snow. Following the Harwich lifeboat's rescue involving the Radio Caroline ship *Mi Amigo* in 1979, Coxswain Mechanic Charles Bowry and his crew were called to the sinking ship in March 1980. The crew made thirteen runs to the ship's side in order to take the survivors off in gale force easterly winds.

The present coxswain, Robin Castle then took over from Charles Bowry and during the famous hurricane of October 1987 was awarded a silver medal for the rescue of two people from a small boat on the Yantlet Flats while the wind was exceeding 90 knots from the south-west. On this occasion the thanks of the RNLI inscribed on vellum was also awarded to Second Coxswain Dennis Bailey and crewman Richard Rogers. The lifeboat became stranded on the flats during the rescue. The two crewmen clambered into the sea to lay an anchor in order to hold the lifeboat head to wind until she could be floated off the mud.

The longest call made on Sheerness came in January 1986 when the crew put out to the new Radio Caroline ship, the converted trawler *Ross Revenge*. The radio ship had lost engine power and was drifting some 44 miles out from Sheerness. The Margate lifeboat was also called out at 3 am on a cold stormy morning to stand by the vessel until the crew of the *Ross Revenge* managed to restore power and replace the anchor cable which had broken during the storm. No-one was taken from the radio ship but the lifeboat was at sea for 16 hours.

Since a lifeboat station was opened for evaluation in 1969, the all-weather and inshore boats have been launched over 1,200 times saving over 550 lives. Many of those rescued were from yachts and pleasure craft, some out in the Thames Estuary, others in the marshes that surround the Isles of Sheppey and which lie in the Medway and River Stour estuaries. The crew also appreciate that Sheerness is a busy commercial port and ferry terminal.

While the Sheerness crew are hoping to be sent a new Fast Afloat offshore lifeboat within the next few years, **Margate**, 30 miles east of Sheerness, awaits the earlier arrival of a new tractor launching Mersey class boat to replace their Rother class boat, *Silver Jubilee (Civil Service No 38)*. The Margate lifeboat was launched from a slipway near the pier until 1978 when the pier was swept away in a storm, the lifeboat making its last launch from the wrecked lifeboat house in order to save itself!

The Margate lifeboat *Lord Southborough* was one of three RNLI lifeboats manned by RNLI crews that sailed for Dunkirk. Nineteen boats went altogether but sixteen were manned by Royal Navy crews. The Margate boat, commanded by Coxswain Edward Parker, transferred over 600 men from the beaches to larger vessels offshore before returning to the Kent coast loaded with soldiers.

Margate lifeboat alongside Pamir *January 1952. The German sail training ship was lost with all hands in 1958.*

Coxswain Parker was awarded the Distinguished Service Medal for gallantry and determination. The other coxswain awarded the same medal was Harold Knight from the **Ramsgate** station around the North Foreland from Margate.

Margate and Ramsgate are close stations both geographically and socially. There have been many occasions when they have co-operated at sea but during one rescue, in 1952, when Dennis Price was coxswain of the lifeboat *North Foreland*, he took the boat over 30 miles across the Thames Estuary almost to the Essex coast. The Essex lifeboats were already at sea effecting rescues in a north-westerly November gale when red flares were seen from the Mid-Barrow lightship.

Coxswain Price and his men launched at 3 am straight into the storm and headed north, reaching the casualty, the auxiliary barge *Vera* which had sunk on the sands. Two men were clinging to the rigging half way up the mast amid icy squalls. Realizing that they must be almost at the end of their tether and probably unable to climb into the lifeboat he drove the

boat over the deck of the barge near the mast so that men could slide down the rigging and onto the lifeboat. Both were recovered safely and taken below to be wrapped in blankets and given rum. They had been on the rigging for nearly five hours.

It was decided aboard the lifeboat that their condition warranted making for nearby Brightlingsea on the Essex coast where they were landed. The lifeboat then returned to Margate where it arrived after almost 12 hours at sea. Coxswain Price was awarded the silver medal for gallantry for this rescue.

In 1966 a fast inflatable was placed at Margate, a reflection of the increasing numbers of pleasure boats and other small craft in the area and the associated increase in the numbers of them getting into trouble near the shore.

The inshore boat was soon busy taking the strain off the all-weather boat, replaced in 1977 by the Rother class boat *Silver Jubilee*. The nearby RAF station at Manston now operates the sophisticated Sea King helicopters which has also eased the task of the local lifeboats although co-operation between the RNLI and the RAF is close.

Around North Foreland lies the port of Ramsgate, converted over the years from quiet fishing harbour to busy ferry port and yachting centre. It also faces the busy Straits of Dover to the south and the Downs, between the cliffs of North and South Foreland. The Goodwin Sands are just a few miles offshore from Ramsgate. The Ramsgate station has recently had its 1976 Waveney class boat replaced by a new Tyne class, the *Kenneth Thelwall II* paid for by the same legacy as that which funded the new Arun at Spurn Head and the extension of the RNLI headquarters at Poole.

Lifeboat operations at Ramsgate are very varied and range from the rescue of yacht crews offshore to swimmers at nearby beaches. With the withdrawal of the all-weather lifeboat down the coast at Walmer at the end of the 1980s, more operational work has fallen on both the inshore and all-weather boats based at Ramsgate, although there is still a fast Atlantic 21 inshore rigid inflatable at Walmer

for local work.

Because operations from Ramsgate were being carried out further and further offshore, the station requested the new Tyne class boat. There is a feeling in the town that an even faster larger boat may be needed soon, although the arrival of the Tyne, with a best speed of 17.6 knots may put Ramsgate down the list of stations that can expect the first of the new larger Fast Afloat Boats (FABs). Whether or not Ramsgate receives a FAB is still in the balance and, unlike other stations, undefined by the RNLI.

Down the Kent coast at **Dover** lies a lifeboat station that has had a history of opening and closing. Today it is very much open, operating a Thames class lifeboat, *Rotary Service*, which was delivered there in 1979 and named by the Queen Mother during the same year. The station first opened in 1837 and joined the RNLI fold in 1855. By any standards, and by virtue of its position in the busiest shipping area in the world, Dover is a busy station and has been since its conception.

One notable rescue attempt occurred

The Dover lifeboat, Thames class Rotary Service, *towing a German yacht to the safety of Dover Harbour.*

in 1910 when the sailing cargo ship *Preussen*, from Hamburg, collided with a mail steamer off Newhaven and was then driven up the Channel before a severe gale. The ship ran ashore below cliffs near Dover and the lifeboat *Mary Hamer Hoyle* was launched. The lifeboat approached the stranded vessel where many crew members could be seen huddled on deck. Tugs were also sent to the ship in the hope that they might be able to tow her back out to sea. The crew therefore refused to board the lifeboat which was close enough for the tug crews to hail them. The seas were too rough for the tug crews to pass lines to the ship which was starting to break up as 19 lines were fired to the deck from the cliffs by coastguards. The German crew were rescued by breeches buoy while the lifeboat returned to Dover.

Due to the demands of the armed services during the First World War the station was closed in 1914, Royal Navy vessels taking over the work of the lifeboat.

The station reopened in 1919, the steam lifeboat *James Stevens Number 3* being placed at Dover but three years later, in 1922, it was closed once more until 1930 when the number of aircraft using the short sea crossing between Dover and France increased. A fast large lifeboat, *Sir William Hillary*, was sent to Dover to meet the new requirement, but the rescue of an aircraft did not occur until 1938 when a small aeroplane ditched off Dover and was taken in tow by a cargo ship and the crew of two saved.

In 1940 the lifeboat was taken over by the Royal Navy and in 1941, with many Royal Navy and Royal Air Force rescue craft in the Straits of Dover, the RNLI station was closed once more. This was not before the lifeboat had saved the crew of a Royal Navy auxiliary vessel which had suffered engine failure in the middle of a minefield. All the crew of the naval vessel, as well as ship's papers and secret anti-submarine detection

equipment, were transferred to the lifeboat during a full south-westerly gale and in the midst of the minefield before the naval vessel, a converted Brixham trawler, was scuttled.

Dover reopened again in 1947 when the Watson class lifeboat, *J B Proudfoot*, was based there for two years, being replaced in 1949 by the Barnett class boat *Southern Africa*, a gift from the South African equivalent of the RNLI. It was not until 1952 that the lifeboat *Southern Africa* was involved in a major rescue of a merchant ship crew when the American ship *Western Farmer* collided with a Norwegian oil tanker off Dover in severe weather.

The Ramsgate lifeboat, *Prudential*, put out and made for the ship while the Dover lifeboat also put to sea but called at Walmer to collect a doctor requested by the American ship's master. The lifeboats arrived as the ship began to break into two pieces and the crew abandoned the ship for their lifeboats. The Ramsgate boat rescued some crew from one ship's lifeboat and then took more from the bow section while the Dover lifeboat repeated the performance with another ship's boat. The Ramsgate boat then took remaining crew from the broken and sinking stern section which earned the lifeboat's coxswain, Douglas Kirkaldie, a bronze medal while both lifeboat crews received a commemorative plaque from the American Seafarer's International Union.

The epic attempt to rescue the crew of the South Goodwin lightship during a winter storm in 1954 has already been mentioned but during a summer storm in 1956 RNLI crew received over fifty calls in a weekend, saving more than a hundred lives. Most calls were to the assistance and rescue of crews aboard yachts and motor cruisers caught out by the storm. The Dover lifeboat was called out three times rescuing a dozen people from several small craft and earning Coxswain John

Walker a bronze medal.

Lightships off Dover called for the help of RNLI crews on several occasions during the 1950s and 1960s. During a storm in 1961 the East Goodwin lightship broke adrift from her anchors. Her crew managed to drop an emergency anchor while the relief lifeboat *Cunard*, on station at Dover while *Southern Africa* was being refitted, took turns with lifeboats from Walmer and Ramsgate to stand by the vessel until the weather moderated.

In December 1966 it was the turn of the Varne lightship to break adrift. The Trinity House vessel *Siren* was at anchor not far from the scene sheltering from the storm that was raging. Her master tried to close with the lightship but was unable to do so. The Dover lifeboat was called out in the early morning under the command of Coxswain Alf Cadman who had taken the task over from John Walker. The Trinity House master, fearing that the lightship would run onto the bank it was meant to be guarding, asked that the lifeboat took the crew off. Coxswain Cadman made six runs alongside the lightship taking one man off on each of the first five passes and two, including the master of the lightship, on the final one.

The following year Dover received a new Waveney class lifeboat, *Faithful Forester*, donated by the Ancient Order of Foresters and named by the President of the RNLI, Princess Marina of Kent. Coxswain Mechanic Arthur Liddon took over from Alf Cadman and the new boat was at sea saving the crew of a yacht within a few days of going on service.

In 1971 an incident occurred off Dover which the RNLI and others had often feared. The oil tanker *Texaco Caribbean* collided with a smaller merchant vessel, the tanker being sliced in two. The bow section sank almost immediately while the Dover and Dungeness lifeboats were called out to search for survivors. Those on the floating stern section were rescued

by another merchant ship and later transferred to the Dover lifeboat to be taken ashore. A total of 21 people were saved and the search for others missing was called off after ten hours.

The work of the *Faithful Forester* continued through the 1960s varying from the rescue of yachtsmen to assisting fishermen, saving canoeists and taking doctors to larger vessels. As mentioned, in 1979 the lifeboat was replaced by a 50 foot Thames class boat, *Rotary Service*. The most memorable recent rescue service by this lifeboat station according to today's crew, was of those aboard the cross-channel hovercraft *Princess Margaret* which, in March 1985, was swept against the southern breakwater of Dover harbour in strong south-westerly winds. The relief lifeboat, the Arun *A J R and L G Uridge* was at Dover at the time.

There were passengers in the water who were saved by the lifeboat crew and the crew of a harbour tug, *Dextrous*, and harbour launches. These were taken ashore and the disembarkation of the remaining passengers aboard began. The tug took off 185 people and the lifeboat 115, a record number to be carried by a lifeboat on service. A search was made for two passengers not accounted for, in which the Dover inshore boat, the Walmer boat and the Atlantic 21 inflatable from Ramsgate assisted, sadly without success.

The hurricane of October 1987 kept many lifeboat stations in southern England busy and Dover was no exception. The Bahamian registered bulk carrier *Sumnia* was drifting near the harbour's Admiralty pier with both anchors down. A harbour tug was unable to put a line aboard because of the terrible state of the seas. The lifeboat was called out but collected a rope around the starboard propeller and shaft so returned to its berth to attempt to clear the rope, but two local divers failed after many gallant attempts.

The coxswain, Tony Hawkins, was on leave at the time, his place being taken by Second Coxswain Mechanic Roy Couzens. He decided to take the boat to sea in spite of the rope still around the propeller and closed with the *Sumnia*. As they neared the ship, which was beginning to break up on the pier, they saw two men on deck who were suddenly swept overboard as a wave broke across the vessel. Both men were in the sea close to the wreck. Second Coxswain Couzens managed to manoeuvre the lifeboat close to each man. They were snatched from the sea by two of the lifeboat crew. More survivors were reported to be outside the harbour entrance so the lifeboat coxswain decided to head out to sea. Twice the lifeboat was almost overwhelmed by immense seas, on the first occasion dropping 60 feet from the top of a wave.

The crew then sighted a life jacket, hauled it aboard and found a man beneath it. They brought him aboard and began resuscitation restarting the casualty's pulse and breathing. With the two survivors and the recently rescued man aboard they returned to harbour, Acting Coxswain Couzens complaining of pains in his chest. Once the survivors had been landed the lifeboat put back out to sea to search for two men still missing. Couzens began to feel his legs becoming weak and his pain worsening. He handed the helm to Acting Second Coxswain Michael Abbott before becoming unconscious. The crew returned ashore and landed the stricken coxswain who was hurried to hospital where his trouble was diagnosed as a heart attack. Happily he recovered, to be awarded the RNLI silver medal while the rest of the crew received bronze medals.

As can be clearly seen, Dover, as with the other nearby lifeboat stations that face out into the eastern English Channel and the Thames Estuary, is a

The 1974 Dover lifeboat, Waveney class Faithful Forester, exercising with a Bristow WS-55 Whirlwind from HM Coastguard's Manston SAR helicopter unit off the cliffs of St Margaret's Bay.

busy station handling a wide variety of problems.

Dungeness, south-west of Dover completes the Kentish chain. Dungeness is a unique station on the Kent coast. The lifeboat house stands out on the long promontory that forms the single headland bearing the name. The other Kent stations are based in towns, but not Dungeness. The headland is bleak, beset with small wooden chalet-like houses owned by local fishing families whose names and homes go back far beyond the days of the first lifeboat based there in 1826. Local people suspect that this date, established by RNLI research, is wrong. They are sure that there was some sort of rescue craft there for years before the Napoleonic war just as there have been fishermen working from the beach for centuries.

The Dungeness lifeboat is beach-launched from a trailer moved by

Dungeness lifeboat on service.

tractor over the shingle. During 1856 the station was used for trials with the first trailer fitted with what would today be described as caterpillar tracks. In those days it was described as Boydell's patent self-laying or endless railway. In view of this development it is surprising that the military, who were very much in the Dungeness area then as now, did not see the value of the system and produce a tank much sooner than during the latter part of World War I.

The Dungeness crew have been the proud operators of a Rother class boat, apt, perhaps, as the Rother Levels are not far away. Their previous boat was the Watson class 42 foot boat *Mabel E Holland* which adventurer David Scott-Cowper bought from the RNLI and took round the world in both directions as well as traversing the notorious North-west Passage. The station keeps in touch with Scott-Cowper who has brought the old boat back to Dungeness on several occasions and sends photographs of his exploits.

Until 1979 Dungeness shared another rare feature with only one other station. Before the advent of the launching tractor that takes the trailer and boat to the sea the lifeboat was launched by a team of local ladies. This system stopped in 1979 when the tractor arrived but the reason for this rare state of affairs was that there were simply not enough able-bodied menfolk in the small community to man the boat and launch it. These lady launchers, as they were known, were led in the final years by Doris Tart, wife of Coxswain Ben Tart who was forty years with the Dungeness boat, ten as coxswain and eighteen as second coxswain before retiring. During operations with the old *Mabel E Holland* he would take photographs with a Box Brownie camera and send them to the London newspapers from which he proudly tells visitors he was paid £3 per picture.

The Rother lifeboat *Alice Upjohn*, beginning to show her years, will be replaced by a Mersey class boat. The Mersey is not new to the station which carried out trials with a Mersey boat prior to its delivery in 1989 to the station down the coast at Hastings.

The lady launchers of Dungeness hauling the lifeboat Mabel E Holland *up the steep shingle beach before a tractor was placed on the station. The photograph was thought to have been taken during the 1960s. There were too few men at Dungeness to both man the boat and launch it so the wives formed part of the launching crew for which they received awards. Amelia Tart was a launcher for 50 years until the age of 72.*

A visit to the station at Dungeness, modernized with its new Mersey class lifeboat in the 1990s, is worth the trek down the long headland. The history of gallantry, shared among a few fishing families, certainly goes back as far as the RNLI itself. Visitors from the United States of America, and there are many who travel there by the Romney, Hythe and Dymchurch Railway, which has its southern station at Dungeness, may be fascinated by the old English names that survive at one of the oldest lifeboat stations. Today the Richardsons, the Tart family, the Oillers and Paines still compose the make up of the crew as they have since the War of Independence. Dungeness is a gallant, self-contained station, making the remainder of the south-east of England seem many a mile away, but right in the thick of the rescue business of the busy waters of the English Channel. Proud people, living on and by the sea.

Sussex by the sea

The coast of Sussex is guarded by eight RNLI stations, five carrying all-weather boats, three fast inflatables and four of the all-weather boat stations also operating fast inshore inflatables. Sussex is a hub of the private leisure seafarers in a wide variety of small vessels and this is reflected by the work of the Sussex lifeboatmen. At the eastern end of the Sussex chain, lying between the Kent station at Dungeness and the station at Hastings is the Rye inflatable. Rye is sadly remembered for the 1928 disaster when the entire crew of their boat was lost. Seventeen men drowned and the event is still remembered to this day every November by a special church service. Such a loss from a community of fishermen and boatbuilders was, and is, catastrophic. Today the small inflatable based at sad Rye keeps the tradition of the RNLI alive in the town while along the coast at **Hastings** a new beach-launched Mersey class boat and a 'D' class inflatable are, in the words of the crew, busy. They expect around thirty launchings a year from everything from passing merchant ships with sick crew needing to be taken ashore to board sailors and amateur yachtsmen who, literally, get out of their depth.

Positioned on the seafront among fishing boats owned and manned by many of the lifeboatmen, the Hastings station is justifiably proud of their new boat, the *Sealink Endeavour* but along the coast westwards at **Eastbourne** life was not quite so assured for the lifeboat crew at the beginning of the decade. Since 1978 the Eastbourne crew had operated a slow Rother class boat which was still there in 1990. Plans were then announced to build the largest sailing centre on the south coast, bigger even than the Brighton Marina, a short distance along the coast from the present Eastbourne lifeboat station. This would enable the station to carry a new Fast Afloat Boat, rather than the beach launched type. Hopes of a new beach-based boat faded to be replaced by hopes for a new, larger fast boat perhaps due in 1993 or 1994. All will depend upon the completion of the new harbour.

Eastbourne is a busy station often having to attend casualties beneath the cliffs at nearby Beachy Head where, for one reason or another, people decide to leap from the top. In 1990, when a mother drove herself and two young children over the cliff in her car the inshore boat was itself in trouble, being overturned when trying to recover the bodies from the car. The station is also a fund-raising flagship for the RNLI. The old lifeboat house, on the attractive promenade near the old Martello Tower, is now a museum and shop selling almost £100,000 per year of gifts, souvenirs and other items. Meanwhile the Rother class boat, *Duke of Kent*,

named by His Royal Highness in 1978, attracts visitors to its base along the beach in the area used by local fishermen. The many retired people living in Eastbourne also keep busy organizing fund-raising events for their own boat as well as the RNLI as a whole.

The next station westwards from Eastbourne along the coast of Sussex is at **Newhaven**. Newhaven, a busy commercial port and ferry terminal, is a sharp contrast to the quiet elegance and peace of Eastbourne. Rescue operations at sea have been performed by Newhaven crews ever since the earliest seafarers put to sea in the Channel. The station as such was established in 1803 when a boat designed by Henry Greathead was placed at Newhaven but the crew seemed unhappy with it as, as far as is known, it was never used on service.

Today Newhaven is the proud possessor of the 1985 built 52 foot Arun, the *Keith Anderson*, a gift in its entirety, at a cost of about £450,000, from Esmé Anderson. Her husband Keith had died so she decided to sell her jewellery and buy the RNLI a lifeboat as a memorial to him. Though from the London area, the Andersons had connections with Newhaven so it was appropriate that the new boat should go there where Esmé Anderson named it on a fine summer's day. There is also a relief fleet Tyne class boat at Newhaven kept in the old boathouse.

Newhaven is a busy station attending everything from small yachts to large merchant ships. Sick crew have been landed from passing shipping on a number of occasions. The lifeboats from Newhaven and Eastbourne co-operate regularly, the two stations being separated by 14 miles of coastline and the massive cliffs of Beachy Head.

Past the crumbling white cliffs of Peacehaven to the east of the town lies the massive Brighton Marina yacht harbour and leisure complex, but in spite of the size of the harbour, originally designed to provide berths for 1,400 boats but now a little smaller, there is no all-weather boat at Brighton. However, there is an Atlantic 21 rigid inflatable to meet the demands of a leisure harbour and the swimmers, board sailors and others who set out from the nearby beaches and the yachtsmen and women sailing to and from the marina.

The next all-weather boat, a brand new Tyne class lifeboat *Hermione Lady Colwyn*, named in memory of the past chairman and president of the station, was placed on station at **Shoreham** in the autumn of 1990 and officially named during the spring of 1991. It replaced an ageing Watson class boat, the *Joseph Soar*. The slipway launched Tyne lies in its shed at the junction of the two long arms of Shoreham harbour that stretch east and west from the entrance, the east arm having a tidal basin and used as a commercial port where gravel and scrap iron is handled. The western arm of the harbour is more dedicated to pleasure craft and this situation, with the lifeboat stationed between the two activities, sums up the scope of its work and that of the 'D' class inflatable also on station at Shoreham.

During the two hurricane force storms of October 1987 and January 1990 the Shoreham boat was at sea. During the first storm the crew successfully stood by a trawler which had lost engine power but during the second hurricane, they were called out in winds of 100 knots to what transpired to be a hoax call.

One must wonder about the mentality of anyone who will make a hoax call to the lifeboatmen during a storm such as that or, indeed, at any time. What might the hoaxer have felt if the lifeboat had foundered while on duty, perhaps with loss of life? Hoaxers must live in the same world as those who follow the increasingly common habit of stealing RNLI and other charity collecting boxes from

public houses. The clarity of detail about the vessel in trouble during the second storm was enough to convince the coastguards who took the call that it was genuine and later convince them that it was not.

The new lifeboat at Shoreham and the appointment of John Landale as coxswain at about the same time has launched the station into the 1990s well prepared for the years ahead. Westward from Shoreham the small port of Littlehampton is the base of one of three Atlantic 21 fast inflatables paid for by the efforts of watchers of the children's television programme 'Blue Peter'. This boat is a link in the Sussex chain between Shoreham and the next all-weather boat based out on the headland of Selsey Bill, the last lifeboat on the Sussex coast.

Selsey has an impressive boathouse for the Tyne class lifeboat *City of London* which launches from a slipway. This boat, on the station since 1982, was the first of this class to be built and was paid for by money raised in the City of London with which the station crew maintain close links, receiving frequent visits from people who helped fund the boat.

The present boathouse and slipway was built in 1961, the third boathouse to be built there partly due to the fact that erosion and the changing shape of the coastline is a serious problem on the promontory. The waters off Selsey, which are beset with rock ledges either side of the Looe Channel and the Owers Sands, marked by a light buoy, further offshore, are also a problem.

Selsey is a busy station, particularly in the summer months when the amateur sailors are about. While the Selsey boats have, over the years, attended larger vessels, the majority of their work today is leisure craft and fishing vessels, the former being in the majority. Selsey co-operates regularly with the Atlantic 21 rigid inflatable based to the west at the entrance to

Chichester Harbour at Sandy Point, Hayling Island. The entrance to Chichester Harbour is notorious for its sand bar where extremely awkward seas can build up when strong winds blow from seawards.

From Eastbourne in the east to Selsey in the west there are, apart from Newhaven, virtually no safe havens in severe onshore winds unless crews are prepared to chance the narrow entrances of the Brighton Marina, Shoreham or Littlehampton. This point was proved when Edward Heath's yacht *Morning Cloud* was wrecked in just such weather while sailing from the east coast back to the Solent, being driven aground to break up on shoals between Littlehampton and Selsey. No flares were seen on that occasion, no radio call made from the yacht and the survivors came ashore after hours at sea in a life raft before the alarm was raised. Such are typical dangers off the Sussex coast, and therefore the vital need of the lifeboats.

Isle of Wight and Hardy Country

The two inflatable lifeboats based at Hayling Island and at Portsmouth are ideal for the demands of large areas of sheltered shoaling waters, both in Chichester and Langstone harbours, as well as the vast tidal expanse of Portsmouth. Obviously with the activities of the Royal Navy in Portsmouth, where the harbour is controlled by the Queen's Harbour Master, an officer in the Royal Navy, there are plenty of small craft afloat day and night that could effect a rescue if required. These vessels range from harbour tugs to launches running from one side of the harbour to the other, but Portsmouth has now become the second busiest ferry terminal on the English side of the Channel after Dover.

Facing the eastern end of Spithead,

the waters outside Portsmouth, is the **Bembridge** lifeboat station, the lifeboat house perched above its slipway at the end of a long narrow pier and housing a modern Tyne class boat, the *Max Aitken III*, paid for by the Beaverbrook Foundation. It is right that a lifeboat from this fund should be based on the Isle of Wight as Sir Max Aitken enjoyed some of his happiest moments racing his various yachts in the Solent and around the island waters as well as entertaining his many sailing friends at his waterfront home at Cowes.

Bembridge itself is a curious collection of ageing houseboats that never move in the inner tidal harbour, a busy sailing centre, old fishermen's cottages, Victorian houses and a leisurely pace of life.

The lifeboat is manned primarily by local fishermen headed by Coxswain Archie Henley, a man with a fine reputation and many friends in the harbours of the south-east. The station is busy. Ferry traffic has had the boat called out on occasions when passengers have been reported overboard and when an engineroom fire aboard a French ferry led to the strong possibility of all the passengers having to be evacuated south of the Isle of Wight. No such evacuation eventually proved necessary but the Bembridge lifeboat stood by the ferry for many hours ready to assist with transferring the passengers to other larger ships also waiting to help.

On another occasion, in January 1968, the submarine *HMS Alliance*, heading back to Gosport, failed to pass outside the Bembridge Ledge buoy, a mark at the end of a ridge of rock stretching out from Bembridge eastwards. The submarine was well aground on the ledge. The lifeboat put out to stand by, lying close to the stranded submarine awaiting the tide to rise. It is told on the Isle of Wight that the coxswain, then Peter Smith, asked the submarine commanding officer, who was standing unhappily

The Bembridge, Isle of Wight lifeboat, Tyne class Sir Max Aitken III undergoing pre-acceptance capsize, self-righting, trials at Cowes.

The submarine HMS Alliance aground on the Bembridge Ledge with the Bembridge lifeboat standing by. The submarine was later successfully refloated using an Admiralty salvage vessel, a tug and the submarine's own engines.

on the bridge at the top of the conning tower, what he intended to do next. The submariner replied that he planned to buy a farm. Whether or not the tale is true (the original is attributed to a young destroyer captain who rammed the Admiral's flagship in the Mediterranean during World War II) it seems apt. The submarine eventually floated free of the rocks and was escorted to Portsmouth Harbour by an Admiralty tug and salvage vessel.

Yachts regularly hit the infamous ledge, some, remarkably, in broad daylight and in good visibility. They often sink. Among more recent casualties were Graham Walker's Admiral's Cup yacht *Indulgence*, which hit the wreck that lies inside the Bembridge Ledge buoy and is therefore guarded by the buoy. The wreck is of an old ship, the *Empress Queen*, which also hit the ledge. Another Admiral's Cup owner, Robin Aisher, managed to hit the ledge in *Yeoman XXV* while the ebullient yachting journalist Bob Fisher, top international sailor and technical advisor to the television series 'Howard's Way', managed it aboard the star yacht of the early part of the series, *Barracuda of Tarrant*, a very successful competitive yacht sailed by a top class crew. The yacht sank and was later salvaged by local fishermen including the lifeboat crew. No lives were lost on any of these occasions, all attended by the Bembridge lifeboat.

Oil tanker fires, notably *Pacific Glory* and other ferry fires, one aboard the Sealink ferry *Earl Granville*, have all been attended by the Bembridge crew. Second Coxswain Martin Woodward, also station historian, is proud of the fact that he has acquired and is restoring an 1886 rowing lifeboat while the Watson class boat *Jesse Lumb*, on station at Bembridge between 1939 and 1970, has been taken to the museum at RAF Duxford and restored. The lifeboat rescued many airmen of all nationalities during World War II. Coxswain Woodward is busy writing a full history of the Bembridge station, established as a RNLI station in 1867, and is unearthing new information all the time. Like every RNLI station there is a book of history lurking in the lifeboat house and surrounding area.

There are no lifeboat stations on the south coast of the Isle of Wight. It is under 30 miles from Bembridge to the next station westwards at the small port of **Yarmouth**. Bembridge and Yarmouth, both with boats capable of 18 knots, can reach the halfway point between them in under an hour while the waters south of St Catherine's Point, the island's southern-most headland, are too treacherous in bad weather for an inflatable to operate safely. Strong tidal currents and overfalls prevail.

Yarmouth's coxswain, Dave Kennett, is typical of the type of person one expects of a coxswain. After twenty-five years service with the RNLI he retires in 1994, handing over the helm of the Arun class lifeboat *Joy and John Wade* to his second coxswain, David Lemonius. Dave Kennett took over at Yarmouth when the lifeboat *Earl and Countess Howe*, an Oakley class boat, was on the station, changing to the faster Arun in 1977.

In 1975, after several years as coxswain, Dave Kennett and his crew received a call to a yacht, the *Choyka of Ardgour*, in trouble between the Channel Islands and the Needles on passage from Cherbourg to Hamble, near Southampton. The crew were six Metropolitan policemen later described by Coxswain Dave Kennett as being young and fit. The yacht had sailed from the French port in a south-easterly wind, ideal for the passage northwards across the Channel for the 60 nautical miles from Cherbourg to either the Needles Channel to the west of the Isle of Wight or the slightly further distance to pass the island to the east.

The yacht was making good progress north from Cherbourg on the following breeze when the wind backed to the north and increased to gale force. A run home with fair winds became a battle into a storm, the crew hard pressed even to make the Needles Channel let alone the eastern approach to the Solent which might have been unwise anyway with the wind driving from the north. The Yarmouth crew set out for the given position in their 9 knot Oakley, perhaps achieving a little more with the following wind helping them.

The yacht was found off the Channel Islands having been driven back by the storm, the crew totally exhausted. Coxswain Kennett used the word 'overwhelmed'. It was in itself amazing that they found the yacht. They began their approach to take off the crew. Apart from the physical condition of the crew it was obvious that the yacht itself was damaged by the weather, possibly eventually going to founder but the mast was still standing. The lifeboat made a pass alongside, taking off crewmen, grabbed by the lifeboat crew on the pass. The 27 ton lifeboat could easily have damaged the already flooded yacht if there had been a hard impact or a prolonged time pounding alongside. It was a delicate business. During the several runs alongside the yacht one of the police officers fell between the two vessels narrowly missing being crushed. He was snatched by one of the lifeboat crew and with the help of another he was bodily thrown onto the very top of the lifeboat that covers the cabin and engineroom. He lay there until a further run was made to take off the remaining crew. All were safe, the lifeboat headed for home and the yacht sank.

All returned safely to Yarmouth aboard the worthy Oakley lifeboat. The storm may have passed but the publicity had not. The RNLI awarded Coxswain Kennett a silver medal for gallantry while several trusts, set up by people in order to make financial awards for deeds of this type, sent award money to Yarmouth. All this was followed by Dave Kennett being made one of the Men of the Year during the 1976 presentations in London and he graduated to the list of people invited to the garden parties given at Buckingham Palace by Her Majesty the Queen.

None of these excitements changed Coxswain Kennett and his crew, who continued to save lives in the difficult waters not far from peaceful Yarmouth. When strong tides run out through the Hurst Narrows against a westerly gale wild steep seas can quickly build up catching out the unwary or inexperienced sailor. It was in the autumn storm of 1989 that Coxswain Kennett admits that just such seas further out in the Channel almost caught him out and there can be no more wary or experienced seaman on that coast.

The roll-on/roll-off cargo ship *Al Kwather* had anchored for shelter from the storm about 3.5 miles from Peveril Point to the east of Swanage on the Dorset coast. The Maltese registered ship was on passage from Felixstowe to Limassol, Cyprus, when the cargo of motor vehicles shifted and a severe list developed. Coxswain Chris Haw, at Swanage, put to sea in the relief Rother class lifeboat *Horace Clarkson* and made for the casualty in a severe gale.

At 11.31 am the Swanage lifeboat arrived at the scene to learn by radio message from the ship's master that he was worried that cars sliding about the deck would injure his crew so was unable to send men forrard to raise the two anchors that had been dropped. Coxswain Haw was having trouble in keeping station on the ship as winds rose to a recorded 88 knots at nearby coastguard stations and waves of 25 feet were also recorded.

The Yarmouth lifeboat, a relief Arun, *Margaret Russell Fraser*, was on

The scene on the deck of the Al Kwather I *after the storm when cars broke free and the ship developed a list.*

The relief fleet Arun class lifeboat Margaret Russell Fraser, *on temporary duty at Yarmouth, Isle of Wight, heading for the car carrier,* Al Kwather I *off the Dorset coast where the crew, along with that from Swanage, stood by the ship in hurricane force winds after the cargo had shifted.*

duty while the station boat *Joy and John Wade* was away for refitting. The Arun left Yarmouth at 1.15 pm and took almost two hours to cover the 15 miles from the station to the casualty so severe was the weather. It was during this passage that the Yarmouth crew almost met disaster. Coxswain Kennett, watching the seas ahead carefully, suddenly saw what can only be called a rogue wave approaching. It towered over the lifeboat which rose to meet it, the bow pointing skywards. Realizing that the boat was about to be flipped bow over stern in a backward somersault capsize, Coxswain Kennett ran both engines full astern pulling the boat back from the concave wave shape and breaking crest which then crashed down on the lifeboat causing superficial damage and smashing the windscreen wipers. The Swanage lifeboat returned home after taking a considerable beating while standing by the casualty and the Yarmouth lifeboat, a fuel tank split by the violent movements, took over the vigil.

The wind was now at hurricane force, gusting at almost 100 knots but the ship had engine power and was not listing any more than earlier so after an hour the Yarmouth crew put into the shelter of Swanage to make temporary repairs. They stayed there with their colleagues from Swanage until just after midnight when the master of the *Al Kwather* reported that he had engine trouble and wanted to have the crew taken off the ship. The weather had moderated enough to allow a coastguard helicopter to take off from the Royal Naval Air Station at Lee-on-the-Solent.

The two lifeboat crews put back out to sea, the faster Yarmouth boat arriving at the casualty first to find her without electric lights and listing as much as 55 degrees, while the lifeboatmen could hear the cars crashing about on deck above the roar of the storm. They approached the stern of the ship using the lifeboat's own searchlight for illumination. A cargo net had been lowered over the stern. Two of the Yarmouth crew, Joseph Lester and Brian Miskin, were forward on deck as Coxswain Kennett approached the ship, trying to avoid a damaging collision in the 25 foot swell. The first survivor then slid down the net rolling onto the deck of the lifeboat, another followed but he trapped a foot in the net and was at one time below the level of the lifeboat when Lester and Miskin grabbed him and hauled him aboard at considerable risk to themselves.

The helicopter then arrived so the Yarmouth lifeboat stood to windward of the *Al Kwather* in order to provide the helicopter pilots with a point of reference while the Swanage boat stood by downwind in case of trouble.

The helicopter crew managed to lift off the remaining six men of the eight man crew after some skilful flying at night above a heavily rolling ship. This task completed the two lifeboats set out for their home ports while a tug arrived the next day and took the badly damaged cargo ship to safety in Southampton, the storm having abated. For this operation Coxswain Dave Kennett received a bronze medal, Coxswain Chris Haw an official thanks on vellum while his crew all received a certificate stating that they had been on an award-earning service as did the crew of the Yarmouth lifeboat.

This operation is a first class example of co-operation between two adjacent stations.

The two 33 foot long Brede class boats on the Hampshire and Dorset coast are at **Calshot**, on the western shore of the entrance to Southampton Water, and at Poole. The Calshot crew, out on the long promontory that was once headquarters of Royal Air Force seaplane operations and now houses a large adventure centre, are often busy with yachting people, board sailors, dinghy sailors and swimmers. The Bramble Bank, which can easily be crossed at high water in a moderate sized yacht, dries at extra low tides and cricket matches have been played on it on these occasions. In recent times the Calshot boat was called out to a large sailing vessel being 'sailed' by two gentlemen. The engine of the yacht failed so, unable to sail the yacht with a following wind and tide back to safety, they summoned the lifeboat to tow them to Cowes. The Calshot men never cease to be amazed at the lack of basic proficiency of some of those who put out to sea, though they seldom comment upon it.

The Brede based at **Poole** lies afloat next to the inner harbour lifting bridge and a new lifeboat crew house that adjoins the harbour police office and the harbour pilotage centre. Poole also has a Boston Whaler fast planing boat adapted to RNLI specification which is used for rescue work in the many creeks and coves of Poole Harbour, the second largest expanse of natural enclosed tidal water in the world after Sydney Harbour. Local people and visitors alike are always impressed at the local knowledge of the inshore crew. None of the more remote parts of Poole Harbour have lit channel marks, more often than not being indicated by a succession of poles. On a number of occasions the inshore boat has found its way in rain, darkness and poor visibility to a casualty stranded somewhere down in the shallow southern reaches of the harbour among the smaller islands that are scattered there.

The larger intermediate boat, with a speed of just over 18 knots, works both in the confines of Poole Harbour as well as further afield, often co-operating with the Swanage station. During the spring of 1990 the Coastguard informed the Poole station that a yacht had reported being off Old Harry rocks, south-east of the Poole Bar buoy, with steering trouble. As dusk fell the Poole lifeboat, *Inner Wheel*, set out into strong easterly

winds which may well have been driving the yacht onto the eastern headlands of the Dorset coast.

After checking several yachts sailing off Studland Bay, Coxswain Steve Vince and his crew were joined by the Swanage boat while the Coastguard reported that they had sighted a yacht steering erratically off St Aldhelm's Head. A rescue helicopter was on the scene and lowered a diver onto the yacht, *La Mouette*, where the diver found three people aboard and the yacht's steering badly damaged. The wind was now gale force and the seas rough. The faster Poole lifeboat reached the yacht and put a crewman aboard while taking the diver off. The Swanage boat then arrived and assisted with the passing of a towline from the yacht to the Poole boat which then towed the yacht back to Poole, accompanied by the Swanage boat which also put into Poole as, by then, it was too rough to rehouse the Swanage boat on its exposed slipway. The tow parted several times during the long haul but was made good on each occasion in spite of the bad sea conditions. All returned safely to the Poole station at 3.25 am.

Being right on the doorstep of the RNLI headquarters, "outside the headmaster's study door" as one RNLI employee put it, might make it seem that Poole has advantages over other stations, but this is not the case. The station is handled in exactly the same way from headquarters as any other. Poole fund-raising activities are managed by local people just as in any town or city around the country and, while proud to be the centre of RNLI operations and have the headquarters in the town, the people of Poole are just as proud of their own local lifeboat station. Obviously there is social contact between 'local' supporters and crew with those at headquarters but that is about the total strength of it.

At about the time of the *Al Kwather* rescue it was decided to put **Swanage** on the list of stations to be modernized and equipped with a fast new lifeboat. This would mean widening the existing lifeboat house to take a Mersey class slipway launching boat. Work at Swanage involves every sort of service, cliff falls being a common one as holiday-makers fall over the many high cliffs in the area and cliff climbers have accidents. Ferries operate from nearby Poole which is also one of the busiest yachting centres on England's south coast. Divers get into trouble, underestimating the strength of local tides that run off the headlands where ridges of rock tempt them to dive in the area. Coxswain Chris Haw is a local dentist so his crew reckon they have the best teeth in the RNLI.

Swanage keeps watch over a rugged piece of coastline stretching from Old Harry rock at the headland south of the entrance to Poole Harbour across

Swanage Bay and out from the dangerous Peveril Ledge where in light weather and an ebbing tide many a small boat sailor finds that he or she cannot get back to the north and shelter of Swanage Bay. South and south-west lie Durlston Head and St Aldhelm's Head with their respective tidal overflows and eddies that can cause problems even in moderate weather if not avoided.

The next station on the Dorset coast is at **Weymouth** where over half the calls are to help vessels in trouble in the notorious Portland Race which runs off the southern point of Portland Bill. Here at the times of the biggest rises and falls of tide, spring tides, the waters in the race run at up to 7 or 8 knots producing fearsome seas while the position of the race moves depending upon the state of the tide. The Weymouth crew were at sea in the October storm of 1987 in

Weymouth: On Friday 2 March 1984, the 68 foot yacht Constellation *was crossing Lyme Bay on passage from Hamble to Falmouth when, the weather deteriorating, the north-westerly winds rose to storm force 10. She turned about to return to Hamble under power. As she approached West Shambles Buoy, however, her fuel pipe fractured; then, while her crew were trying to make sail to get into Weymouth Bay, her boom was found to be broken. The 54ft Arun lifeboat* Tony Vandervell, *under the command of Coxswain Victor Pitman, came up with* Constellation *east of the Shambles Bank and took her in tow. The return passage to Weymouth, in winds which had by now moderated to gale force, took two hours.*

winds of almost 100 knots, at night, rescuing the crew of a 58 foot catamaran, the *Sunbeam Chase*, a brand new sailing vessel on a delivery passage from the Solent to the Mediterranean. They were at sea for 9 hours and saved the lives of six people but could not save the vessel.

Apart from the hazards of the race off Portland, Weymouth is a busy seaside resort, ferry terminal, sailing centre and fishing port. One rare rescue was of the 12 metre sailing yacht *Constellation*, the American yacht that defeated the British challenger *Sovereign* in the 1964 America's Cup. Converted to a cruising yacht and fitted with an auxiliary engine, she was in difficulties near the Portland Race and towed to safety when the engine broke down.

Weymouth also lies close by the Portland Royal Navy base. The lifeboat crew exercise with the naval helicopter crews, practising search and rescue. Their 54 foot Arun *Tony Vandervell* is a familiar sight for local people, one of whom thought he saw the lifeboat towing a helicopter like a kite. He was mistaken. The helicopter had lowered a diver to the lifeboat deck who was then about to clip a lifeboatman to the wire and send him back up to the helicopter, familiarizing both the naval airmen and lifeboatmen with winching.

Once past Portland Bill and sailing to the west the coastline changes from the towering headlands of St Aldhelm and Old Harry, the shallow waters of large tidal harbours and the wealth of places affording shelter to the barren expanse of Chesil Beach, the graveyard of many a ship driven ashore in the prevailing westerly winds. Portland is something of a gateway in the English Channel both tidally and geographically. The waters of the Channel seem clearer west of Portland but apart from the small harbour at Bridport, where the pilotage manuals describe the entrance as dangerous in even moderate onshore winds, there is no shelter for 20 miles or more until one reaches Lyme Regis where vessels of over 36 feet are prohibited from entering the small harbour, The Cobb. Between Portland and Lyme Regis the massive mound of gravel that forms Chesil Bank offers nothing except

Weymouth lifeboat, 54 foot Arun class Tony Vandervell *goes to the aid of a fishing boat sinking off Portland Bill, 15 November 1982.*

danger to the mariner in trouble in south-westerly and westerly winds. There is an Atlantic 21 rigid inflatable at Lyme Regis which is kept busy in the summer months when the amateur sailors emerge on the sail boards and dinghies while there is the occasional winter call to fishing boats. While a Dorset station Lyme Regis is often more concerned with the coast of Devon to the west.

The West Country stations

The peninsula that is formed by Devon and Cornwall sticks out into the Atlantic like a stone-age granite arrowhead pointing towards the worst that the ocean can throw at it. At the point of the arrowhead lies the lifeboat station on the Isles of Scilly but at the point where the arrowhead joins the shaft formed by the rest of southern England lies the **Exmouth** station. Here a Brede class boat, the *Caroline Finch*, covers the offshore waters between the west of Portland Bill and Torbay sharing the task with

the **Torbay** lifeboat which is based at the fishing port of Brixham. The mouth of the River Exe is beset with shoals that often trap the unwary visiting yachtsman, dinghy sailor and board sailor while falls from the cliffs both to the east and west of the station have produced many calls on the boat. The Exmouth station was established in 1803, at the same time that a lifeboat began work from Plymouth.

Being a larger boat and close by the regional coastguard station at Brixham the Brixham lifeboat, the 54 foot wooden Arun class boat *Edward Bridges*, handles more calls than Exmouth though it is common for the two crews to work together. Arthur Curnow, coxswain of the Brixham boat who retired in 1991, describes the Brixham station as busy, handling everything from pleasure craft and fishing boat casualties to transferring injured crew from cargo vessels that shelter in Torbay or put in there for help.

Coxswain Curnow, who continues to operate his harbour tug at Brixham, relates with some relish the rescue of a crew of nine young ladies and an

Torbay lifeboat crew on board their lifeboat Edward Bridges (Civil Service No 37).

embarrassed man from a yacht that came ashore near Berry Head, east of Brixham, one night in November 1989. The ferro-concrete boat hit the rocks with a crash that damaged its steering gear, propeller and hull. While emergency services were alerted by the Coastguard three of the girls, thinking they were on the mainland shore, jumped from the vessel to find themselves stranded on a small cluster of rocks surrounded by the sea. The yacht slipped back from the rocks as the pilot boat and lifeboat approached. The pilot boat crew took the damaged yacht in tow, stern first, while the lifeboat crew launched the small 'Y' class inflatable and rescued the three stranded ladies from their eyrie. Meanwhile the towline to the yacht had parted so the lifeboat crew took over the towing and all arrived back safely at Brixham at about 3 am.

The damaged yacht was secured safely near the lifeboat station and the yacht's crew escorted to the lifeboat house and crew room for hot drinks and, its seems, hospitality. Normally after a midnight call lasting three hours the crew are soon home to their beds, but for some inexplicable reason they did not return home until well after daybreak while an unhappy local television reporter and his cameraman spent a damp night on the town quay awaiting the return of the lifeboat and survivors of the yacht. Like them, the wives of the gallant Brixham lifeboatmen wondered what on earth, or sea, could have kept the crew away so long.

Life was not quite so easy or amusing for the Brixham crew some ten years earlier when, early in the morning of a December day in 1979, the cargo ship *Butaseis,* of Spain, radioed the Coastguard that there was a fire aboard their ship which was anchored in Torbay. The lifeboat was launched and headed for the burning ship. The ship's crew had already taken to their own lifeboat and were furiously rowing away from the ship.

Coxswain Curnow asked by radio what the ship was carrying. He was told that it was loaded with 740 tons of liquid butane gas.

The lifeboat crew approached the ship while the local pilot boat and a coaster stood by. There was no power aboard the *Butaseis* to raise the anchor so the lifeboatmen had to collect oxyacetylene cutting equipment to break the anchor cable having been unable to break the cable at a slip-shackle that is in the anchor chain for this purpose. Once the anchor cable was cut the coaster *Deneb* then took the burning ship in tow and headed out to sea. If the gas had blown up in Torbay the explosion would have caused considerable damage ashore in Brixham, Paignton and possibly Torquay.

The lifeboat escorted the coaster and the casualty eight miles out to sea when a Royal Navy minesweeper came round Start Point, her captain greeting the procession with a cheery ''Good morning, gentlemen'' before putting a party of firefighters aboard the *Butaseis*. They managed to control and eventually extinguish the fire, but they lost their inflatable dinghy during the operation.

The Spanish ship was then towed to a safe anchorage by an Admiralty tug. Later the courageous crew of the coaster *Deneb* claimed salvage for their part in the saving of the ship, but it had been a very dangerous business for all concerned, particularly those who stayed close to the burning ship and even more for those who boarded her. This was typical of the type of calls made on the Brixham crew but certainly one they would rather not have to face again.

During a severe storm in the winter of early 1990, the Pakistani registered container ship *Murree* reported that she was in trouble off Start Bay, near Dartmouth. The Brixham lifeboat was launched into the gale and found the ship to be sinking, her cargo having shifted in the storm. They approached

Sea King 5 of 771 Naval Air Squadron hovering over the MV Murree *in October 1989.*

the ship as helicopters arrived from RNAS Culdrose. The crew were lifted off by the helicopter crew, the lifeboat crew asking whether the helicopter crews needed them to stand by. The reply was very positive, the American Coast Guard pilot, on exchange with the Royal Navy, explaining that in view of the weather he felt much happier to have a lifeboat nearby in case anything went wrong with the difficult business of winching in the severe weather. All were saved from the ship which sank shortly after the rescue.

The two Royal Navy divers, who were lowered from the two helicopters to the steeply angled deck of the ship, worked in awesome conditions to ensure that the forty people aboard the *Murree* were all saved. Among the survivors were a number of women and children. Petty Officer Aircrewmen Dave Wallace and Steve Wright stayed aboard the ship during the rescue, the winds gusting to over 50 knots. Almost as soon as the last survivor was on the way up to a helicopter the ship began to sink bow first with the naval men still aboard. As the stern rose they both jumped 90 feet into a debris-strewn sea to be picked up by the helicopters as the ship vanished. For this rescue Dave Wallace and Steve Wright both received the George Medal from Her Majesty the Queen in November 1990. On the preceding day they were presented with a special gallantry award during the Silk Cut Awards luncheon at the Savoy Hotel, London, the presentation being made by round-the-world yachtswoman Dame Naomi James. It is perhaps worth remembering that while the two men leapt into the sea knowing that their helicopter pilots would do everything possible to winch them to safety, they also knew that a RNLI lifeboat was standing by.

Brixham is a busy fishing port. In 1990 three trawlers sank in waters off the port, Coxswain Curnow adding a vellum award to a bronze medal he already held for taking an injured man off another local fishing boat in bad weather.

The sinking of the Pakistani container ship MV Murree, *in October 1989 which was attended by Sea Kings of the Royal Navy's Sea King helicopters from 771 Squadron, RNAS Culdrose and the Torbay lifeboat. Having rescued all 40 people from the ship Petty Officer Aircrewmen Steve Wright and Dave Wallace, pictured left and right, had to jump 90 feet into the sea as the ship foundered. They were each awarded the George Medal for their courage.*

As long ago as July 1968 the crew of the Brixham lifeboat established a record that they think has never been broken by one boat working alone. The pleasure cruiser *Western Lady* that plied between Torbay and the River Dart carrying tourists ran ashore in bad visibility between Berry Head and the entrance to the Dart. In calm weather the lifeboat rescued 126 people and a dog.

Salcombe, the next lifeboat station westwards along the coast of Devon from Brixham, has a Tyne class boat, *The Baltic Exchange II*, moored afloat in the picturesque harbour. The narrow entrance to the harbour is straddled by a sand bar that can be dangerous in strong southerly winds but this has never stopped the Salcombe crew from putting to sea, which they do about thirty times a year. In October 1916 thirteen out of a crew of seventeen local men were lost when the rowing and sailing lifeboat capsized on the bar but it was more recently, in April 1983, that the Watson class lifeboat, also named *The Baltic Exchange*, capsized out at sea during a storm but self-righted. One of the crew was swept overboard during the capsize and spent an agonizing time struggling in the sea watching the propellers of the upturned boat still turning as they pointed skywards. The lifeboat self-righted and the man overboard was recovered. The Brixham lifeboat, which was also at sea, escorted the Salcombe crew to safety, a fine example of co-operation between adjacent stations.

More recently Coxswain Frank Smith and his crew had what they describe as a rare experience when a tug towing a barge broke down off Start Point. The tug skipper took a lift ashore from a passing yacht, leaving two crew aboard the tug. He told the harbour master, Peter Hodges, of his problem. The lifeboat was launched as a southerly gale was forecast and the two crew remaining aboard the tug were taken off but put back aboard, with the skipper, next day and the tug and barge towed to Salcombe where the tow parted as the procession crossed the bar. Eventually all was put right and a successful rescue accomplished.

Salcombe, like Brixham and the other West Country stations, has a number of calls directly connected with the tourist industry, be these to save amateur sailors, cliff climbers, walkers, divers or swimmers. They also have their fair share of fishing boat casualties. In October 1990 they were at sea for 16 hours in bad weather looking for a crew member of a trawler who had fallen overboard. They never found him.

There are strong associations between the Salcombe crew and The Baltic Exchange in London who have supplied the funds to buy their last two lifeboats. While members of the Exchange, the centre of shipping cargo brokerage, visit Salcombe and are welcomed by the crew during the holiday season, the crew, in turn, are invited to The Exchange, all travel expenses paid, to a special lunch.

Obviously sufficient crew have to stay at home in case a call comes through.

Plans are in hand to improve the shore facilities of the station, the RNLI acquiring a harbourside property which they will develop to meet the needs of the lifeboat crew and then sell the parts that they do not need to fund the conversion.

Plymouth and Salcombe lifeboats cover the waters from the Salcombe estuary westwards past Bolt Tail and the Eddystone lighthouse towards Cornwall. At **Plymouth** the Arun class lifeboat *City of Plymouth* is based at Sutton Pool, the oldest part of the port of Plymouth close to the famous Barbican and Plymouth Hoe. Retired Coxswain John Dare, who handed the job over to Second Coxswain Pat Marshall at the end of 1990, is philosophical about the work of the lifeboat crews.

The Plymouth lifeboat handles about 100 calls every three years though recently the call rate has dropped. Coxswain Dare puts this down to the greater sophistication of equipment aboard every type of vessel that puts to sea and a greater awareness of weather forecasting, use of modern communications and navigational aids

Plymouth lifeboat the Arun class City of Plymouth.

by seafarers. The busy local fishing fleet, as well as trawlers from further afield, provide a number of the calls made on the Plymouth lifeboat, which was paid for out of funds raised locally in a massive effort. A 'shopping list' was published offering everybody from corporate companies to individuals to buy anything from one of the two engines to the VHF radio whip aerials. It was typical of many similar efforts that have taken place over the years around the country.

West of Plymouth, past Rame Head and Whitesand Bay lies the little Cornish port of **Fowey** where, in 1990, the Waveney class boat *Thomas Forehead and Mary Rowse II* was kept busy by every type of rescue from fishing boats and yachts to cliff falls and divers.

Fowey lifeboat house is best approached from the sea, particularly in the summer months when the very narrow steep streets of the little town are crammed with tourists. Prime Minister Margaret Thatcher may have appreciated this when she visited the station in the summer of 1990 when, accidentally, she made lifeboat history.

Mrs Thatcher was making a call on the Fowey lifeboat station during which she was invited to take a short trip round the harbour aboard the boat. Coxswain Mathew Stuart, a Northumbrian from the lifeboat port of Amble, put to sea with his crew and the Premier plus entourage of detectives and other followers. In the midst of the cruise a call was received from the crew of the yacht *Slipshod* who reported that the keel fastenings of their yacht had become loose and that the yacht was taking in water. There was no time to put the Prime Minister ashore so she was taken along for the ride where the lifeboat crew expected to put a pump aboard the yacht to keep the incoming water in check. It was not needed. The call was a success, no awards for gallantry were handed out to the crew or anyone else, although it was a call on

their services that they will not forget.

Fowey is not a great distance from RNAS Culdrose and is often co-operating with the Search and Rescue helicopters, as much as 50% of their calls involving work with the naval pilots. Also all local lifeboats work with the naval crew on exercises involving helicopters. Links with Fowey and RNAS Culdrose are strong, as they are with Falmouth, the next station to the west along the Cornish coast.

Falmouth, once more an active shipyard, is as busy as a sailing centre, fishing port and holiday resort. This combination of activities makes Falmouth, with its Arun class lifeboat *Elizabeth Ann*, a busy station. Lifeboats from the western area of operations are refitted at the port.

A typical operation involving three West Country stations occurred in February 1985. The French trawler *St Simeon* began to take in water during a violent easterly storm while off the coast of Cornwall. The Falmouth lifeboat stood by the vessel followed by the Penlee boat *Mabel Alice* which stayed with the St Simeon for over ten hours in storm force winds. The Plymouth lifeboat, then the Waveney class boat *Thomas Forehead and Mary Rowse II* which is now at Fowey, took over from the Penlee crew. Eventually it became apparent that the trawler was going to sink. Her crew abandoned ship and took to their life raft. Coxswain John Dare made several approaches to the raft managing to save all five of the French crew. Coxswain Dare, together with Coxswain Ken Thomas of Penlee and Coxswain Vivian Pentecost of Falmouth all received the thanks of the RNLI inscribed on vellum for this rescue.

Nothing stays in the minds of the lifeboat crew at **The Lizard**, in its remote promontory station, more than the night of the loss of the lifeboat from Penlee in December 1981. They were called out to sea aboard their lifeboat *The Duke of Cornwall* into winds gusting at over 100 knots, seas

Torbay lifeboat and station.

of 60 feet and a night as black as pitch. Before they reached the area of the search south from Mousehole they heard by radio that wreckage from both the motor ship *Union Star* and the Penlee lifeboat *Solomon Browne* was coming ashore at Lamorna Cove. They spent a day at sea, accompanied by the St Mary's lifeboat from the Scilly Isles, searching.

Their lifeboat was badly damaged by the seas. The deck area in front of the wheelhouse was cleared of stanchions and mooring bollards. The bilge keels were strained beneath the hull. The centre part of the lifeboat was flooded. The lifeboat had to be taken to Falmouth for repair next day, a relief lifeboat being put on the station. The calls on The Lizard station are generally long, varying from six to eighteen hours in duration simply due to the geographical location of the station.

In July 1984, the lifeboat *Duke of Cornwall* was replaced by another lifeboat, the *James and Catherine MacFarlane* which was soon busy. In September that year two yachts, the *Bass* and the *Alto*, were driven ashore

on the nearby Wellow Reef. The *Bass* was taken in tow as the Penlee lifeboat arrived to assist the other yacht. Both yachts were then taken under tow to Newlyn, near Penzance, and safety.

The rescue of these yachts earned Coxswain Peter Mitchell a bronze medal from the RNLI but in some opinions an even more dramatic rescue was to follow. The motor vessel *Caroline*, registered in Honduras, radioed that she was sinking close to The Lizard. The lifeboat was launched and found the vessel awash. A Royal Navy helicopter from nearby RNAS Culdrose had taken off all the crew except one who remained in a ship's lifeboat firmly secured to the sinking ship. Lifeboatman Phil Burgess, now coxswain of The Lizard station lifeboat, leapt aboard the ship's boat and told the crewman that unless he left the boat and came aboard the lifeboat he would lay him flat and carry him off. An axe was passed from the lifeboat and the ship's boat cut free, the lifeboat being above the sinking ship during the whole operation. The man was taken aboard the lifeboat without the future coxswain having to administer drastic first aid.

After a succession of the old slower relief lifeboats The Lizard received its present lifeboat, the Tyne class *David Robinson*, in August 1988, named after the man who paid for this lifeboat and also the *Mabel Alice* which replaced the *Solomon Browne*, lost at Penlee. Peter Mitchell retired as coxswain, to be awarded the British Empire Medal by Her Majesty the Queen for his services to the RNLI, his place as coxswain being taken by fighting Phil Burgess. The Tyne has proved popular with the crew at The Lizard and has been busy. In April 1989, the 80 foot schooner *Southern Cross* was in difficulty, short-handed with a crew of three, 35 miles off The Lizard. A helicopter took off an exhausted woman leaving two men aboard. Lifeboatmen then boarded the yacht and assisted rigging a tow to haul the yacht to the shelter of Falmouth Harbour.

The 1989 Fastnet yacht race is an event described by The Lizard honorary secretary, John Jones, known by all as J J, as the bane of the lifeboatmen's life. The lifeboat was out all night on 7 August assisting three yachts which were in trouble while competing in the race. Another yacht had to be helped in May 1990, when, sails blown out off The Lizard, it was coming ashore in strong winds, the crew exhausted. The lifeboat crew managed to reach the yacht in strong easterly winds and put a line aboard before the long hard towing job back to safety in Falmouth. Later, during the same summer, they put out to a yacht that had completed a transatlantic crossing from the Caribbean and become becalmed off Cornwall having already run out of food and water. The Lizard lifeboat took out the necessary supplies to the hungry and thirsty sailors before offering a welcomed tow to Falmouth. Not listed as an operation of daring-

do it was simply listed as having given help, but that is exactly what the lifeboat service is all about.

Around Lizard Point from Church Cove and across Mount's Bay the emotive station at Penlee Point lies on the little headland between the small village of Mousehole and the commercial fishing port of Newlyn where the present **Penlee** boat, the Arun class *Mabel Alice* lies. The terrible disaster and loss of the entire crew in 1981 has been described, but while memories certainly linger the Penlee station is very much back in business. While the old lifeboat house still stands out on Penlee Point, occasionally filled by a slipway boat, a new lifeboat centre has been built at Newlyn where the Arun lies on moorings.

Coxswain Ken Thomas, a big man in every way, has moulded a crew together from eighteen men, ten of them from Mousehole, the community which has always traditionally manned the Penlee lifeboat, and eight from Newlyn. Shortly after receiving their Arun class boat in 1983 the Penlee crew had the unenviable task of going to the Isles of Scilly to collect seventeen bodies of those killed when a helicopter operating a passenger service between Penzance and the islands had ditched in the sea. In the same year the French ferry *Amorique* caught fire north of the Isles of Scilly while on passage between France and Ireland. Lifeboats were launched to meet the ship as she steamed at full speed for Mount's Bay where emergency services were being prepared. The ferry had 700 passengers aboard. While the ship's own lifeboats could certainly have accommodated everyone it was obvious that the RNLI lifeboats would be needed to assist those adrift in them. The Penzance to Isles of Scilly ferry, *Scillonian III*, was also put on stand-by for an evacuation.

In fact there were three fires burning on the ferry that had been started, it was suspected, by an arsonist. By the time the ferry reached Mount's Bay, pursued by several lifeboats and other vessels, the fire was under control. One passenger died in the fire but apart from some problems caused by the inhalation of smoke everyone else was safe.

Recently the Penlee men have faced a new but particularly odious task. There are now undertakers in the West of England offering burial at sea to their customers but, unfortunately, several bodies reappeared on the surface of the sea following 'burial' and had to be recovered by the lifeboat. Coxswain Ken Thomas was not happy with the situation, forcefully pointing out that their prime task was to save life and not to go to sea to recover the remains of people who were already dead and buried.

While Newlyn is one of the busiest fishing ports in Britain, nearby Penzance and the surrounding coast is a major holiday area so the work of the lifeboat is as busy and varied as any station. In recent years the crew

have reported that life has been relatively quiet when compared with earlier times.

The most westerly station on the English and Welsh mainland is at **Sennen Cove**, a small fishing village tucked into a bay a mile north-east of Land's End. The lifeboat house, with its two slipways, one for launching and one for recovering the boat, is the largest in Britain. The slipways, protected by a pier from the worst of the westerly weather, present a fearsome prospect for the crew when entering and leaving the cove.

There are two ways in and out of Sennen, north-east and then west, passing north of off-lying rocks, or due west, passing south of the same rocks and close to others near the shore. It is not a place for the faint hearted in a westerly gale and a dark night. Until 1990 Sennen operated with an ageing Rother class boat but in 1991 a Mersey class boat was to be put on the station for evaluation. The present coxswain, Terry George, looks forward to the arrival of the new boat

The Sennen Cove lifeboat being launched.

but has no adverse thoughts about the slower boat, the *Diana White*.

Under the command of the previous coxswain, Maurice Hutchens, the crew rescued seven men from an Icelandic grain carrier, the *Tungafoss,* in September 1981. In bad weather the cargo of maize had shifted while the ship was just south of the Longships light, just off Land's End and not far from Sennen Cove. A helicopter was called from RNAS Culdrose and succeeded in winching three of the crew from the ship before the naval diver, the man who is lowered to the deck of the casualty, was injured. The lifeboat went alongside the ship and took off seven more men, leaving the master aboard. It then became apparent that the ship was about to sink. The lifeboat closed in once more as the helicopter lowered the winch wire and strop to the deck but without the diver. As the ship began to go under the master managed to put one arm through the strop at the end of the wire and hang on as he was hauled to safety aboard the helicopter. It was a brave move by the helicopter crew as, without the diver, the strop could have easily snagged on something aboard the ship causing a serious disaster.

This rescue earned Coxswain Hutchens and his crew a special Icelandic award and an Icelandic medal for gallantry for him. The Royal Navy helicopter crew were similarly rewarded by the President of Iceland who came to Britain specially to make the presentation. Earlier, in 1979, the lifeboat crew received a letter of thanks from Prime Minister Margaret Thatcher following their efforts during the Fastnet storm. In 1983 the ferry *St Killian* was hit by a massive sea that damaged her bridge and steering gear. The lifeboat was launched into terrible conditions but by the time it reached the ferry matters had been put right.

One problem faced at Sennen Cove is recovering the lifeboat on to the

slipway in bad weather. The nearest shelter along to coast is at Newlyn, round Land's End to the south or St Ives Bay about the same distance, 16 miles, to the north-east. It is not uncommon for the Sennen boat to make for one of these ports after a call and return home when bad weather has moderated.

During the *Amorique* ferry fire the Sennen boat was called out and later received a letter of thanks from the head of Brittany Ferries although with a speed of only 8 knots, the crew had trouble in keeping up with the ferry as it began its frantic dash south to the shelter and help awaiting off Penzance.

The point of the West Country arrowhead is the Isles of Scilly where, until a few years ago the Lethbridge family were synonymous with the RNLI just as Henry Blogg and the Davies family are synonymous with Cromer on the Norfolk coast.

Until Matt Lethbridge retired as coxswain in the mid-1980s after forty years with the boat and thirty of these as coxswain there had been a Lethbridge as coxswain of the **St Mary's** lifeboat continuously for seventy-one years, Matt having taken the job over from his father who, in turn, had inherited it from Matt's grandfather. His father took the Prince of Wales, later to abdicate as Edward VIII, aboard the St Mary's lifeboat before the Second World War and Matt took the present Prince of Wales, Prince Charles, to sea aboard the Arun class boat *Robert Edgar* fifty years later.

The 1979 Fastnet Race and the resultant loss of both lives and yachts on the doorstep of the St Mary's lifeboat house produced some very strong thoughts from Matt Lethbridge. He felt that much of the gear aboard modern yachts was not up to the strength required and that insurance companies should enforce standards to be met. If the standards were not met then insurance cover would not be

The legendry coxswain of the St Mary's, Isles of Scilly, lifeboat, Matt Lethbridge BEM. He holds three RNLI silver medals.

given. Insurance should be compulsory as is the case with motor vehicles. He was also critical of those who abandoned yachts for the life rafts. Several abandoned yachts were recovered while members of their crews died having taken to the life rafts. He regards a life raft as a step between a floating boat and swimming.

During the *Amorique* ferry fire Matt Lethbridge and his crew pursued the ferry at full speed in the 18 knot Arun all the way to Mount's Bay, receiving thanks from the ferry company for his effort even if help was not needed. In 1983, when a Penzance to Scilly Isles helicopter ditched off the islands in bad visibility several survivors told later that the most wonderful sound was that of Matt Lethbridge's voice calling through the swirling mist.

The prototype Arun class boat, now

at Barry Dock in South Wales, was put on trials at St Mary's in the hands of Matt Lethbridge who admits to never driving a boat at anything less than full speed. At the time of the loss of the Penlee lifeboat he covered the 30 miles from St Mary's to the Runnelstone Rocks in one hour forty-five minutes into the teeth of the storm force south-easterly winds that were blowing at the time. Asked his opinion of retirement at fifty-five years old and how he felt while still driving a fast offshore boat at the age of sixty-two when he retired, he commented that he was often still standing at the wheel when younger men were tiring. Three silver medals and a British Empire Medal mark his years as a lifeboatman. Today he is still busy at his home in Hugh Town, St Mary's. He is a painter of note, many of his works showing lifeboats, ferries and other ships in intricate details and with an eye for sea and sky that cannot be taught at art school. He makes models of ships using bronze from scrapped engines or brass from the many shipwrecks around the Isles of Scilly. He is often at the ferry dock when the boat arrives from the mainland greeting old friends who have come to see him or seeing friends off. Prince Charles is among those who call in at his neat cottage when on the islands.

Today the Arun lies at mooring between the old lifeboat house and the end of the harbour pier. Coxswain Rodney Terry, who operates the inter-island medical boat, has a hard act to follow treading in the footprints of the Lethbridge era but local opinion is that at one of the wildest and more remote RNLI stations he and his crew are managing well.

St Ives, the first station east from Land's End along the north Cornish coast, has problems because of the tide and a harbour that dries. A new Mersey class lifeboat arrived on the station in late October 1990 and was named *The Princess Royal (Civil Service No 41)* in 1991. A new boathouse is planned on the promenade to house the boat, its trailer and the Talus tractor. There is also an inflatable at St Ives which is kept busy during the summer months. During the summer of 1990 it was called upon twenty-one times in twenty days, mainly to holiday-makers falling off sail boards, being cut off by the tides and getting into difficulties while swimming.

During a March storm in 1989 the Oakley class lifeboat, that preceded the Mersey now at the station, battled in massive seas to answer a call from a timber ship *Secil Japan* that had run on rocks in a severe north-westerly storm along the coast north-east of St Ives. Helicopters were at the scene, saving all the crew but one who fell from the winch wire during lifting. Helicopter crews received commendations for their gallant

efforts. The *Secil Japan* broke up and her cargo of a variety of exotic timbers swept from her onto the shore. The baulks of timber vanished as soon as they hit the beaches and rocks, old Cornish traditions apparently prevailing.

The **Padstow** lifeboat is not at Padstow but out on the north-east side of Trevose Head some miles from the small fishing port that lies at the entrance to the estuary of the River Camel. The Padstow lifeboat, the Tyne class *James Burrough*, also went to the assistance of the *Secil Japan* and covered the distance to stand by the casualty, 23 miles, in one and a half hours suffering superficial damage, though little could be done other than lie off the cliffs while the Royal Navy and Royal Air Force helicopter crews set about lifting the Greek and Korean crew. As the Padstow men lay off, the wind threatening to drive them ashore if they had a mechanical failure, their thoughts, unspoken, were being cast back to the loss of the Penlee lifeboat in similar conditions and circumstances eight years earlier. The Padstow lifeboat was at sea for a total of eleven hours in terrible conditions, the crew exhausted from the buffeting on return to the station.

The Padstow crew have, in recent times, helped everything from a yacht crew who were lost without engine, sails or compass off the north coast of Cornwall, to five local fishing boats threatened by trouble when trying to cross the bar off Padstow harbour in a storm. Coxswain Trevor England is himself a local fisherman so they could have had no better pilot to help them.

If Padstow is a remote station perched out on Trevose Head then by contrast the station at **Appledore** is a sheltered one, the new Tyne class lifeboat lying afloat off the boat house at the junction of the rivers Taw and Torridge close to the village of Appledore. The lifeboat, the *George Gibson*, was donated by the

Padstow lifeboat station.

Gibson Charitable Trust set up by George Gibson, OBE. Since the station was first opened in 1825 Appledore crews have earned twenty-three silver medals, three bronze medals and saved almost 600 lives. In earlier times the casualties were fishing vessels, cargo ships plying the waters of the Bristol Channel to the north or making to and from the entrances of Barnstaple and Bideford harbours.

Today calls are divided fairly equally between fishing boats and pleasure craft. An Atlantic inflatable is housed in the old boathouse which is busy in the summer when visitors become stranded on the miles of sand that are uncovered at low water but which are covered again, very rapidly, when the tide floods. The rise and fall of the water along this part of the Cornish and North Devon coast is one of the largest in the country and can be a considerable danger to the unwary.

Several inflatables are positioned along this coast between the all-weather boat stations, at St Agnes in Trevaunance Cove, Newquay, Port Isaac and Bude. The closing of the lifeboat station at Clovelly put extra weight on the Appledore station although the Search and Rescue helicopters from nearby RAF Chivenor compensate for this to some extent.

Ilfracombe is the only all-weather lifeboat station on the North Devon coastline between Bull Point, west of the town, and the Severn Bridge, 80 miles to the east but it must be remembered that the south coast of Wales is only 15 miles from the northern-most point of the Devon and Somerset north coast at Lynmouth. This narrow part of the Bristol Channel is covered by the Ilfracombe station to the south, The Mumbles station near Swansea to the north and the station at Barry Dock, near Cardiff, to the east.

The new Mersey class lifeboat *Spirit of Derbyshire*, funded by the Derbyshire Lifeboat Appeal and local fund-raising in North Devon, went on station in the summer of 1990 and during the first five months there twenty-six lives were saved. The previous lifeboat was the Oakley class *Lloyds II* which had served Ilfracombe since 1966 and among many rescues earned Coxswain David Clemence a bronze medal in September 1984, for the rescue of one person from the yacht *Liberty* that was dragging her anchor close to the shore in a north-

Old and new. The old Ilfracombe lifeboat, Oakley class Lloyds II, *on station since 1966, on the right alongside the new lifeboat* Spirit of Derbyshire, Mersey class, *on station since 1990.*

westerly gale. The skipper of the yacht had died aboard during the storm and his crew of one had little or no yachting experience. The trailer launched lifeboat put to sea, her crew managing to secure a towline to the yacht, by then grounding in 20 foot high seas and only yards from rocks. The yacht was dragged into the outer harbour where it took two minutes for one of the lifeboat crew, who had boarded the yacht, to cut the anchor cable before the yacht could be taken to safety and her one survivor taken ashore.

Three years earlier, in April 1981, a storm struck Ilfracombe. The owner of the yacht *Springtide* decided to move the yacht to a safer berth as force 9 to 11 winds battered it against the harbour wall. Unfortunately, because of the violent movement of the yacht the owner was unable to embark but an experienced sailor aboard decided it would be safer to put to sea and ride out the storm offshore. The crew consisted of a girl of sixteen and a

boy only twelve years old. Watched by coastguards the yacht seemed to be safely clear of the coast when she suddenly began moving towards the shore again.

The *Lloyds II* was launched as a helicopter arrived from RAF Chivenor. After 30 minutes the helicopter crew managed to winch the girl from the yacht while the lifeboat was disappearing from the sight of those ashore in monstrous seas. Once in hospital the girl reported that the other two people aboard had apparently abandoned the yacht after a fire broke out aboard caused by a leak from a gas cylinder, probably wrenched free from its place by the violent movement. Neither the adult nor the boy were ever found.

Ilfracombe handles everything from holiday-makers stranded on cliffs and in the many small coves and bays along the coast to yachts, fishing boats in difficulty and medical evacuations from passing ships which have included the Sail Training

Association's flag ship, the 300 ton topsail schooner *Sir Winston Churchill*. Because of the tides, which are extreme, launching by tractor and trailer is somewhat akin to the situation at Llandudno, the boat being taken along the town streets to the slipway from the boathouse.

One of the last tasks of the old lifeboat *Lloyds II* was the rescue of international yachtsman Tony Bullimore's multihull yacht *Spirit of Apricot* which capsized in the Bristol Channel with the loss of one life, while the new boat was soon in action, her crew saving fifteen people from a fishing boat in trouble off Combe Martin along the coast to the east.

Along this coast to the east of Ilfracombe there are two Atlantic class rigid inflatables at Minehead and Weston-super-Mare mainly dealing with tourists in trouble, these two stations completing the chain of stations around the coast of the West of England.

The Channel Islands

The geographic nature of the Channel Islands, the massive rise and fall of the tides that flow round them and the strong currents that these tides produce are only three of the problems that face the local lifeboat crews. Add to these thousands of rock outcrops that surround the islands, the often inhospitable coastlines and an almost total lack of shelter from anything the Atlantic Ocean can throw at them and one begins to understand why the Channel Island lifeboatmen are among the highest scorers in terms of gallantry awards.

The most northerly station is at **Alderney** where, on a rough day, one looks from the harbour office at Braye northwards across a mass of white breaking water swirling over razor-sharp rocks and moving at speeds of 8

knots or more. That is the hunting ground for the Alderney lifeboat crew led by Coxswain Steve Shaw. Their boat is a Waveney but Coxswain Shaw, harbour master at Braye, openly admits that he would appreciate having a larger faster boat to cope better with both the seas around the islands and the tidal currents.

Traffic through Braye harbour is as varied as anywhere. Fishing boats and yachts use the harbour almost continuously, some 7,500 pleasure yachts calling at Braye each year. Ferries pass either side of the island while to the north lies the traffic separation zone off the Casquets rocks, one of the busiest stretches of water in the world after the Straits of Dover.

During a storm in the late summer of 1986 the Alderney lifeboat was on call for a total of 36 hours escorting one sailing yacht to the safety of the harbour, attempting to save a large motor yacht that had broken its moorings inside the harbour and saving an eighty-six year-old man from another yacht that had broken from moorings and was lying in the dangerous overfalls to the east of the sheltered area. While the lifeboat crew saved both the old gentleman and his boat they could not save the large motor yacht, which was smashed to pieces on the rocks. At the time the Alderney men were using a 33 foot Brede class boat, *Foresters Future*. The Brede, an intermediate boat between the Tynes, Merseys and the Atlantic 21 rigid inflatable inshore boats, was only just boat-enough for that effort in the prevailing weather.

Apart from the marine traffic passing Alderney the island lies close to the Ortac rock which is a busy 'way-point' for air traffic using both European and transatlantic routes. In addition, Alderney has its own small busy airline, Aurigny Air Services, which flies regularly between Southampton and Alderney and operates a busy inter-Channel Island service and flights from the islands to France. Although they seem almost oblivious to the bad weather that often strikes the islands in winter from the Atlantic, Aurigny has never had a serious accident, certainly not a passenger fatality, and has never needed to call on the RNLI for help.

One particular rescue modestly recalled by Coxswain Steve Shaw was that of the yacht *British Bullfrog*, from Hamble, one of the yachts from the Hamble-based fleet of the Britannia Sailing School. In October 1989, when a severe storm struck the south-west the yacht, with a crew of an instructor and trainees, was off Alderney. The wind was blowing at force 10 to 11.

The Alderney lifeboat crew set out and found the yacht but not without difficulty. Such was the sea state and the flying spray that it was not until they were only 15 metres from the yacht that they were able to see it.

The crew of the yacht had been overwhelmed by the weather and were suffering from seasickness and hypothermia. The yacht was about 15 miles from Alderney when found. The lifeboat crew managed to pass a line aboard and the long haul back to Braye harbour and safety began, but the new towing pennant, made from braided man-made fibre, continually broke and had to be re-attached. The mystery of the parting of the line was not solved but since then the lifeboat has carried a normally laid rope (but has had no long towing work with which to test it before the end of 1990). The yachtsmen were safe. That is what it is all about.

One of the more remarkable facets of the Alderney station is the work of the Ladies Guild and the local fund-raisers. Although there are only a little over 2,000 people living on Alderney, during the year 1989-90 £13,000 was

St Helier's RNLB Alexander Coutanche, *Tyne class.*

raised on the island of which £11,000 was sent to the central fund at Poole headquarters. Sadly there has been a recent new development, that being the theft of lifeboat collecting boxes during the holiday season. The second unusual feature, Coxswain Shaw boasts, is that when the crew hold their social evenings they have a special treat . . . they fly, by courtesy of Aurigny Airlines, a Chinese take-away supper for 100 people in from Guernsey, tiring, no doubt, of their local diet of fresh fish, lobster, crab and other delicacies.

While the most northerly lifeboat station in the whole RNLI chain is at Aith, in the Shetland Isles, the most southerly is in Jersey in **St Helier** harbour. Here, during the winter of 1990, Coxswain Mike Berry retired, his second coxswain, Bob Vezier taking over the lifeboat, a new Tyne class, the *Alexander Coutanche*. The new boat, built in 1989, was funded by the local lifeboat appeal fund-raisers, the money they raised being matched by the States of Jersey Government. In spite of the donation by the Jersey authorities they take no part in the operations of the lifeboats, although the inflatables used by the States of Jersey Fire Service often work on inshore work in close co-operation with the RNLI boats on the island.

In addition to the Tyne class lifeboat based in St Helier there is now, since 1990, an Atlantic class inshore boat based in the new boathouse at St Catherine on the north-east point of the island. The boathouse is the largest ever provided for an inshore boat and replaces the old inshore station that was a short way along the coast.

During his twenty years with the lifeboat Coxswain Berry earned two silver and a bronze medal for gallantry as well as several words of thanks on vellum. Many calls are made on the rescue services by tourists stranded on rocks having walked there at low tide and not realizing that the tide would

Jersey/St Helier Coxswain Mike Berry.

cut them off.

Other common calls on the Jersey station come from French charter yachts where a curious law allows Frenchmen with no sailing experience to put to sea in a yacht or motor cruiser as long as the engine is no more than 10 horsepower. Unfortunately an engine of such low power is no match for the strong currents that swirl between Jersey and the nearby coast of France. It was the rescue of one such yacht that earned Coxswain Berry one of his silver awards. The yacht was stranded among rocks to the south-east of the island known as The Gutters. These are long banks of rock with trenches of sand between them that stick out from the coast like long fingers.

Coxswain Berry took the boat into the rock-strewn area in bad weather while the yacht lay in comparative safety in one of the trenches of sand. The lifeboat was badly damaged, one

The St Helier, Jersey, lifeboat Alexander Coutanche, *assisting the crew of the local fishing boat* Port de Hurel, *which sank. This was one of the last operations carried out by Coxswain Mike Berry before his retirement.*

rudder being driven up into the hull and a propeller ripped off but in spite of this the French crew were brought to safety. It was certainly a brave effort but Mike Berry was not overjoyed by the damage to the lifeboat although it was virtually unavoidable under the circumstances. It came as a surprise to him when, sometime later, he was nominated for a Silk Cut Award for Seamanship. These awards are made each year by a panel of judges from the maritime world who select award winners from votes sent in by amateur sailors and others such as marine journalists, coastguards, RNLI members and harbour masters.

During the hurricane of January 1990 the Jersey crew were called out to help the French trawler *Antaeus* that was adrift 16 miles from St Helier with her propeller fouled. Winds of over 70 knots were recorded at Jersey while the lifeboat crew encountered waves of 60 feet as they searched for the casualty which they located after two hours at sea. The lifeboat stood

by the trawler until the French crew managed to free whatever was fouling the propeller. They then proceeded towards the French port of Granville with the lifeboat still in attendance until it was released to return to St Helier.

In contrast to this rescue one of the last lifeboat operations carried out by Coxswain Mike Berry was to save the crew of a local fishing boat that had run aground on rocks in thick fog a few miles from St Helier. Visibility was officially described as 'nil' but the Jersey lifeboat arrived on the scene within an hour and put pumps aboard the fishing boat, the *Port de Hurel*. In spite of this effort it became apparent that the boat was going to sink. The crew were taken off minutes before it foundered.

At the time of his retirement Mike Berry recalled a time when one of the employees of the garage he manages was in trouble in a small boat off Jersey. After a night search the casualty was found and brought back to Jersey in the early hours. On return

The Arun class lifeboat Sir William Arnold, of St Peter Port, Guernsey pacing the relief fleet lifeboat (at that time), the Thames class lifeboat Rotary Service. Rotary Service is now stationed at Dover.

to the lifeboat station, a converted German bunker, Mike Berry told the survivor that as he, Mike, would be at the garage at 8 o'clock that morning so would he, the man rescued.

Jersey has strong connections with nearby France, often co-ordinating and co-operating with the French lifeboats at Cap de la Hague, Granville and St Malo where the lifeboats are government funded.

The most western of the Channel Islands is Guernsey where the Arun class lifeboat Sir William Arnold is based in **St Peter Port**. Peter Bisson is coxswain; he holds two bronze awards for gallantry. One of these was for his part in the rescue of twenty-nine people from the Ecuadorian cargo ship Bonita adrift and listing in hurricane force winds far out in the middle of the English Channel during the winter of December 1981. Mike Scales was coxswain of the lifeboat while, at that time, Peter Bisson was then one of the crew, all of whom received bronze medals.

During the early afternoon of Sunday 13 December the Danish vessel Charlottenburg radioed the coastguards that she was going to the aid of the Bonita which, in severe southerly winds, was listing heavily at a position not far north of the Channel Lightship some 35 miles north of Guernsey and on the north side of the traffic separation zone. The Brixham coastguard station received the signal which was also heard at the St Peter Port signal station. The Torbay lifeboat, based in Brixham, was already out on a call to a yacht. Brixham coastguards had suffered a power failure because of power lines falling in the storm. At 2 pm prepared for a long duty, the Guernsey lifeboat put to sea and headed north through the treacherous Little Russel Channel, to the east of the island. Driving snow and sleet stopped the radar being effective so navigation was done by Decca. The wind was still southerly, gusting from between force 10, storm, to force 12, hurricane. At that time there was no lifeboat station on the more northerly Alderney island.

The lifeboat broached in the following seas several times while travelling at full speed to the area of the casualty. Two and a half hours after leaving St Peter Port and after being knocked over eight times, the lifeboat arrived close to the *Bonita* while several other ships were standing by. Helicopters from RNAS Culdrose and Portland, which had been unable to reach the scene earlier, had arrived and a Sea King from Culdrose had managed to winch four people from the ship. No other helicopter rescue attempt was successful because of the sea state, the listing of the ship and the wind that had backed from south to south-east.

The seas were breaking right over the ship which was lying with a list of 45 degrees to starboard, the wing of the bridge dipping in the water while the high side of the ship was facing the wind. Debris littered the water on the downwind side. Coxswain Scales realized that he could only effect a rescue over the stern of the *Bonita* so signalled his intention to the crew. One man made his way aft but slipped, breaking his leg. His crewmates grabbed him and lashed him to a hatch before making their own way aft. The lifeboat approached the stern rising and falling a height of 50 feet on the waves, level with the ship's deck on the crests and level with the bottom of the ship's rudder in the troughs. Coxswain Scales risked damaging the lifeboat on the protruding rudder but lay against the ship while three men jumped. They mistimed the jump, falling over 20 feet to the deck of the lifeboat, one man being seriously injured.

The lifeboat then ran off the ship and back again, this time bow on to the stern of the ship with Second Coxswain Peter Bougourd standing on the bow and the remainder of the crew on deck clipped on to lifelines. A light line was then passed from the lifeboat to the ship. It was by now dark. Two women tied themselves to the line and jumped into the sea to be hauled aboard the lifeboat by the crew. Three others were taken off by this risky method, but it worked.

The eye of the storm then passed over the area, the wind backing from south-east to north-west and increasing. This turned the sea into a turmoil. One of the *Bonita* crew then fell from the ship. After having rescued another who had jumped, the lifeboat crew set out to find the man who had fallen but were told by the crew of a cargoship standing by that they could see him lying dead in the water. The heaving line method of rescue continued, while some attempts were abandoned when it was obvious that serious damage to the lifeboat might have resulted. Many runs were made to the ship, ten being needed before one man could be persuaded to tie himself to the light line and jump. Sixteen people were rescued during this first stage of the operation. The lifeboat then stood back from the ship to give the crew a short rest.

Rescue work with the heaving line continued until all the crew except the man lashed to the hatches were off the ship, the master leaving last. A helicopter was returning from refuelling at Portland to try and lift off the remaining man but before it arrived he fell from the deck into the sea to be picked up by the French tug *Abeille Languedoc* which was among the ships standing by.

During the rescue work Motor Mechanic Robert Vowles had been in the wheelhouse or below deck helping the injured as well as attempting to keep the uninjured survivors as warm as was possible in the prevailing conditions. One survivor had been brought aboard unconscious and not breathing. Crew Member John Webster had immediately cleared his airways and started resuscitation. The Torbay lifeboat *Edward Bridges* was now on its way having successfully taken a French yacht, the *Talvez*, to safety in the lifeboat's home port of Brixham. The Torbay boat had been requested before the French tug crew had rescued the last man from the *Bonita* in case a helicopter rescue was to be attempted. The helicopter crew had felt it provident to have a lifeboat standing by in case of mishap.

Coxswain Michael Scales decided to make for Brixham at reduced speed into force 11 headwinds in order to prevent the possibility of further injury to the survivors, who were packed into the stern and cabin as well as the wheelhouse. There were twenty-nine survivors aboard the lifeboat which took just over three hours for the 40 miles back to the shelter of Brixham harbour. Coxswain Scales insisted that the survivors stayed aboard the lifeboat until blankets and dry clothing had been provided before exposing themselves to the fierce winds raging outside. The interior of the lifeboat was reasonably warm due to the heating system aboard and heat rising from the engineroom.

The St Peter Port crew stayed in Brixham for the night, returning to Guernsey next morning. Sadly the injured crew member from the *Bonita* who fell on to the deck of the lifeboat died two days later. The *Bonita* eventually sank early in the morning of the day following the rescue, a few miles north-west of the Channel light vessel that marks the centre of the western approach to the traffic separation zone to the north-west of the Channel Islands.

Coxswain Scales received the top RNLI award, the gold medal, for this rescue while his entire crew received bronze medals, presented to them by HRH Princess Alice at the RNLI annual meeting held at the Royal Festival Hall, in London, in May 1982. Coxswain Scales was also nominated as one of the twelve Men of the Year. It is difficult not to over-dramatize an event such as the rescue of the people from the *Bonita*, but in this case there was little scope for exaggeration of

the awfulness of the weather conditions, the plight of the survivors or the selfless gallantry of the lifeboat crew.

A silver plate was also presented to the Guernsey station at St Peter Port by the Norwegian agents for the ship.

Two other notable rescues occurred in the Channel Islands during the few years before the *Bonita* affair. In 1975 the coastal tanker *Point Law* ran onto rocks off the Alderney coast. Astonishingly the ship, 1,500 tons, was surrounded by rocks and a 300 foot cliff. Coxswain John Petit, predecessor to Coxswain Michael Scales, was in command of the lifeboat *Sir William Arnold*.

The St Peter Port lifeboat reached the stranded ship very early on a July morning and stood by. The ship's master thought it wise to have half of the crew of twelve taken off the ship but Coxswain Petit suggested that they waited until daylight. Local pilots were nearby aboard another vessel to advise the lifeboatmen about the positions of covered rocks. Another party of rescuers had assembled with a breeches buoy apparatus on the cliff top above the ship. The wind was blowing at around gale force but the tide was low and the ship well aground. Eventually six of the crew were transferred to the lifeboat using the ship's own life raft and the lifeboat's dinghy, a difficult business as the dinghies were covered in diesel oil and the engine on the lifeboat dinghy failed to start. Crew Member John Robilliard volunteered to row it back and forth through rough seas. He transferred four men, one at a time, from the ship to the lifeboat but the last two, one injured, presented a problem as the injured man needed to be transferred in a stretcher. This rescue was eventually completed, the injured man being accompanied by the sixth survivor. A French coastguard helicopter was now standing by at nearby Alderney airport and a French tug was on the scene so the coxswain took the six survivors to Braye harbour, Alderney, and landed them. Three local firemen had boarded the ship from the cliff to help with pumping out flooded compartments.

The rising tide, the close proximity of rocks and an increase in wind and swell prevented the tug from achieving a tow. The ship was pounded and threatening to break up so the French helicopter crew lifted the remaining five crew, the master and the three firemen one at a time, to the cliff top. The lifeboat departed for Guernsey. Coxswain Petit was awarded a bar to his bronze medal having earned his first bronze while serving under his father during the rescue of a Norwegian crew in 1965, for which his father received a gold medal. Crew Member John Robilliard also received a bronze medal while the rest of the lifeboat crew earned medal service certificates.

Another extraordinary rescue was effected by the Guernsey lifeboat in February 1978 when the oil rig Orion broke adrift in the English Channel to the west of the island while being towed by an ocean-going tug from Holland to Brazil. At the time the boat on station was the Barnett class *John Gellatly Hyndman*, replacing the *Sir William Arnold* which was away for refit. The lifeboat, with Coxswain John Petit in command, set out in darkness into west-north-westerly winds of storm force. The crew sighted the lights of the rig, which was 250 feet high and built on to a tanker hull. The windage caused by the massive legs was driving the rig at a speed of almost 6 knots towards the west Guernsey shore. When the rig crew were told they were within thirty minutes of running ashore they asked to be taken off.

Waves were breaking clear over the stern of the tanker as the rig's master told the lifeboat crew that he would lower a net from the helicopter platform that extended out from one side of the rig and tanker hull. The

Barnett class boat had a maximum speed of only 9 knots, 3 knots better than the drifting rig. Two men managed to get to the net as the lifeboat came in. The crew grabbed one man before the lifeboat anchor caught in the net throwing the second man into the sea. A swell then threw the lifeboat under the overhanging platform breaking the mast and damaging the radio aerials and radar scanner. The crew then extricated the lifeboat from the net and managed to throw a line to the man in the sea who was hauled aboard. As the rig was now firmly aground further rescues via the net were abandoned. Helicopters were on their way from RNAS Culdrose. The lifeboat crew were told to remain nearby in order to illuminate the scene with flares.

The helicopters reached the rig in terrible conditions, their rotor blades only feet from its towering legs. Twenty-five men were taken off before it was decided that the conditions were too dangerous to continue. The lifeboat made for St Peter Port with the two survivors that the crew had saved still aboard. Next morning, in daylight, two of the rig crew were taken off by breeches buoy operated by a team from the St John Ambulance Brigade and the remaining four were lifted off by helicopter.

Nine days later, the rig now free of the tanker hull, an attempt was made to tow it from the shore but this failed. In storm force winds and snow the lifeboat returned to the rig to take off the six men aboard. This rescue earned Coxswain John Petit a silver medal for gallantry and the crew thanks on vellum. Coxswain Petit was also named as a Man of the Year at the reception in London where he met the two Royal Navy helicopter pilots, Lieutenant Tilsley and Lieutenant Eagles.

When he retired in 1980, Coxswain John Petit had won a silver and four bronze medals for gallantry. His successor, Michael Scales, ably followed in his footsteps, handing over to the present coxswain, Peter Bisson. Coxswain Bisson added a bar to the bronze medal he earned during the *Bonita* rescue in 1986 when he saved the crew of a French yacht aground under cliffs on the south shore of the island. He drove the lifeboat *Sir William Arnold* bow first over hidden rocks and managed to put a crew member aboard the yacht using the lifeboat's rubber dinghy to take a line aboard. The yacht was then towed back out to sea in severe gale force 9 winds from the south. This was very typical of the present day work of the Guernsey lifeboat.

Guernsey's 'territory' stretches far to the north and west. Co-operation with Brixham, as was seen in the *Bonita* rescue, marks the northern limits, while to the west the Guernsey men will go as far as a line from the Lizard to the north-west coast of Brittany. There is fierce but friendly rivalry between the islands in many spheres, from business to tourism. The lifeboats are no exception.

There was a fine example of this when it was suggested to Coxswain Peter Bisson that his Arun class lifeboat, the *Sir William Arnold*, might replace the Alderney boat, a Waveney, while a new Fast Afloat lifeboat be placed at Guernsey. Coxswain Bisson's reply, made with a menacing smile, was short and sharp. He would burn and scuttle his lifeboat rather than let the men of Alderney get their hands on it! In spite of the rivalry, there is not a lifeboatman on any of the islands who would not willingly risk his own life if one of the other island crews sailed into difficulty. It would be a sad day if it was ever, in any way, different.

The Irish Stations

There have been special boats for the purpose of saving life based in Ireland since the start of the nineteenth century. By the time Sir William Hillary founded the National Institution for the Preservation of Life from Shipwreck in 1824, there were five lifeboat stations on Ireland's east coast while two more, one at Newcastle, County Down, and another at Courtmacsherry, County Cork, were independently established in 1825. The first station established by what was to be the RNLI was at Arklow, set up in 1826.

Financial troubles in the RNLI in Britain during the 1840s and the famines in Ireland at about the same time meant that the Irish lifeboats, whether affiliated to the RNLI or not, were in a sorry state by 1860. A year later, the RNLI took several of the independent Irish lifeboats into its fold. From then on the situation improved and by 1911 there were thirty-five RNLI stations in Ireland. It was as well that the RNLI was a voluntarily-supported organization when the Irish Free State was formed in 1922. While the Coastguard and the lighthouses were taken under the wing of the newly-formed Irish Government the lifeboats remained attached to the London-based RNLI which over the years ahead was essential to the operation of the Irish stations. The Coastguard service was promptly closed. The relatively small population of Eire, when compared with that of Britain, meant that fund-raising could never have supported the vital modern needs of the Irish crews.

The fact that the Irish stations in Eire remained part of the RNLI family makes considerable sense. The traffic at sea around the Irish coast is entirely international but a great part of it flies the British flag. The main routes from large ports and many fishing harbours on the west coasts of England, Scotland and Wales pass through the Irish Sea. Many of the more epic of rescues by Irish crews have been of vessels from nations worldwide.

The stations in northern Ulster, notably Portrush, are linked with those on Scotland's south-west coast, while those further south in Ulster, and as far south as Wicklow in Eire, are part of the wheel of stations of which those on the Isle of Man form the hub. The headquarters of the Irish lifeboat operation is at Dublin so perhaps it makes sense to start describing the Irish stations at Howth and Dun Laoghaire, north and south of the entrance to Dublin harbour and the estuary of the River Liffey.

The crew at **Howth** proudly operate the Arun class lifeboat *City of Dublin*, which arrived on the station in 1986. It was paid for from funds raised locally following an appeal by the City of Dublin. The Government of the Republic of Ireland make an annual donation to the RNLI in order to help finance the services in the Republic.

Dun Laoghaire, which operates the Waveney class lifeboat *John F Kennedy*, has the unhappy honour of being at the scene of Ireland's worst lifeboat tragedy.

During a storm on Christmas Eve 1895 the Finnish steamship *Palme* was in difficulty off the harbour. As the lifeboat, one of two stationed at Dun Laoghaire, approached the casualty the lifeboat capsized drowning all fifteen of the crew. The second lifeboat at the station then put out with nine lifeboatmen aboard and six volunteers from *HMS Melampus* but this too was capsized while under sail though the entire crew managed to regain the lifeboat. They all survived. Next day, Christmas Day, a steam tug, the *Tearsight*, put out under command of Captain Thomas McCombie. The tug crew managed to rescue all twenty people from the *Palme*, a feat which earned Captain McCombie the RNLI gold medal for his skill and gallantry.

The next station southwards on the east coast of Eire is at **Wicklow** where a Tyne class lifeboat, the *Annie Blaker*, is based having arrived at the station in 1989. Almost half the services are

to the assistance of pleasure craft. Down the coast at **Arklow** the services to pleasure craft, although few in recent years by comparison with some other stations, were more than 50% of the total.

Perhaps the most memorable service provided by the **Rosslare Harbour** lifeboat was that to the oil tanker *World Concord* which broke in two during a storm in 1954 and which has already been described. Years earlier, in February 1914, the Norwegian ship *Mexico* ran ashore in a storm at South Keeragh Island. The nearest lifeboat stations were, in those days, at Fethard and inside Wexford Harbour close to the modern ferry port of Rosslare. The lifeboat from Fethard put out with a crew of fourteen men aboard.

The Fethard crew reached the island but the boat was swept onto the rocks and was totally destroyed, nine of the crew being carried away to sea and drowned while five managed to scramble onto the island from where they assisted some of the crew of the *Mexico* already ashore. The news of the disaster reached London from where Commander Thomas Holmes, Chief Inspector of Lifeboats, set out for the area, arriving twenty-four hours after the loss of the Fethard boat. The Dunmore East lifeboat was already at sea trying to reach those on the island as were lifeboats from Wexford and Kilmore accompanied by a tug from Rosslare. The Dunmore East crew managed to save two men by dragging them off the small island with lines, but this method was considered to be too dangerous to be continued. The Wexford boat arrived at the island with the tug on the morning of Sunday 21 February. The lifeboat crew borrowed a strong dinghy, a punt in Eire, from the tug. One of the crew of the *Mexico* had died on the island.

Two lifeboatmen manned the dinghy which, attached to the lifeboat, was steered on lines towards the island from which survivors of the *Mexico* and the Fethard lifeboat were taken off two at a time. Commander Holmes was aboard the lifeboat. During these operations the dinghy struck the rocks and was holed but the crew stuffed the hole with packing and a loaf of bread before continuing the work of rescue. The Fethard survivors and those from the *Mexico* were then transferred to the tug which towed the lifeboat to land the Inspector and five Fethard men at Fethard before towing the Dunmore East boat back to her station and the Wexford boat to shelter in Waterford Harbour.

The RNLI Committee subsequently awarded a silver medal to Commander Holmes. Medals were also awarded to Coxswain Edward Wickham, of Wexford, and silver medals to Coxswain Walter Power of the Dunmore East lifeboat as well as to James Wickham and William Duggan, both of Wexford, who manned the dinghy during the final rescue. A memorial was later erected at Fethard to the lost lifeboatmen but in February 1982, sixty-eight years after the event, a further memorial, a sculpture of a lifeboatman, was unveiled in memory of all who took part in the rescue including the tug crew and master. The tug master had received a letter of thanks on vellum at the time of the rescue, but the Rosslare memorial, recorded typical co-operation between lifeboat crews.

Rounding Carnsore Point on the south-east corner of Ireland and just south of Rosslare, where the Arun class lifeboat *St Brendan* is stationed, one comes across the first of four Irish stations that were involved in one of the most dramatic and tragic events in more recent maritime history, the 1979 Fastnet Race. **Kilmore Quay** houses an Oakley class lifeboat but a Mersey class boat has been designated for the station, where much of the work involves rescues of fishing craft and other vessels among the dangerous rocks and shoals offshore from the

harbour. This part of the Irish coast has the densest number of lifeboat stations in Ireland simply due to the nature of the coast, traffic passing it and using it.

Dunmore East, which still operates the Waveney class boat *St Patrick*, was the most easterly of all lifeboats to be called out during the three days from 13-15 August 1979. Their call came from the Marine Rescue Co-ordination Centre at Shannon on the morning of 15 August when Acting Coxswain John Murphy and his crew set out on a long seven hour passage into strong westerly winds to search for the yacht *Wild Goose* which had lost its steering. That yacht was already being taken care of by a gas rig service vessel. The lifeboat crew contacted another yacht, the *Korsar* and then the yacht *Autonomy* which had lost its steering, before they met up with the yachts *Juggernaut* and *Locomotion*. *Autonomy* was taken in tow to Dunmore East while the lifeboat also escorted *Juggernaut* and *Korsar* to safety. They then helped *Locomotion* to safety, spending in all over fifteen and a half hours at sea.

Further west along the coast at **Ballycotton** Coxswain Tom McLeod and his crew put to sea in the early hours of 14 August into a severe gale, heading for two yachts in trouble off nearby Roche's Point. Before meeting the yachts, *Scaldis* and *Accento*, they were asked to search further offshore for the Irish yacht *Golden Apple of the Sun*. This yacht was nearer to the Cornish coast than to Ireland so they were diverted once more to the yacht *Wild Goose*, already being helped by the rig service vessel.

Frustrated, they stayed at sea continuing their search for casualties aware that there were many yachts out at sea in difficulties, that rescue services from Britain were reporting that people had drowned, and aware that a further storm could be expected. Eventually they found the small French yacht *Ossian* dismasted some six miles offshore from the Irish Alpha gas platform. They towed the yacht back to the safety of Ballycotton station. The Irish lifeboatmen had been at sea in severe weather for a total of over sixteen hours.

Ballycotton is best remembered in the history of the Irish lifeboats for the gallant rescue in February 1936 of the crew of the Daunt Rock light vessel by Patrick Sliney and his crew. This has already been described, the occasion leading to the presentation of the gold medal to the coxswain as well as the lifeboat itself rather than to individual crew members. Another rare event in RNLI affairs was announced early in 1991 when the station's honorary secretary, Donie O'Sullivan, was to receive the RNLI gold badge for twenty-five years of service to the station and the RNLI. Unwilling to fly, let alone to London, he received it in Dublin in 1991.

Donie O'Sullivan recalls rescues which took place well before the time of the 1979 Fastnet storm, but being a superstitious man, he remembers the night of Friday 13 January 1985 when a French trawler with a crew of twelve people came ashore on rocks under cliffs on the Waterford coast east of Ballycotton.

The rescue services had called for a helicopter from RAF Brawdy across the St George's Channel in South Wales. The wind was so ferocious that Donie O'Sullivan, his superstitions apart, was unhappy about putting the lifeboat out to sea. As the final decision rests with the coxswain he asked Coxswain Tom McLeod to decide for himself as to whether to launch. The assistance of the lifeboat had been requested to back up the Sea King helicopter crew in case there was difficulty during the winching of the trawler crew. Not only did Coxswain McLeod decide to put to sea, but the entire team from which the crew are picked volunteered to sail.

At night, its rotor blades only yards from the cliff face in winds of over 60

knots, the RAF aircrew lifted the twelve Frenchmen to safety to the admiration of the Irish lifeboat crew. Two years later, in April 1987, the Ballycotton crew were called out to a local trawler in trouble with a fouled propeller nine miles east of the station. The seas were very rough and the wind very strong from the north-east, the worst for Ballycotton's small east facing harbour.

The Ballycotton men found the casualty after an hour at sea, took a towline and began towing it back westwards. The tow parted several times in the big seas and it was decided too dangerous to take the fishing boat into Ballycotton. It was agreed to make for Crosshaven, a creek inside Cork Harbour to the west of the entrance, some fifteen miles from Ballycotton. The tow took a long five and a half hours before the lifeboat could head for home, having been, in all, ten and a half hours at sea.

Ballycotton's least happy task in recent years occurred in July 1990 when the lifeboat was called out to recover the bodies of three government fishery inspectors whose 23 foot work-boat had capsized in bad visibility off Ballycotton Island. One, the only one wearing proper survival clothes, survived after being in the sea for two and a half hours. The other three were dead. A public enquiry was ordered by the government following the incident.

There is great happiness at Ballycotton in spite of events such as this recent incident. The lifeboat Mary Stanford, in which the Ballycotton men saved the Daunt Rock lightship crew has been recovered from the Shannon where it was used as a pilot launch. It is being restored to its original state, stopping at Ballycotton to be escorted by the current lifeboat, the Arun class Hyman Winstone, before heading east for refurbishment in Dublin.

The next lifeboat station involved in the Fastnet storm rescue is at

Above: The Ballycotton Arun class lifeboat *Hyman Winstone* at speed off the coast of south-west Ireland.

Below: The lifeboat *Mary Stanford* in which the Ballycotton crew saved the Daunt Rock lightship. The boat was stationed at Ballycotton from 1930 to 1959, during which time she saved 101 lives, and is now being restored.

Courtmacsherry, in West Cork, twenty miles west of the entrance to Cork Harbour. During the storm the relief Watson class lifeboat *Sir Samuel Kelly* was put to sea. The honorary secretary had to drive from his home in nearby Bandon as the local telephone exchange had been struck by lightning. The maroons were fired and the lifeboat put out at 2.40 am on 14 August 1979 to search for the yacht *Wild Goose* which was in fact, as we now know, already being helped. They were then asked to search for the yacht *Pepsi* and although they failed to find her, they did find the British yacht *Casse Tete V*.

The yacht, sailed by a top offshore crew, had lost her rudder 26 miles off Galley Head. The yacht was taken in tow at about 11.30 am on 15 August and, for Coxswain Sammy Mearns and his crew, a long haul of ten hours duration in heavy seas and strong north-westerly winds began to take the yacht back to Courtmacsherry. The lifeboat and yacht reached safety at 9.30 pm where there was no lack of appreciation from Dave Johnson and his crew. The yacht and lifeboat secured, the party rumbled on late into the night.

The Courtmacsherry station, along with those at Dunmore East, Ballycotton and Baltimore, received letters of thanks from the Commodore of the race organizer's club, the Royal Ocean Racing Club as well as from Prime Minister Margaret Thatcher. Today plans are in hand for a massive and expensive dredging operation to be carried out at the entrance of Courtmacsherry Harbour to allow a larger faster lifeboat to be placed on this station where, during the 1989 Fastnet Race, they were called out to a yacht called *Shady Lady*, dismasted off the Irish south-west coast. Never, recalls Honorary Secretary Desmond Bateman, had there been such a willing and rapid turn-out by the crew who thought the boat might be that of Tracy Edwards and her all-girl

round-the-world race crew sailing with an unsponsored name for the yacht.

Perhaps the worst time for the crew at Courtmacsherry occurred on 7 May 1915 when the liner *Lusitania* was sunk off the Old Head of Kinsale by a German submarine with the loss of 1,198 lives. The lifeboat crew from Courtmacsherry worked with local fishing boats in recovering the hundreds of bodies that littered the sea and continued to surface for weeks afterwards in various stages of decomposition and destruction.

In June 1985 the Courtmacsherry lifeboat was put on alert when an Air India Boeing 747 airliner was blown up while approaching the west coast of Ireland. The lifeboats at Ballycotton, Courtmacsherry, Baltimore and Valentia were all launched but only the Valentia lifeboat, the nearest to the last known position of the aircraft, went to a scene of awful carnage. The other three lifeboats were recalled as they would probably not have had fuel for the outward passage, a search and then the return passage.

The most southerly lifeboat station in Ireland lies at the small harbour of **Baltimore** in Baltimore Bay. It is the closest station to the Fastnet Rock and was therefore very much in the centre of events during the 1979 storm. The Marine Rescue Co-ordination Centre alerted the Baltimore men via the Mizen Head lighthouse that *Wild Goose* was in trouble 30 miles south of Galley Head. The lifeboat crew had already received a call from the Fastnet Rock lighthouse keeper that a yacht was in trouble nearby so when the MRCC call reached them the Baltimore crew had already been at sea for several hours searching for another unidentified yacht that had reported trouble but was not found. They left the search for the *Wild Goose* once she was reported to be in the care of the rig service vessel and headed off to find the rudderless yacht *Regardless*, which was found and towed to Baltimore. No sooner had they towed this yacht to safety than another call was received that the yacht *Marionette*, owned by Chris Dunning, was in trouble without a rudder south-east of the Fastnet Rock.

Without hesitation, indeed without a change of clothes from their wet foul-weather gear or even a cup of tea, the Baltimore crew, with Christy Collins in charge as coxswain, set out once more in weather that was at last starting to moderate, to assist the crew of the *Marionette*. They found her well south of Galley Head and towed her back to Baltimore reaching their home port with the damaged yacht and tired crew after five minutes short of 12 hours at sea.

Baltimore is one of the more recent additions to the RNLI Irish chain, and a chain it certainly is, stretching as far as Baltimore and Valentia in the far south-west. Baltimore was established in 1919 but local people earned medals for rescue work before then, often saving crews of ships who were washed ashore from wrecks on this ferocious coast using local boats and even lines from ashore. A leader of these activities among those who were often involved in these rescues, was the Venerable Archdeacon John Becher. In 1916 he led a rescue party with lines and rescue equipment over hillsides to the wreck of the steamship *Alondra of Liverpool* saving twenty-three of the forty crew and earning a silver medal before the area had been established as a station in the RNLI framework.

Today Baltimore operates a Tyne class lifeboat, built in 1987 and named *Hilda Jarrett*, with Kieran Cotter as coxswain. The majority of the Baltimore work is with commercial trade, the fire aboard the bulk tanker *Kowloon Bridge* in Bantry Bay emphasizing this point.

The *Kowloon Bridge* was anchored in Bantry Bay for inspection of her hull and probable repair in November 1986 when her anchor cable broke. The tanker had 250,000 tons of fuel cargo aboard, described by the master, Captain Roa from India, as a floating bomb. Surveyors were still aboard when he decided to put to sea in a full gale rather than risk being driven into other tankers in the bay. Later, the hull of the ship fractured in mighty seas off the south-west coast of Ireland releasing many thousands of tons of crude oil into the sea. It was a major ecological disaster. While the lifeboat stood by it was not until the *Kowloon Bridge* was away from Bantry and Baltimore to the west that the lifeboat put out in fearsome weather only to be recalled. The crew of the *Kowloon Bridge* were lifted from the ship by helicopter and taken to Cork while ecological mayhem followed.

A remote station, Baltimore calls are mainly to fishing vessels working in the waters between the southern Irish coast and the northern coast of Cornwall. Spanish fishing boats are becoming more and more common among casualties as their crews sweep further and further afield from the Spanish Atlantic fishing ports. Some of these fishing boats are actually based in western British ports.

On the coast of Kerry, which shares the long finger-like peninsulas sticking out into the Atlantic with County Cork, lies the island of Valentia and the **Valentia** lifeboat station where the Arun class lifeboat *Margaret Frances Love* is based. Valentia first operated an RNLI lifeboat in 1864 and closed in 1895, but rescues continued from the island in spite of the lack of support from the RNLI. In 1908 the King, Edward VII, sent a message of congratulations and bronze medals for gallantry to men of Valentia who, in their own boats, rescued the crew of two seine net fishing boats in trouble off the island. The station reopened under the RNLI flag in 1946 and has been involved in some courageous rescues since that time.

Among operations still part of Valentia folklore is that of the rescue of the crew of the Irish coaster

Oranmore which suffered engine failure off the north-west coast of Kerry at Brandon Head. The Barnett class lifeboat *Rowland Watts*, with Coxswain Dermot Walsh in command, left Valentia during the evening of 20 February 1970 for the long slog through storm force winds and seas northwards on the forty mile passage to the casualty which was being driven towards the coast. The crew of the *Oranmore* failed to restart the engines and had dropped anchors so the master signalled to the lifeboat that he wanted some of the crew taken off. The waves were rising to great heights but with great skill Coxswain Walsh made several runs alongside the ship and took the crew off one and two at a time. The master then decided to abandon the ship completely. The seventh man to leap from the ship fell into the sea, was grabbed by a boathook from the lifeboat and brought aboard but could not be revived.

Slipping the head rope attaching the lifeboat to the coaster, the lifeboat then gathered a line around its port side propeller. The lifeboat radio had failed early in the operation and since the storm was still severe, Coxswain Walsh decided to head for Kilrush in the Shannon Estuary on only one engine early in the morning of 21 February. After being at sea in terrible conditions for twelve hours the Valentia lifeboat reached Kilrush to land ten survivors and, sadly, the body of Joseph Lennon, the mate of the coaster. This rescue earned Coxswain Dermot Walsh a silver medal for gallantry while the rest of his crew received the thanks of the RNLI on vellum. Coxswain Walsh received his medal at the Royal Festival Hall, London after the annual general meeting of the RNLI in the spring of 1971.

Alongside that of the rescue of the crew of the Daunt Rock light vessel, this was regarded as one of the epic rescues by Irish lifeboats which has featured in both a film and radio broadcast made by the Irish Broadcasting Authority, RTE. The *Oranmore* stayed safely beached for several days after the rescue causing some to wonder whether the crew might not have been safer staying aboard. It is easy to be wise after an event, particularly an event taking place on a dangerous lee shore at night on one of the wildest nights that the Irish coastal weather could produce.

Rescues continued at Valentia, often of fishing boats working off the west coast of Ireland. In 1983 a new Arun class lifeboat was placed on station at Valentia and was named *Margaret Frances Love*. Two years later the boat was involved in the awful Air India flight 182 disaster.

As already mentioned four Irish lifeboats were sent to sea when the dot that was the Air India airliner disappeared off radar screens at the Shannon Airport Air Traffic Control Centre. Other ships were also directed to the area but only the Valentia lifeboat, under the command of Coxswain Seanie Murphy, set out to the west. The coxswain estimated, with Second Coxswain Richard Connolly and Mechanic Joseph Houlihan, that they could reach the area, make a search to assess the situation and return to the Irish coast, though fuel conservation was to be essential and the best but most economic running speed had to be selected.

This is a type of job the lifeboat crews openly admit that they dread. The results of a major air crash are always quite horrific in terms of damage to passengers. The Air India disaster was no exception. The sea was red with blood with only a few bodies afloat. Many had sunk with the aircraft but were to re-surface later after the lifeboat had been forced to leave the area due to a shortage of fuel. The Valentia crew gathered the remains of five people aboard the lifeboat including one of a five year-old child and with heavy hearts they headed home. In his book on the history of the Valentia lifeboat station Dick Robinson tells of how those among the crew who were parents were unashamedly weeping. It was a terrible homecoming. Short of fuel the lifeboat stopped at the Skellig Rock lighthouse, then still manned, to collect enough fuel for the final sad miles to Knightstown Quay where the bodies were examined before being taken ashore by Irish Army personnel and the Garda, the Irish Police.

In November 1985 the lifeboat at Valentia took part in a rare rescue that involved not only the lifeboat but the police, the local Kerry Mountain Rescue team, the local fire brigade and people from the surrounding area. Seventeen year-old Dolores O'Connor, helping her father round up sheep on a cliff top, was walking a route she knew well when struck by large rocks that fell down the hillside from above. She was trapped by a massive boulder which was eventually lifted off her by a local plant-hire operator. The only way out was to move her by sea, so she was lowered in a cage stretcher accompanied by the Kerry Mountain Rescue experts. The inflatable boat carried on the cabin top of the Arun lifeboat was waiting to take her to a spot where she could be landed, taken to an ambulance and then to Tralee Hospital where she recovered completely from her ordeal.

Most operations at Valentia are concerned with the fishing vessels that are prevalent in the area between the Fastnet Rock and the Aran Islands ninety miles to the north, where the next lifeboat is based on the Galway Bay station. During 1989 the Valentia lifeboat reported only one service to a fishing boat, a quiet year. They subsequently reported that their business for that year was 100% commercial, 0% pleasure craft. There seems to be something somewhat Irish about that profound observation! The

rescue in question, or the call to assist in a rescue, occurred on 13 January 1989 when the Brixham trawler *Big Cat* was driven ashore on Beginnis Island close to Valentia. The wind was blowing from the south at severe gale strength and the fishing vessel was hard on the rocks beneath cliffs. It was breaking apart when the lifeboat station received the call for help, but there was a problem.

The Valentia lifeboat had one of its two Caterpillar engines under repair. In spite of this Coxswain Seanie Murphy decided to put to sea on one engine but was unable to get to the trawler which was lying under steep cliffs. Using a fishing boat and the lifeboat's inflatable a shore party were landed on the island. They managed to haul eleven survivors up the oil covered cliff where, once on the top, they were taken to the mainland by helicopters from the Irish Air Corps and RAF Brawdy. Three men were still missing so the now single-engined lifeboat, an anchor ready in case there was trouble with the remaining engine, continued to search, at sea in all for nine hours. One body was found, that of the engineer of the *Big Cat* but nothing was ever seen of the other two missing people. The trawler was a total wreck.

There was great celebration in Valentia early in 1991 when it was announced from the RNLI headquarters at Poole that long serving and popular Valentia station honorary secretary, Paddy Gallagher was to receive the Institution's gold badge for long service, to be presented to him at the 1991 annual general meeting at London's Festival Hall by HRH the Duke of Kent. The happy news was soon sent up the coast to the lonely station at Galway Bay and published in the local Kerry newspaper.

The **Galway Bay** lifeboat station is surely, with those at Ballyglass to the north and Arranmore off the coast of Donegal north-west of Ulster, one of the remotest in the RNLI chain both in

Britain and Ireland. The Galway Bay station, which proudly accepted the new Arun class lifeboat *Roy and Barbara Harding* in the summer of 1988, is at Kilronan on the largest of the Aran Islands, Inishmore. The lifeboat was named at a splendid ceremony attended by Lord Killanin, Vice President of the Irish section of the RNLI, Brian Miles, making his first visit to Ireland since his appointment as Director of the RNLI and, happily, by Mrs Barbara Harding who came with family and friends from Seaton, Devon, to name the boat.

Naming ceremonies of RNLI lifeboats follow a traditional pattern and that at Kilronan was no exception. The lifeboat was formally handed over to the station by Lord Killanin, Mrs Harding was given a souvenir Aran sweater by Nessa Flaherty, daughter of Coxswain Michael Flaherty and the Service of Dedication, with two Irish hymns being sung, was led by the Right Reverend John Neil, Bishop of Tuam, Killala and Achonry. Tea and Irish dancing by local children followed. One can possibly assume that other less-formal celebrations followed later. Roy and Barbara Harding had been involved with the RNLI for many years, Roy as Operations Trials Officer of the RNLI during the trials of the prototype Arun lifeboat and his wife as honorary secretary of the Seaton, Beer and District branch for forty-eight years. The £500,000 boat was paid for from RNLI funds.

During November 1986, before the new Arun class lifeboat was on station at Galway, the crew were called by the Marine Rescue Co-ordination Centre at Shannon to go to the aid of a 2,000 ton fish factory ship *Cornelius Vrolijk* from Holland, which had run ashore on Lower Gorumna Island in south-easterly winds of up to storm force 10. A British oil tanker, *Shell Technician*, was unable to do more. The Galway lifeboat put out into enormous seas at 7.15 am on Sunday

9 November and made for the casualty under the command of Coxswain Mechanic Bartley Mullin. The ship's master had decided that twenty-one of the crew should be taken off while a party of six remained aboard to try and refloat the ship, which was holed, when the weather moderated. The lifeboat managed to lie alongside the ship without sustaining any serious damage and those to be taken off climbed down to the safety of the lifeboat, though they may well have wondered just how safe they were in the violently tossing lifeboat. The Solent class vessel *R Hope Roberts* and the crew coped admirably, landing the Dutch crew at Rossaveal, on the Irish mainland, one and a half hours after taking them off. The factory ship was successfully floated off later, with her pumps running flat out, and beached in Galway Bay.

The Galway Bay station is very much an ambulance centre, taking injured islanders from the many islands to the mainland for medical treatment. This work is similar to that of the stations off the west coast of Scotland, which in many ways resembles that of the coast of Galway. Many feel that there is also a great similarity between the peoples of the island-strewn coasts.

Galway Bay is one of only two stations opened in the Irish Republic since the creation of the Irish Free State in 1922. While the station in Galway Bay was established in 1927, the other all-weather lifeboat station was opened up the coast of Eire at Ballyglass, County Mayo, in 1989. Several stations manning inflatable lifeboats have been opened since 1922, including the small station at Clifden, which lies between Galway Bay and Ballyglass.

Clifden, which is the home of a 'C' class inflatable, was established in 1988 primarily to deal with the increase of pleasure craft on the western coast of Eire. Northwards from there lies another new station, that at **Ballyglass** which was opened in

1989 for evaluation and which operates the 52 foot Arun class lifeboat *Mabel Williams*. The Ballyglass crew underwent the week-long training programme at Poole before taking their temporary station lifeboat proudly home to a rapturous welcome and subsequently a handing-over and religious service of dedication attended by Lord Killanin and Michael Noonan, Minister of State for the Department of the Marine for Ireland as well as two thousand well-wishers from every part of Ireland. The evaluation period proved to be successful and the station is now firmly established.

Arranmore Island, off the coast of County Donegal, is home to a new Tyne class lifeboat, *William Luckin*, placed there in 1985 as part of the rationalization of the Irish lifeboat chain to provide the whole coast with modern fast lifeboats. One incident at Arranmore did not involve the lifeboat but did involve the then coxswain, Francis Bonner. He was making his way along the quay around midnight when he heard a hooter being sounded from a yacht anchored offshore. The yacht, from County Down, Ulster, was drifting towards rocks in strong winds. Realizing the danger and that there would be no time to launch the lifeboat he called out John O'Donnell, the lifeboat mechanic, and manned the yacht's own inflatable dinghy which those of the crew of the yacht, who were ashore, had left nearby.

Coxswain Bonner and Mechanic O'Donnell started the outboard of the tender and headed for the yacht managing to take a mother and young daughter into the dinghy and landing them ashore just before the yacht hit the rocks and sank. It was fortunate that the alarm hooter from the yacht was heard by the one person who knew exactly what to do. One can only wonder what sort of yachtsman leaves his yacht at anchor on a lee shore in a near gale with a woman and young girl aboard and is still

ashore at midnight without, apparently, having checked the wellbeing of the yacht or those aboard. Thanks to RNLI men the yachtsman was lucky not to have lost more than just the yacht.

Around the Irish coast from the stations off Dublin lies the seasonal inshore inflatable station at Lough Swilly before one crosses the border into Ulster and finds the offshore station at **Portrush**, at the east side of the estuary entrance of Lough Foyle, which has operated a busy Arun class lifeboat, the *Richard Evans (Civil Service No 39)* since the early 1980s. Before that, during October 1960, the Greek cargo ship *Argo Delos* ran ashore on the small island of Torbeg, north of Malin Head, the most northerly mainland point of Ireland. The Watson class lifeboat *Lady Scott (Civil Service No 4)* was launched in the early hours of a rough night and made for the scene in very confused seas.

Coxswain Samuel Cunningham had made contact with the warship *HMS Leopard* which was standing by near the casualty and decided, after several dummy runs alongside the Greek ship, to stand off until the seas had moderated a little. He then made a run in towards the ship while a helicopter from *HMS Leopard* put men aboard to set up a communication link and managed to take off some of the Greeks while others climbed backwards down a shipside ladder and jumped into the arms of waiting lifeboatmen. All were saved. This rescue earned Coxswain Sam Cunningham the RNLI silver medal while Second Coxswain Robert McMullan was awarded the bronze medal. The crew of *HMS Leopard* were so impressed with the effort of the lifeboat crew that they sent inscribed silver tankards to each crew member.

More recently the Portrush crew were called out when Richard Branson's transatlantic balloon flight seemed doomed to a premature

Above: The Watson class lifeboat Lady Scott *(Civil Service No 4).*

Below: The Portrush lifeboat Richard Evans *exercising with a Royal Navy Wessex helicopter with the guided missile destroyer* HMS Glamorgan *in the background. The picture was taken by a photographer from* HMS Osprey, *Portland, indicating that the lifeboat was probably on her maiden voyage back to Northern Ireland.*

ending close to the station. During 1990 the station received two calls to ditched aircraft, one an RAF Turcano prototype trainer that crashed, killing the test pilot working from the Shorts Aircraft factory airfield near Belfast, the other a private light aircraft. Many of their calls are to pleasure craft but a number are to fishing vessels off the Eire coast of Donegal to the west of the station.

Donaghadee is the next offshore station southwards from Portrush, separated from Portrush by two inshore bases at Red Bay and Bangor. The Donaghadee lifeboat, under Coxswain Hugh Nelson was very much involved with the disaster of the ferry *Princess Victoria* already described, which earned the coxswain the British Empire Medal. Although it occurred forty years ago the disaster still seems fresh in the memory of older local people. Having rescued the few survivors, the lifeboat crew had the awful task of putting to sea several times more once the weather had abated to recover many bodies.

Today most of the lifeboat work involves pleasure craft as the north-east coast becomes increasingly popular with the leisure industry and the fishing quotas take their toll of the once-prosperous fishing fleet that operated from Donaghadee and other local fishing ports. The Arun class lifeboat *City of Belfast* was funded by an appeal in the city and put on station in 1985.

Donaghadee is the most northern lifeboat station in Ireland that forms part of the Isle of Man Wheel already described. When trouble brews in the northern part of the Irish Sea it is likely that this lifeboat will be co-operating with those from Portpatrick across the water near Stranraer and those on the Isle of Man itself.

Bangor, at the top of the Ards Peninsula facing Belfast Lough, now has an Atlantic 21 class semi-rigid inflatable but in 1987 operated a 'D' class inflatable. An incident from that

time emphasizes the worth of these fast inshore craft. Three men fell from a motor boat off Bangor Harbour. The local yacht club rescue launch and the RNLI inshore boat put out recovering all three but one man seemed close to death. While the rescue boat from the club took two survivors ashore, the fast inshore lifeboat, its crew calling ahead by radio to be met by an ambulance, took the sick man ashore as fast as was possible. The casualty survived. This is a typical rescue by the many small inshore inflatable lifeboats around the coast of Britain and Ireland, the crew becoming unsung heroes.

Newcastle, County Down, was awaiting a new Mersey class lifeboat during 1991, replacing their veteran Oakley class boat *Jane Hay*. In the autumn of 1990 the Newcastle crew were out and back to port over a period of three days during a combined search by helicopters and lifeboats from the Isle of Man and northwards. A local fishing boat had disappeared but after an extensive search just one body was recovered.

The **Clogher Head** station is the most northern on Eire's east coast, very much part of the Manx Wheel and one of the few beach launching stations in Ireland. Older Oakley class boats have served the station during recent years but a new beach launching Mersey class boat is expected in 1992, when the crew will go to Poole for training prior to bringing their new boat proudly home. Honorary Secretary Paddy Hodgins has said that he might go with them to attend a course for station secretaries but, like others in Ireland who are proud home-bound people, he may well have other thoughts on the matter when the time comes. He drives the local harbour crane that, among other things, places the boom in position during easterly winds.

Clogher may have one of the older slower lifeboats until the new fast

Mersey arrives but they have had their share of calls. They, with their friends at northern Newcastle, were out for many hours looking for the crew of a missing local lobster fishing boat in 1990, while in January 1991 they were called to Carlingford Lough to stand by a coaster aground in bad weather off Warren Point.

No sectarian, political or nationalistic problems affect the work of the lifeboat crews in Ireland, Ulster or Eire. There are strong links between stations north and south of the border that divides the Republic from Ulster. Crews, fund-organizers and others involved with the operations of the RNLI are often old and close friends while, as in mainland Britain, a sense of friendly rivalry prevails between stations. Certainly British people who visit the stations in Eire find a welcome as warm as anywhere.

AN EPILOGUE

During the early months of 1991 work was completed ashore at Littlehampton on the newest design of lifeboat, the Fast Afloat Boat Type 3. This is a scaled-up version of the Arun class, being 57 feet in length and powered by two 1,000 horsepower Caterpillar turbo-charged diesel engines. The top speed is expected to be better than 25 knots. Following builder's, engine manufacturer's and RNLI acceptance trials from the yard of William Osborne at Littlehampton, the new boat, not yet officially commissioned as a lifeboat, will be sent round lifeboat stations for evaluation by lifeboat crews, inspectors and others. During trials in May 1991, the prototype lifeboat went to the assistance of a yacht in Lyme Bay, off the Dorset coast.

If the trials are successful and the new lifeboat joins the RNLI fleet the first steps will have been completed in what may become further rationalization of RNLI operations in the next century. The last Arun class lifeboat was built at a cost of around £500,000. The new lifeboats will cost £1 million. The slipway and tractor/carriage launching Tyne and Mersey class lifeboats cost a little less than the Arun class. The latest arrivals of these lifeboats on stations mean that these stations have been equipped with lifeboats for two decades ahead. Meanwhile it seems, subject to the FAB 3 class coming up to requirements, they will replace the

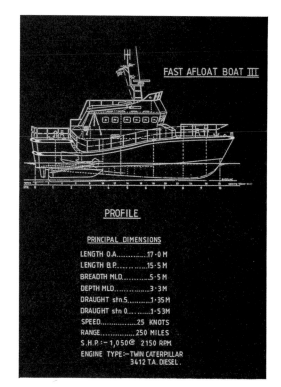

FAB III – Diagram profile.

older Arun class boats, and some of these are now twenty years old. For example, the original Arun, based at Barry Dock, South Wales, was commissioned in 1971.

During 1990 the all-weather and inshore lifeboats of the RNLI were called out 4,937 times. A total of 1,601 lives were saved, a record for the RNLI in any one year. The total running cost of the RNLI during 1991

Lifeboat launches, lives saved and people landed 1981 – 1990

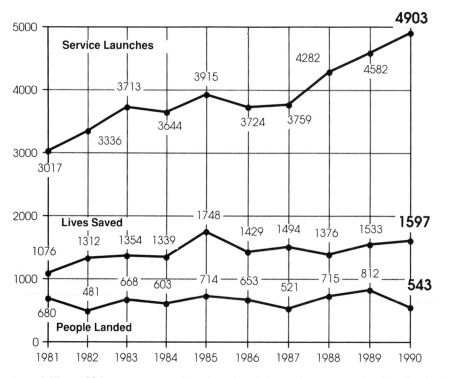

Service Launches

3017, 3336, 3713, 3644, 3915, 3724, 3759, 4282, 4582, 4903

Lives Saved

1076, 1312, 1354, 1339, 1748, 1429, 1494, 1376, 1533, 1597

People Landed

680, 481, 668, 603, 714, 653, 521, 715, 812, 543

1981 1982 1983 1984 1985 1986 1987 1988 1989 1990

An additional 30 lives were saved by shoreboats in services recognised by the Institution.

is expected to be £44 million or, if one prefers, £5,022 an hour, £83 per minute, day and night, 365 days a year. It is a massive amount of money, but it seems obvious that the British public would have it no other way as they continue to support the RNLI through flag days, specially-organized events and other chances for people to contribute to one of Britain and Ireland's favourite charities. Should it remain a charity? This was a question asked of the public during 1990. The answer came as some surprise to the staff of the RNLI at Poole. Of those questioned a majority thought that it was wrong that the Institution should rely on charitable funds. The RNLI counteracted by admitting that there

was not enough public awareness of the benefits of the voluntary status of the Institution. Crews of lifeboats were more adamant. They thought that if government funds were to be available they would never put to sea in all but the best of weather and then only after filling in copious forms!

It will be remembered from earlier pages of this book that the lifeboat stations in Eire receive some financial help from their own Government but in England, Scotland and Wales there is none and hopefully none will ever be needed. Apart from the staff at Poole, the paid coxswains and coxswain mechanics on stations and the regional staff, the whole RNLI

Lifeboat launches in 1990

Analysed by type of casualty

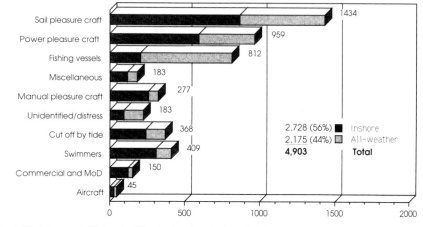

Sail pleasure craft	1434
Power pleasure craft	959
Fishing vessels	812
Miscellaneous	183
Manual pleasure craft	277
Unidentified/distress	183
Cut off by tide	368
Swimmers	409
Commercial and MoD	150
Aircraft	45

2,728 (56%) ■ Inshore
2,175 (44%) ▨ All-weather
4,903 **Total**

Service statistics for the year ended 31 December 1990 are based on returns of service received at headquarters by 18 March 1991

operation runs happily on the magic word VOLUNTEER. Ever since those early days when Sir William Hillary watched the fishing fleet being wrecked outside Douglas harbour on the Isle of Man, the people of the RNLI have worked for nothing apart from the small fee that crews earn from the RNLI when called out, a fee, as an Irish lifeboatman put it, that hardly pays for the well-earned glass of stout that they may enjoy on their return.

New boats are being built, new equipment being supplied and even new lifeboat houses and crew rooms being constructed. The RNLI is as strong in heart, if not stronger, than ever. It is a unique anachronism that could probably only ever be devised and allowed to survive by the British and Irish. Anywhere else it would probably have foundered for one reason or another. Sir William Hillary's dream has surely grown to something quite extraordinary. The refuge tower that he built outside Douglas harbour on the Isle of Man remains on St Mary's Rock, but his real memorial is dotted along the coast of Britain and Ireland, the stations of the RNLI.

INDEX